Lecture Notes in Computer Science 6093

Commenced Publication in 1973
Founding and Former Series Editors:
Gerhard Goos, Juris Hartmanis, and Jan van Leeuwen

Editorial Board

George T. Heineman Jan Kofron
Frantisek Plasil (Eds.)

Research
into Practice –
Reality and Gaps

6th International Conference
on the Quality of Software Architectures, QoSA 2010
Prague, Czech Republic, June 23 - 25, 2010
Proceedings

 Springer

Volume Editors

George T. Heineman
Worcester Polytechnic Institute
Department of Computer Science
Worcester, MA 01609-2280, USA
E-mail: heineman@cs.wpi.edu

Jan Kofron
Charles University in Prague
Faculty of Mathematics and Physics
Malostranske namesti 25
118 00 Praha 1, Czech Republic
E-mail: jan.kofron@d3s.mff.cuni.cz

Frantisek Plasil
Charles University in Prague
Faculty of Mathematics and Physics
Malostranske namesti 25
11800 Prague 1, Czech Republic
E-mail: plasil@d3s.mff.cuni.cz

Library of Congress Control Number: 2010928915

CR Subject Classification (1998): D.2, C.2, F.3, H.4, D.3, D.4

LNCS Sublibrary: SL 2 – Programming and Software Engineering

ISSN	0302-9743
ISBN-10	3-642-13820-9 Springer Berlin Heidelberg New York
ISBN-13	978-3-642-13820-1 Springer Berlin Heidelberg New York

springer.com

© Springer-Verlag Berlin Heidelberg 2010
Printed in Germany

Typesetting: Camera-ready by author, data conversion by Scientific Publishing Services, Chennai, India
Printed on acid-free paper   06/3180

Preface

The goal of QoSA is to address aspects of software architecture focusing broadly on quality characteristics and how these relate to the design of software architectures. Specific issues of interest are defining quality measures, evaluating and managing architecture quality, linking architecture to requirements and implementation, and preserving architecture quality throughout the lifetime of the system. Past themes for QoSA include Architectures for Adaptive Software Systems (2009), Models and Architecture (2008), and Software Architecture, Components, and Applications (2007).

In this, the sixth incarnation of QoSA, researchers and practitioners demonstrated how specific sub-elements within an architecture lead to measurable quality in the implemented system. While clear challenges remain, the theme for QoSA 2010 was "Research into Practice – Reality and Gaps."

There were 32 submissions to QoSA 2010 from which the Program Committee selected 11 long papers, for an acceptance rate of 34%. To further foster collaboration and exchange of ideas with the component-based software engineering community, QoSA was held as part of the conference series Federated Events on Component-based Software Engineering and Software Architecture (COMPARCH). These federated events were QoSA 2010, the 13th International Symposium on Component-Based Software Engineering (CBSE 2010), the 15th International Workshop on Component-Oriented Programming (WCOP 2010), and the First International Symposium on Architecting Critical Systems (ISARCS 2010), a symposium dedicated to dependability, safety, security and testing/analysis for architecting systems. Because of the close relationship between the CBSE and QoSA communities, COMPARCH 2010 once again integrated these technical programs to further promote discussion and collaboration.

We would like to thank the QoSA Steering Committee and the members of the Program Committee for their dedicated and valuable work during the review process. We thank Alfred Hofmann from Springer for his continuing support in reviewing and publishing this proceedings volume.

April 2010

George T. Heineman
Jan Kofroň
František Plášil

Organization

QoSA 2010 was organized by the Department of Distributed and Dependable Systems, Charles University in Prague, Czech Republic as a part of COMPARCH 2010.

General Chair

František Plášil   Charles University in Prague, Czech Republic

Organization Committee Chair

Petr Hnětynka   Charles University in Prague, Czech Republic

Program Committee Chairs

George T. Heineman   WPI, USA
Jan Kofroň   Charles University in Prague, Czech Republic

QoSA Steering Committee

Steffen Becker
Ivica Crnkovic
Ian Gorton
Raffaela Mirandola
Sven Overhage
František Plášil
Ralf Reussner
Judith Stafford
Clemens Szyperski

Program Committee

Danilo Ardagna	Politecnico di Milano, Italy
Colin Atkinson	University of Mannheim, Germany
Muhammad Ali Babar	Lero, Ireland
Len Bass	Software Engineering Institute, USA
Steffen Becker	Forschungszentrum Informatik (FZI), Germany
Jan Bosch	Intuit, USA
Ivica Crnkovic	Mälardalen University, Sweden

Rogerio De Lemos	University of Kent, UK
Antinisca Di Marco	Università dell'Aquila, Italy
Carlo Ghezzi	Politecnico di Milano, Italy
Anirüddhā Gokhālé	Vanderbilt University, USA
Ian Gorton	Pacific Northwest National Laboratory, USA
Vincenzo Grassi	Università di Roma "Tor Vergata", Italy
Jens Happe	Forschungszentrum Informatik (FZI), Germany
Darko Huljenic	Ericsson Nikola Tesla, Croatia
Samuel Kounev	University of Karlsruhe, Germany
Heiko Koziolek	ABB, Germany
José Merseguer	Universidad de Zaragoza, Spain
Raffaela Mirandola	Politecnico di Milano, Italy
Robert Nord	Software Engineering Institute, USA
Boyana, Norris	MCS Division, USA
Sven Overhage	University of Augsburg, Germany
Dorina Petriu	Carleton University, Canada
František Plášil	Charles University in Prague, Czech Republic
Marek Procházka	ESA/ESTEC, Noordwijk, The Netherlands
Sasikumar Punnekkat	Mälardalen University, Sweden
Ralf Reussner	University of Karlsruhe, Germany
Roshanak Roshandel	Seattle University, USA
Antonino Sabetta	ISTI-CNR PISA, Italy
Raghu Sangwan	Penn State, USA
Jean-Guy Schneider	Swinburne University, Australia
Judith Stafford	Tufts University, USA
Clemens Szyperski	Microsoft, USA
Petr Tůma	Charles University in Prague, Czech Republic
Hans van Vliet	Vrije Universiteit, The Netherlands
Wolfgang Weck	Independent Software Architect, Switzerland
Michel Wermelinger	Open University, UK

Co-reviewers

Etienne Borde	Pavel Jezek
Franz Brosch	Thomas Leveque
Fabian Brosig	Josip Maras
Senthil Kumar Chandran	Pierre Parrend
Akshay Dabholkar	Diego Perez
Aleksandar Dimov	Ricardo J. Rodriguez
Antonio Filieri	Nilabja Roy
Matthias Huber	Viliam Simko
Nikolaus Huber	Sumant Tambe

Table of Contents

Case Studies and Experience Reports

Intrinsic Definition in Software Architecture Evolution

Jeffrey N. Magee

Imperial College London
Huxley Building
South Kensington Campus
London SW7 2AZ, U.K.
j.magee@imperial.ac.uk

Abstract. Incremental change is intrinsic to both the initial development and subsequent evolution of large complex software systems. The talk discusses both, the requirements for and the design of, an approach that captures this incremental change in the definition of software architecture. The predominate advantage in making the definition of evolution intrinsic to architecture description is in permitting a principled and manageable way of dealing with unplanned change and extension.

Intrinsic definition also facilitates decentralized evolution in which software is extended and evolved by multiple independent developers. The objective is an approach which permits unplanned extensions to be deployed to end users with the same facility that plugin extensions are currently added to systems with planned extension points. The talk advocates a model-driven approach in which architecture definition is used to directly construct both initial implementations and extensions / modification to these implementations.

An implementation of intrinsic evolution definition in Backbone is presented – an architectural description language (ADL), which has both a textual and a UML2, based graphical representation. The talk uses Backbone to illustrate basic concepts through simple examples and reports experience in applying it and its associated tool support to larger examples.

G.T. Heinemann, J. Kofron, and F. Plasil (Eds.): QoSA 2010, LNCS 6093, p. 1, 2010.

A Component-Based Approach to Adaptive User-Centric Pervasive Applications[*]

Martin Wirsing

Institute of Computer Science
Ludwig-Maximilians-University Munich
Oettingenstr. 67
D-80538 Munich
Germany
wirsing@informatik.uni-muenchen.de

Abstract. In the last years computing has become omnipresent and even devices that do not look like computers have computing capabilities. Seamless man-machine interfaces and ad-hoc communication allow for pervasive adaptive control and computer support in everyday activities. So-called pervasive-adaptive environments are becoming able to monitor, diagnose and respond to the cognitive, emotional and physical states of persons in real time.

In this talk we present a new approach for designing and realising adaptive systems that provide assistance to humans in a discrete and personalized manner. The approach is based on a strict component-based framework for controlling pervasive adaptive systems including real-time sensor and actuator control, user and context-awareness, affective computing, self-organization and adaptation. A rule-based domain-specific language simplifies the dynamic creation and modification of system architectures; mechanisms for the transparent distribution of applications, flexible on-line data processing, and early experimentation with data analysis algorithms facilitate the construction of user-centric adaptive systems while a modular assume/guarantee framework allows to compute formal representation of such systems and to verify them against given system requirements. We illustrate our approach by two case studies for detecting cognitive overload and influencing the mood of a user in the way he desires.

---

[*] This work has been partially supported by the EC project REFLECT, IST-2007-215893.

G.T. Heinemann, J. Kofron, and F. Plasil (Eds.): QoSA 2010, LNCS 6093, p. 2, 2010.

Validating Model-Driven Performance Predictions on Random Software Systems

Vlastimil Babka[1], Petr Tůma[1], and Lubomír Bulej[1,2]

[1] Department of Distributed and Dependable Systems
Faculty of Mathematics and Physics, Charles University
Malostranské náměstí 25, 118 00 Prague, Czech Republic
{vlastimil.babka,petr.tuma,lubomir.bulej}@d3s.mff.cuni.cz
[2] Institute of Computer Science, Academy of Sciences of the Czech Republic
Pod Vodárenskou věží 2, 182 07 Prague, Czech Republic

Abstract. Software performance prediction methods are typically validated by taking an appropriate software system, performing both performance predictions and performance measurements for that system, and comparing the results. The validation includes manual actions, which makes it feasible only for a small number of systems.

To significantly increase the number of systems on which software performance prediction methods can be validated, and thus improve the validation, we propose an approach where the systems are generated together with their models and the validation runs without manual intervention. The approach is described in detail and initial results demonstrating both its benefits and its issues are presented.

Keywords: performance modeling, performance validation, MDD.

1 Motivation

State of the art in model-driven software performance prediction builds on three related factors: the availability of architectural and behavioral *software models*, the ability to solve *performance models*, and the ability to *transform* the former models into the latter. This is illustrated for example by the survey of model-driven software performance prediction [3], which points out that the typical approach is to use UML diagrams for specifying both the architecture and the behavior of the software system, and to transform these diagrams into performance models based on queueing networks.

Both the models and the methods involved in the prediction process necessarily include simplifying assumptions that help abstract away from some of the complexities of the modeled system, e.g., approximating real operation times with probability distributions or assuming independence of operation times. These simplifications are necessary to make the entire prediction process tractable, but the complexity of the modeled system usually makes it impossible to say how the simplifications influence the prediction precision.

G.T. Heinemann, J. Kofron, and F. Plasil (Eds.): QoSA 2010, LNCS 6093, pp. 3–19, 2010.
© Springer-Verlag Berlin Heidelberg 2010

Without sufficient insight into the modeled system, a straightforward approach to the question of prediction precision would be similar to common statistical validation: a sufficiently representative set of systems would be both modeled and measured and the measurements would be compared with the predictions. Unfortunately, the fact that the software models still require manual construction limits the ability to validate on a sufficiently representative set of systems. For most prediction methods, the validation is therefore limited to a small number of manually constructed case studies.

To improve the validation process, we propose to automatically generate software systems together with their models and then use the systems for measurement and the models for prediction. That way, we can validate the performance predictions on a large number of systems, and, provided that the generated systems are representative enough, achieve a relatively robust validation of the prediction methods.

The goal of this paper is to explore the potential of the proposed validation process by taking a specific generation mechanism and applying it on a specific performance model. While neither the generation mechanism nor the performance model are the focus of the paper, we describe them in detail so that the reader can form an impression of what the benefits and the issues of applying the approach are. We start by analyzing the requirements on the automatic software system generation in Section 2 and detailing a particular generation mechanism in Section 3. In Section 4, we describe how we transform the architecture model of the generated software system into a performance model based on the Queueing Petri Nets (QPN) formalism [4]. Section 5 presents the initial results of the validation using the generation mechanism and the performance model outlined in the previous two sections. In Section 6, we discuss the broader context of the related work. We conclude by outlining future development directions in Section 7.

2   Requirements on Software Generation

While an automated generation of a fully functional software system would generally be considered infeasible, it is done in limited contexts, for example when generating domain specific editors [9], test cases [1,8], test beds [13], or benchmarks [33]. When generating software systems to validate performance predictions, the context is roughly as follows:

Executability. The system must be immediately executable, so that measurements of its performance can be taken.

Functionality. The system does not have to deliver any particular functionality, because the validation is concerned with other than functional properties.

Applicability. The performance effects observed on the generated system must be applicable to real systems for which the validated performance prediction method would be considered.

These requirements are commonplace when constructing benchmark applications for performance evaluation [28,24]. While not expected to deliver real results, a benchmark is required to exercise the system in a manner that is as close to real application as possible, so that the benchmark performance is directly related to the performance of the corresponding production system.

When our goal is to see how the simplifying assumptions in the performance models influence the prediction precision, we can extrapolate the requirements easily: the generated system needs to be faithful to reality especially in those places where the prediction makes the simplifications. We now list some of the significant simplifications that are commonly performed:

Scheduling approximation. The operating system scheduler is usually a complex module that schedules threads or processes based not only on priorities or deadlines, but also on heuristics based on resource consumption or interactive behavior. Performance models usually simplify scheduling using one of the well defined algorithmic models such as random, first-come first-served, or ideal sharing [11].

Operation duration approximation. Although the individual operation durations tend to be arbitrary, performance models frequently approximate them with statistical distributions, especially the exponential distribution, which maps very well to some of the underlying analytical models. Only sometimes, arbitrary distributions are approximated [7].

Operation dependency approximation. The objects or functions of a software system frequently operate on shared data. This gives rise to a multitude of dependencies that influence performance. Perhaps most notable are dependencies due to locking, which are usually captured by performance models, for example as special tasks in LQN [30] or special places in QPN [4]. Less frequently captured are dependencies due to argument passing, so far only captured in performance models solved through simulation [19]. Otherwise, operation durations are usually assumed statistically independent.

Resource isolation approximation. Sharing of processor execution units, address translation caches, external processor buses and similar features found in contemporary hardware architectures potentially impacts performance. These are only rarely captured by performance models [10], and usually only for evaluating hardware design rather than software system. Typical performance models assume resources are mostly independent.

Although other approximations could likely be found, we focus on the ones listed here. Where the individual approximations are not concerned, we strive to make the generated software system random, to avoid introducing any systematic error into the validation. To provide a practical anchor, we apply our approach in the context of the Q-ImPrESS project [27], which deals with quality-of-service predictions in service oriented systems.

3   Generating Tree Structured Servers

In our experiments, the overall architecture of the generated software system has been influenced by the architectural model of the Q-ImPrESS project [5].

This model is built around the notion of components, whose interfaces are interconnected in a hierarchical manner, and whose behavior is described using the usual notions of operation invocations, sequences, branches and loops.

The generated software system consists of leaf modules, which approximate the primitive components of the architectural model, and interconnecting modules, which approximate the hierarchical interconnections and the behavior description of the architectural model. The leaf modules perform useful work in the sense of generating processing workload. The interconnecting modules arrange other modules in sequences, branches and loops.

In the following, we need to make a distinction between multiple meanings of some terms. We therefore use *module* when we mean a code unit implementing a feature, *component* when we mean an architectural element, and *instance* when we mean an actual state allocated at runtime. The same module can be used to realize multiple components. Multiple instances of the same component can be allocated.

We have opted to generate the system in top-to-bottom order. First, a module realizing the topmost component is selected at random from the set of all existing modules. Then, for any component realized by an interconnecting module with unassigned children, the same random selection is applied recursively to assign the child components. The probability of selecting a particular module is adjusted so that only interconnecting modules are selected at the topmost level of the architecture. Leaf modules are gradually more likely to be selected on the lower levels of the architecture.

The described algorithm generates a tree architecture. This would present an unacceptable restriction since there are no shared components in a tree architecture, and sharing of a component typically influences performance, especially when synchronization is involved. However, our design involves some synchronization between threads, explained later on. In principle, this synchronization resembles synchronization over a shared component, thus making the restrictions of the tree architecture relatively less important.

3.1   Realistic Leaf Modules

In the architecture, the workload that exercises the system is only generated by the leaf modules – the workload generated by the interconnecting modules amounts to the usual invocation overhead and remains trivial by comparison. Since we require the workload to exercise the system in a realistic manner, we use benchmarks from the SPEC CPU2006 benchmarking suite [14], which has been designed to reflect realistic workloads, as the leaf modules.

The use of benchmarks from the SPEC CPU2006 benchmarking suite brings multiple technical challenges related to reuse of code that was not designed to be strictly modular. To begin with, we have manually separated the initialization and execution phases of the benchmarks as much as possible, and wrapped each benchmark in a class with a unified module interface. The interface makes it possible to initialize all benchmarks before commencing measurement, and to execute each benchmark through a single method invocation.

Wrapping the benchmarks in classes is further complicated by the fact that the benchmarks are single threaded and use statically allocated data structures. Creating multiple instances of a wrapper class or invoking methods of a wrapper instance from multiple threads could therefore lead to race conditions. A straightforward solution, namely converting the statically allocated data into dynamically allocated attributes of the corresponding wrapper class, would require further modifications of the benchmarks. Given the size of the benchmarks, performing such modifications manually would not be a feasible approach – the potential for introducing subtle errors into the benchmarks that would disrupt the measurement is simply too high.

To tackle the problem, we have modified the linking process so that every component realized by a module uses a separate copy of the statically allocated data structures. In detail, for every component realized by a module, new copies of the binary object files containing the module and the corresponding wrapper class are created. In these copies, all external symbols are uniquely renamed. The generated software system is then linked with the renamed copies. This ensures that even when the generated software system contains multiple components initially realized by the same module, the individual components will be served by distinct module copies with distinct statically allocated data.

To cover the situation where methods of a wrapper class instance are invoked from multiple threads, each wrapper class is protected by a static lock. Thanks to symbol renaming, this lock synchronizes concurrent accesses to each single component, but not concurrent accesses to multiple components realized by the same module. As an exception, the lock is not used for modules whose correct function without synchronization can be reasonably expected, such as modules written by ourselves or modules explicitly documented as thread safe.

Since the standard execution time of the individual benchmarks can be in the order of hours, and the generated software system can incorporate many benchmarks arranged in sequences, branches and loops, the execution time of the entire system could become rather long. We have therefore also reduced the input data of the benchmarks to achieve reasonable execution times, and excluded some benchmarks whose execution times would remain too long even with reduced input data.

Besides the leaf modules that wrap the benchmarks from the SPEC CPU2006 suite, we have also included leaf modules that exercise the memory subsystem in a well-known manner. These leaf modules, together with the workload that they generate, are described in [2].

Whenever a module accepts arguments, the generated software system provides them as random values from a configurable statistical distribution or value domain. This goes not only for the arguments of the leaf modules, which include for example allocated memory block sizes, but also for the arguments of the interconnecting modules, which include for example loop iteration counts or branch path probabilities.

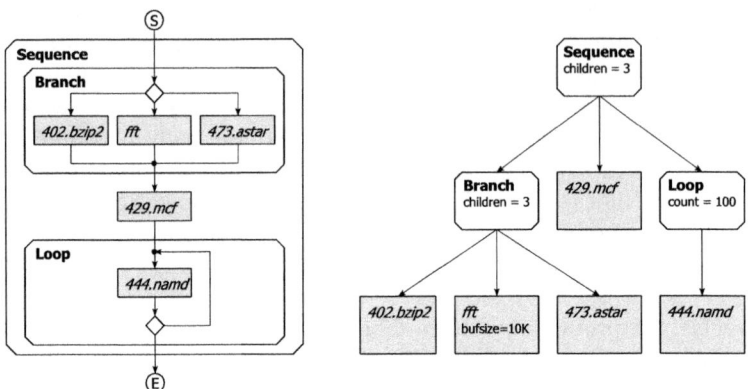

Fig. 1. Example of control flow and architecture of a generated system

3.2   Client Workload Generation

In the adopted architectural model of the Q-ImPrESS project [5], the topmost components represent services used by external clients. In this sense, each generated software system therefore also approximates a service used by external clients – and we need to provide the system with a mechanism for an appropriate client workload generation.

Our tool uses a closed workload model, with client requests handled by a thread pool. Each client request is handled by one thread – the thread invokes the topmost component of the generated software system, which, depending on the particular interconnecting module used, invokes some or all of its child components, progressing recursively through the entire system. The number of clients, the client think time, and the thread pool size are again random values with configurable properties.

To avoid excessive synchronization, threads allocate private instances of components. Coupled with the process of module wrapping and module linking, this makes it possible to execute multiple threads in parallel even in a leaf module that is single threaded by design, provided the module was selected to realize multiple components.

To summarize, the generated software system is a random tree of components that generate realistic workloads, executed in parallel by multiple threads with some degree of synchronization. An example of such a system is depicted on Fig. 1. This meets most of the requirements of Section 2, except for the requirement of faithful operation dependency approximation, which is still simplified because the components do not pass arguments among themselves.

4   Constructing Performance Models

The tool outlined in the previous sections provides us with a way to quickly generate a large number of executable systems together with their architectural models. The next step is transforming the generated architectural models into performance models, and populating the performance models with input values such as operation durations and loop iteration counts. We perform this step in the context of performance models based on the QPN formalism [4].

4.1   Performance Model Structure

The process of constructing a performance model of a component system using the QPN formalism is outlined in [17]. To summarize, queueing places are used to model both client think time and server processing activity, immediate transitions describe the behavior of the component system, token colors are used to distinguish executing operations. Since our approach (implemented as an automated model-to-model transformation) is based on the same principle, we limit the description to significant aspects of the transformation.

The part of the network that is concerned with clients and threads uses a *clients* queueing place to model the client think time and a *threads* ordinary place to model the thread pool size. The tokens in the *clients* place represent thinking clients. The place has an infinite server scheduling strategy with exponential service time representing the client think time, the initial token population is equal to the number of clients. The tokens in the *threads* place represent available threads, with initial population equal to the size of the thread pool.

When a client finishes thinking and a thread for serving it is available, a transition removes one token from the *clients* place and one token from the *threads* place, and puts one token representing the thread serving the client into an ordinary place called *requests*.

The component operations are either active, actually consuming processor time, or passive, waiting without consuming processor time.

To model the execution of active operations, we use a queueing place called *processing*, configured to use the first-come first-served strategy, with the number of servers set to the number of processors available to the system. For each component whose operation is active, a dedicated color is defined, and the service time for that color in the *processing* place is set to reflect the operation duration.

In a similar manner, we use a queueing place called *waiting* to model the execution of passive operations. For each component whose operation is passive, a dedicated color is defined, and the service time for that color in the *waiting* place is set to reflect the waiting duration.

To model components that serialize execution, we use an ordinary place called *mutex*. We define a unique color for each serializing component operation and initially place one token of that color into the *mutex* place. The transition through which the tokens representing synchronized component operation arrive at the *processing* place additionaly removes the corresponding token from the *mutex* place ; analogously for returning the token.

The transitions around the *processing* and *waiting* places capture the flow of control through the individual components as defined by the architectural model. The transformation traverses the architecture model in a depth-first order and defines transitions that reflect the sequence of component operations that a thread serving a client request will perform. Following are the major rules for defining the transitions:

- Each component operation connects to the previous operation by removing the token from where the previous operation deposited it, the first such transition removes the token from the *request* place.
- Each active operation is modeled by a transition that connects to the previous operation and deposits a token of the color corresponding to this operation into the *processing* place.
- Each passive operation is modeled by a transition that connects to the previous operation and deposits a token of the color corresponding to this operation into the *waiting* place.

A component that realizes a branch needs two additional ordinary places, called *split* and *join*. One transition connects the previous operation to the *split* place with a unique color and mode for each child, all firing weights are set equally. Additional transitions to the *join* place connect the child component operations.

A component that realizes a loop needs one additional ordinary place, called *loop*, and two colors, called *looping* and *exiting*, used in the *loop* place to indicate whether the loop will execute the next iteration. Two transitions deposit a token in the *loop* place, one connects the previous operation, one returns the tokens of the finished child component operations. Both transitions leading to the *loop* place have two modes that deposit a token of either the *looping* or the *exiting* color. The number of times a token of the *looping* color is deposited into the *loop* place has a geometric distribution, the firing weights are calculated so that the mean value of the distribution is equal to the loop iteration count.

4.2   Providing Operation Durations

The performance models need to be populated with input values. There are two kinds of input values – values such as loop iteration counts or branch path probabilities, which are available as the arguments of the interconnecting modules, and are therefore obtained directly from the generated software system – and values such as operation durations, which have to be measured.

To measure the generated software system, we employ the advantage of having full control over code generation, and insert the necessary instrumentation directly into the wrapper classes of the individual modules. The executable system therefore reports its own performance, providing us with both the input values of the performance model and the overall performance figures to be compared with the outputs of the performance model.

The instrumentation includes the necessary precautions to avoid systematic measurement errors – the component initialization, buffer allocation, and warmup execution take place before the measurements are collected, reporting takes place after the measurements terminate. Operation durations are measured twice, once for each component executing in isolation and once for each component executing together with the rest of the generated software system. Both the wall clock times and the thread local times are recorded.

5   Validation Results

With both the generated executable systems and the corresponding performance models at hand, we carry out the validation by comparing the outputs of the performance models with the measurements of the executable systems. Before the results of the validation are presented, however, we point out that our goal is not to evaluate the prediction precision of a specific performance model, but rather to explore the potential of the proposed validation process. The result presentation is structured accordingly.

Our measurements were taken on a Dell PowerEdge 1955 system.[1] The executable systems used a thread pool of eight threads. The performance models were solved using the SimQPN solver [18].

Unless specified otherwise, we report and compare client service time, measured from the moment the client request is assigned a thread to the moment the client request is finished.

5.1   Precise Single Client Predictions

As an example of a context where precise performance predictions are expected, we have first generated 228 software systems and configured them for a single client workload, thus minimizing resource contention due to parallel execution. The results are shown on Fig. 2 as a ratio of predicted to measured service times plotted against the predicted processor utilization.

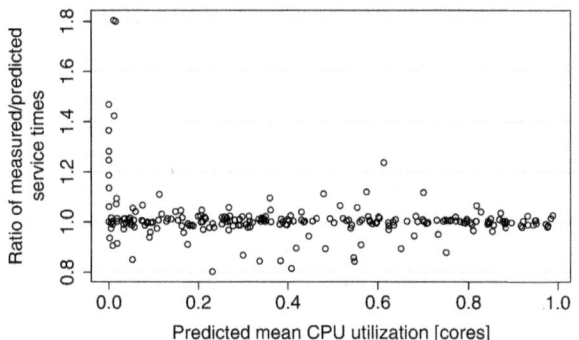

Fig. 2. Prediction precision with one client

We can see that the prediction error is relatively small, except for the errors at very low processor utilization, where the service time is very small compared to the client think time, and the error can therefore be attributed to the overhead of the execution infrastructure. In the following, we avoid this error by selecting

---

[1] Dual Quad-Core Intel Xeon processors (Type E5345, Family 6, Model 15, Stepping 11, Clock 2.33 GHz), 8 GB Hynix FBD DDR2-667 memory, Intel 5000P memory controller, Fedora Linux 8, gcc-4.1.2-33.x86_64, glibc-2.7-2.x86_64.

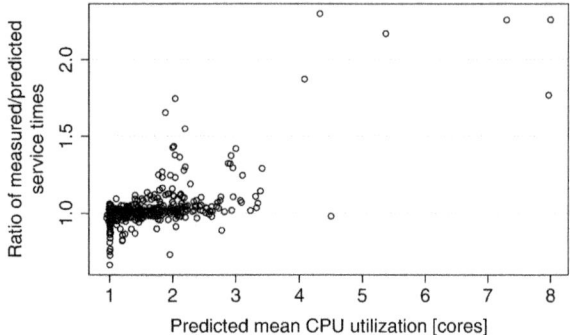

Fig. 3. Prediction precision with multiple clients

only those results with predicted processor utilization for a single client workload above 2 %. On Fig. 2, this would leave 204 remaining architectures, of which 8 % exhibits prediction error over 10 %.

5.2   Multiple Clients Prediction

We move on to a context with multiple clients to assess the prediction error when multiple concurrent threads are involved. For this experiment, we have used the same architectures as in Section 5.1, with the number of clients set to 50. To increase the coverage, additional 600 architectures were generated, with the number of clients drawn from a uniform distribution between 5 and 30, and then restricted to cases where the intensity of requests generated by the clients was predicted to result in mean thread utilization of at least four of the eight available threads. After the filtering described in Section 5.1, 645 architectures remained.

The results are shown on Fig. 3, where the ratio of predicted to measured service times is again plotted against the predicted processor utilization. We can see that the prediction accuracy is lower than in the single client scenario, and that the error tends to increase with growing processor utilization.

5.3   Operation Duration Distribution

Using the same architectures as in Section 5.2, we examine how the approximation of the individual operation durations with statistical distributions impacts the prediction precision. The SimQPN solver uses discrete event simulation and therefore easily supports multiple statistical distributions – for illustration, we compare the results from models that use normal distribution with the results from models that use exponential distribution. For normal distribution, the parameters were set to match the sample mean and variance of the isolated operation durations. For exponential distribution, the mean was set to match the sample mean of the isolated operation durations.

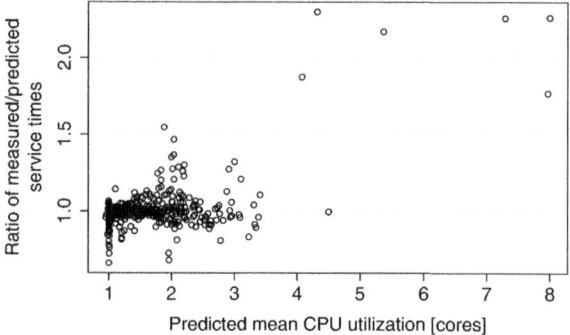

Fig. 4. Prediction precision with multiple clients, using exponential approximation of isolated durations for the service time prediction

The results that use exponential distribution are shown on Fig. 4. By comparing them with the results that use normal distribution on Fig. 3, we can observe that in many cases, the ratio of predicted to measured service times is lower for the exponential distribution than the normal distribution. This can occur both for the optimistic predictions, where the error is thus decreased, and for the accurate predictions, where the error turns them into pessimistic ones.

To explain this effect, we turn to Fig. 5, which shows the ratio between the results for the two distributions, plotted against the mean number of threads that are blocked due to the serializing modules. We can see that in the extreme cases (when there is no blocking, or when a serializing component dominates the execution so much that seven out of eight threads are blocked), both distributions yield the same prediction. When a mix between serialized and concurrent execution is present, using the exponential distribution can yield a significantly more pessimistic prediction than using the normal distribution.

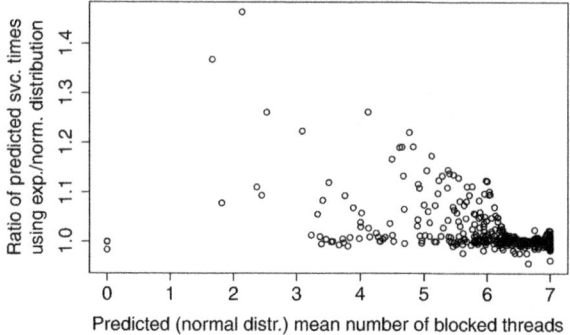

Fig. 5. Difference in prediction with exponential and normal approximation of isolated durations, depending on the mean number of threads blocked due to synchronization

A mix between serialized and concurrent execution is present when a serializing component is close to dominating the execution and threads are starting to block. Due to variations in operation durations, invocations can arrive at the serializing component either sooner or later than usual – but while the invocations that arrive sooner are more likely to be queued, the invocations that arrive later can more likely be processed immediately. In effect, this amplifies variations that lead to pessimistic predictions, because the performance gain due to invocations arriving sooner is masked by queueing, while the performance loss due to invocations arriving later is not. In our experiment, we have chosen distribution parameters that match the isolated operation durations, which resulted in the exponential distribution having higher variance than the normal distribution. The amplifying effect is thus more pronounced with the exponential distribution.

5.4 Resource Contention Impact

Many performance prediction methods involve performance model calibration, where the operation durations are adjusted to fit the model output onto the measurement results. When the operation durations are influenced by resource contention that is not captured in the performance model, such as contention for various memory caches, the calibration incorporates the resource contention effects into the adjusted operation durations. We isolate this effect by populating the performance models with the operation durations measured when the components were executing together, as opposed to the operation durations measured when each component was executing in isolation, used so far. Thread local times are used to obtain the new durations, thus excluding waiting on serialization locks, which is already modeled explicitly in the performance model.

The results where performance model is populated by isolated measurements were shown on Fig. 3, the results of model populated with measurements from combined execution are shown on Fig. 6. We observe that using measurements from the combined execution eliminates most of the cases where the predicted

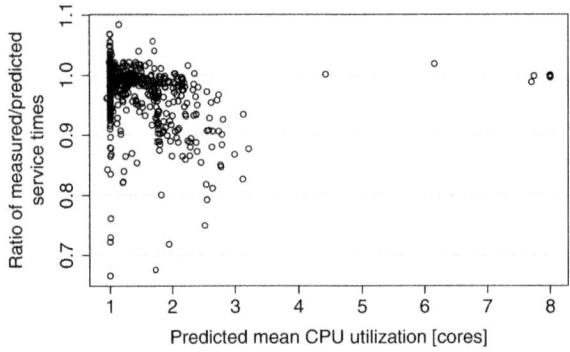

Fig. 6. Prediction precision with multiple clients, using measurements from combined execution to parameterize the performance model

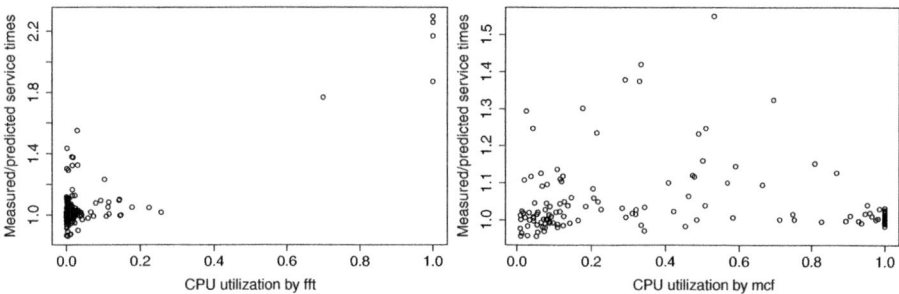

Fig. 7. Prediction error depending on the relative CPU utilization of a module

service times were lower than the actual measured times. Since resource contention depends on the particular choice of components, we also determine how the individual components contribute to this effect. To do this, we plot the prediction error with the operation durations measured in isolation against the relative processor utilization due to a particular component. To conserve space, we only show plots for the `fft` and `mcf` modules, on Fig. 7.

The `fft` module does not serialize execution and is known to be sensitive to cache sharing effects – as expected, the prediction error increases as the `fft` workload dominates the execution time. The `mcf` module serializes execution – when the `mcf` workload usurps the execution time, the serialization limits the competition for resources and the prediction precision is good. In contrast, when the `mcf` workload consumes around half of the execution time, the prediction error is significant for some systems, most likely when the components consuming the other half of the execution time compete with `mcf` for resources.

5.5 Workload Scalability Behavior

Often, the goal of performance prediction is not to predict throughput or response time with a fixed number of clients, but to determine scalability of the system depending on the number of clients. Our approach can be used to validate such performance prediction in a straightforward way, by running both the generated executable and prediction with varied number of clients.

Figure 8 shows an example of such validation for one of the systems which yielded imprecise prediction in Section 5.2. We can observe that the throughput predicted using normal distribution of operation durations is accurate up to six clients, then the error starts to increase. The prediction using exponential distribution of operation durations has a similar trend, but with relatively lower values, pessimistic up to nine clients and optimistic afterwards.

Finally, note that the validation results might be somewhat deceptive because the frequency of occurence of particular system properties might be different between generated and real systems.

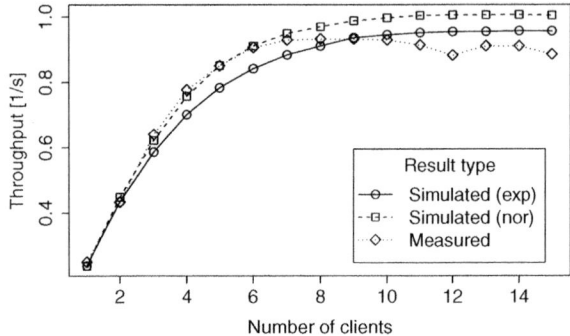

Fig. 8. Predicted and measured throughput depending on the number of clients

6   Related Work

Most works that focus on a particular performance prediction methodology strive to validate it on a case study that is reasonably large and undisputedly realistic. Recent examples of such validation include using the SPEC jAppServer 2004 workload running on WebSphere and Oracle [17], using an online stock trating simulation with two different architectures and two different platforms [21,20], using a generic performance model of an EJB server in various scenarios [32], or using a model of an air traffic control system [12]. While the cited validation examples are without doubt more realistic than our approach, they are also a case in point we are making: the expenses of manually constructing the performance models prevent validation on a large number of case studies.

The situation is somewhat alleviated by the existence of case studies designed to provide a playground for validation activities – besides application benchmarks such as SPEC jAppServer [25], Sun Pet Store [26], or RUBiS [22], we can list the CoCoME competition [23], which provides both the architecture model and the prototype implementation. Even those case studies, however, do not amount to the hundreds of systems which we have used here.

Besides validating a particular methodology, the question of prediction precision is tackled from many other angles, including workload characterization [29,16], or generation of either the executable system [31,13,33,6] or the performance model [15,19]. What these approaches have in common is that they still require manual intervention, either in creating models of application architecture, performance, and workload, or in test execution. We eliminate the need for manual intervention by automatically generating both the executable software system and the corresponding performance model, rather than constructing one from the other.

A pivotal issue of our approach is the degree of realism achieved in the generated software systems. One of the ideas we have investigated to guarantee some degree of realism was to use common software metrics to assess the generated software systems and to exclude those with unusual values.

Interestingly, the common software metrics have turned out to be unsuitable. Some, such as the development effort or the function points, are not suitable for generated software systems with no specific functionality. Others, such as McCabe's cyclomatic number or Halstead's program measures, are focused on human perception of complexity, and thus tell little about whether the generated software system is realistic from the performance modeling perspective. Finally, measures such as lines-of-code count have usual values ranging across several orders of magnitude and therefore do not allow to reasonably exclude the generated software systems.

7   Conclusion

We have presented an approach that makes it possible to validate performance predictions on a large number of executable systems and performance models without excessive manual intervention. We believe the approach has the potential to bring a new type of answers to the important questions of performance modeling, such as "what is the range of prediction precision ?" or "what design patterns or design artifacts make performance difficult to predict ?" ... As a proof of concept, we illustrate the process of providing answers to some of these questions for performance models based on the QPN formalism (here, however, we focus more on the potential of the approach than the specific answers for this particular class of performance models).

Our approach has been implemented in a prototype tool that solves a number of technical issues, especially issues related to safe reuse of code that was not designed to be strictly modular. The prototype tool is available for download at http://d3s.mff.cuni.cz/benchmark.

The presented approach hinges on our ability to generate reasonably realistic systems. Although there might be some alleviating circumstances – for example, when the validation fails on a model that subsequent manual inspection finds unrealistic, we simply exclude the model – the question of realism remains too important to be ignored. In this work, the elements contributing to the overall realism are for example the usage of a real server model and a real workload, but other elements, for example the data dependencies, remain to be tackled.

In the absence of a clearly objective measure or criteria of realism, it might turn out that only more extensive usage of the approach will provide enough practical knowledge to answer the issue of realism to satisfaction.

Acknowledgments

The authors gratefully acknowledge Samuel Kounev for his help with SimQPN and Jakub Melka and Michal Bečka for their work on the random software generator. This paper was partially supported by the Q-ImPrESS research project by the European Union under the ICT priority of the 7th Research Framework Programme, by the Czech Science Foundation grant 201/09/H057, and by the grant SVV-2010-261312.

References

1. Avritzer, A., Weyuker, E.J.: The Automatic Generation of Load Test Suites and the Assessment of the Resulting Software. IEEE Trans. Software Eng. 21(9) (1995)
2. Babka, V., Bulej, L., Decky, M., Kraft, J., Libic, P., Marek, L., Seceleanu, C., Tuma, P.: Resource Usage Modeling, Q-ImPrESS Project Deliverable D3.3 (2008), http://www.q-impress.eu/
3. Balsamo, S., Di Marco, A., Inverardi, P., Simeoni, M.: Model-Based Performance Prediction in Software Development: A Survey. IEEE Trans. Software Eng. 30(5) (2004)
4. Bause, F.: Queueing Petri Nets - A Formalism for the Combined Qualitative and Quantitative Analysis of Systems. In: Proc. 5th Intl. W. on Petri Nets and Performance Models. IEEE CS, Los Alamitos (1993)
5. Becker, S., Bulej, L., Bures, T., Hnetynka, P., Kapova, L., Kofron, J., Koziolek, H., Kraft, J., Mirandola, R., Stammel, J., Tamburrelli, G., Trifu, M.: Service Architecture Meta Model, Q-ImPrESS Deliverable D2.1 (2008), http://www.q-impress.eu/
6. Becker, S., Dencker, T., Happe, J.: Model-driven generation of performance prototypes. In: Kounev, S., Gorton, I., Sachs, K. (eds.) SIPEW 2008. LNCS, vol. 5119, pp. 79–98. Springer, Heidelberg (2008)
7. Becker, S., Koziolek, H., Reussner, R.: The Palladio Component Model for Model-driven Performance Prediction. J. Syst. Softw. 82(1) (2009)
8. Bertolino, A.: Software Testing Research: Achievements, Challenges, Dreams. In: Proc. Intl. Conf. on Software Engineering, ICSE 2007, W. on the Future of Software Engineering, FOSE 2007. IEEE CS, Los Alamitos (2007)
9. Budinsky, F., Brodsky, S.A., Merks, E.: Eclipse Modeling Framework. Pearson Education, London (2003)
10. Cascaval, C., DeRose, L., Padua, D.A., Reed, D.A.: Compile-Time Based Performance Prediction. In: Carter, L., Ferrante, J. (eds.) LCPC 1999. LNCS, vol. 1863, p. 365. Springer, Heidelberg (2000)
11. Franks, G., Maly, P., Woodside, M., Petriu, D.C., Hubbard, A.: Layered Queueing Network Solver and Simulator User Manual (2005), http://www.sce.carleton.ca/rads/lqns/
12. Franks, G., Al-Omari, T., Woodside, M., Das, O., Derisavi, S.: Enhanced Modeling and Solution of Layered Queueing Networks. IEEE Trans. Software Eng. 35(2) (2009)
13. Grundy, J.C., Cai, Y., Liu, A.: Generation of Distributed System Test-Beds from High-Level Software Architecture Descriptions. In: Proc. 16th IEEE Intl. Conf. on Automated Software Engineering, ASE 2001. IEEE CS, Los Alamitos (2001)
14. Henning, J.L.: SPEC CPU2006 Benchmark Descriptions. SIGARCH Comput. Archit. News 34(4) (2006)
15. Hrischuk, C.E., Rolia, J.A., Woodside, C.M.: Automatic Generation of a Software Performance Model Using an Object-Oriented Prototype. In: Proc. 3rd Intl. W. on Modeling, Analysis, and Simulation On Computer and Telecommunication Systems, MASCOTS 1995. IEEE CS, Los Alamitos (1995)
16. Joshi, A., Eeckhout, L., Bell Jr., R.H., John, L.K.: Distilling the Essence of Proprietary Workloads Into Miniature Benchmarks. ACM Trans. Archit. Code Optim. 5(2) (2008)
17. Kounev, S.: Performance Modeling and Evaluation of Distributed Component-Based Systems Using Queueing Petri Nets. IEEE Trans. Software Eng. 32(7) (2006)

18. Kounev, S., Buchmann, A.: SimQPN: A Tool and Methodology for Analyzing Queueing Petri Net Models by Means of Simulation. Perform. Eval. 63(4) (2006)
19. Koziolek, H., Happe, J., Becker, S.: Parameter dependent performance specifications of software components. In: Hofmeister, C., Crnković, I., Reussner, R. (eds.) QoSA 2006. LNCS, vol. 4214, pp. 163–179. Springer, Heidelberg (2006)
20. Liu, Y., Fekete, A., Gorton, I.: Design-Level Performance Prediction of Component-Based Applications. IEEE Trans. Software Eng. 31(11) (2005)
21. Liu, Y., Gorton, I.: Accuracy of Performance Prediction for EJB Applications: A Statistical Analysis. In: Gschwind, T., Mascolo, C. (eds.) SEM 2004. LNCS, vol. 3437, pp. 185–198. Springer, Heidelberg (2005)
22. OW2 Consortium: RUBiS: Rice University Bidding System, http://rubis.ow2.org/
23. Rausch, A., Reussner, R., Mirandola, R., Plasil, F. (eds.): The Common Component Modeling Example: Comparing Software Component Models. Springer, Heidelberg (2008)
24. Standard Performance Evaluation Corporation: SPEC CPU2006 Benchmark, http://www.spec.org/cpu2006/
25. Standard Performance Evaluation Corporation: SPECjAppServer2004 Benchmark, http://www.spec.org/jAppServer2004/
26. Sun Microsystems, Inc.: Java Pet Store Demo, http://blueprints.dev.java.net/petstore/index.html
27. The Q-ImPrESS Project Consortium: Quality Impact Prediction for Evolving Service-oriented Software, http://www.q-impress.eu/
28. Transaction Processing Performance Council: TPC Benchmarks, http://www.tpc.org/information/benchmarks.asp
29. Weyuker, E.J., Vokolos, F.I.: Experience with Performance Testing of Software Systems: Issues, an Approach, and Case Study. IEEE Trans. Software Eng. 26(12) (2000)
30. Woodside, C.M., Neron, E., Ho, E.D.S., Mondoux, B.: An "Active Server" Model for the Performance of Parallel Programs Written Using Rendezvous. J. Syst. Softw. 6(1-2) (1986)
31. Woodside, C.M., Schramm, C.: Scalability and Performance Experiments Using Synthetic Distributed Server Systems. Distributed Systems Engineering 3(1) (1996)
32. Xu, J., Oufimtsev, A., Woodside, M., Murphy, L.: Performance Modeling and Prediction of Enterprise JavaBeans with Layered Queuing Network Templates. SIGSOFT Softw. Eng. Notes 31(2) (2006)
33. Zhu, L., Gorton, I., Liu, Y., Bui, N.B.: Model Driven Benchmark Generation for Web Services. In: Proc. 2006 Intl. W. on Service-oriented Software Engineering, SOSE 2006. ACM, New York (2006)

Statistical Inference of Software Performance Models for Parametric Performance Completions

Jens Happe[1,*], Dennis Westermann[1], Kai Sachs[2], Lucia Kapová[3]

[1] SAP Research, CEC Karlsruhe, Germany
{jens.happe,dennis.westermann}@sap.com
[2] TU Darmstadt, Germany
sachs@dvs.tu-darmstadt.de
[3] Karlsruhe Institute of Technology (KIT), Germany
kapova@ipd.uka.de

Abstract. Software performance engineering (SPE) enables software architects to ensure high performance standards for their applications. However, applying SPE in practice is still challenging. Most enterprise applications include a large software basis, such as middleware and legacy systems. In many cases, the software basis is the determining factor of the system's overall timing behavior, throughput, and resource utilization. To capture these influences on the overall system's performance, established performance prediction methods (model-based and analytical) rely on models that describe the performance-relevant aspects of the system under study. Creating such models requires detailed knowledge on the system's structure and behavior that, in most cases, is not available. In this paper, we abstract from the internal structure of the system under study. We focus on message-oriented middleware (MOM) and analyze the dependency between the MOM's usage and its performance. We use statistical inference to conclude these dependencies from observations. For ActiveMQ 5.3, the resulting functions predict the performance with a relative mean square error 0.1.

1 Introduction

With the rising complexity of today's software systems, methods and tools to achieve and maintain high performance standards become more and more important. Software performance engineering [27] and model-based performance prediction (surveyed in [3] and [18]) provide software architects and developers with tools and methods to systematically estimate the expected performance of a software system based on its architectural specification. Performance engineering of today's enterprise applications entails a high degree of complexity. Enterprise application systems are very large and are rarely developed from scratch. In most cases, a sound base of software exists on which developers build their new applications. Such software bases include middleware platforms, third party components (or services), and legacy software. Up to date performance models for these systems are not available in most cases. Moreover, knowledge about the structure and performance of these systems is limited. However, the software basis of

---

* This work is supported by the European Community's Seventh Framework Programme (FP7/2001-2013) under grant agreement no.216556.

G.T. Heinemann, J. Kofron, and F. Plasil (Eds.): QoSA 2010, LNCS 6093, pp. 20–35, 2010.

an application can have a major influence on its overall performance and thus has to be considered in performance predictions. Most existing approaches use established prediction models [3,18] to estimate the performance of already existing complex software systems. Their main focus lies on the questions: i) "How can we automatically derive or extract the models we need?" and ii) "How can we estimate the resource demands / quantitative data needed for our models?" Approaches addressing the first question analyze call traces [7] or use static code analyses [20] to derive models of software systems. Approaches addressing the second question (e.g. [23,19]) use benchmarking and monitoring of the system to extract model parameters. In order to apply these approaches, software architects have to instrument large parts of the system and conduct precise measurements. Furthermore, they are bound to the assumptions of the prediction model used. For example, if a network connection is modeled with FCFS scheduling, it won't capture the effect of collisions on the network. Another drawback of these approaches is that they do not scale with respect to the increasing size and complexity of today's software systems. Size and complexity can become inhibiting factors for quality analyses. The process of creating performance prediction models for those systems requires heavy effort and can become too costly and error-prone. For the same reason, many developers do not trust or understand performance models, even if such models are available. In case of legacy systems and third party software, the required knowledge to model the systems may even not be available at all. In such scenarios, re-engineering approaches (e.g. [20]) can help. However, re-engineering often fails due to the large and heterogeneous technology stack in complex application systems.

In our approach, we handle the complexity of large scale enterprise application systems by creating goal-oriented abstractions of those parts that cannot be modeled or only with high effort. For this purpose, we apply automated systematic measurements to capture the dependencies between the system's usage (workload and input parameters) and performance (timing behavior, throughput, and resource utilization). To analyze the measured data we use statistical inference, such as Bayesian networks or multivariate adaptive regression splines (MARS) [10]. The analysis yields an abstract performance model of the system under study. The abstractions are similar to flow equivalent servers used in queueing theory where a network of servers is replaced by a single server with workload-dependent service rate. The resulting models can be integrated in the Palladio Component Model (PCM) [6], a model-driven performance prediction approach. For this purpose, we combine the statistical models with parametric performance completions introduced in our previous work [11]. The combination of statistical models and model-based prediction approaches allows to predict the effect of complex middleware components, 3rd party software, and legacy systems on response time, throughput, and resource utilization of the whole software system.

In this paper, we focus on message-oriented middleware platforms which are increasingly used in enterprise and commercial domains. We evaluated our approach using the SPECjms2007 Benchmark for message-oriented systems. The benchmark resembles a supply chain management system for supermarket stores. In our case study, we used MARS and genetic optimization to estimate the influence of arrival rates and message sizes on the performance of a message-oriented middleware (MOM). The comparison of measurements and predictions yielded a relative mean square error of less than 0.1.

The contributions of this paper are i) statistical inference of software performance models, ii) their usage in combination with model-driven performance prediction methods, and iii) the application of our approach to a supply chain management scenario including a validation of predictions and measurements.

The paper is structured as follows. Section 2 gives an overview on our approach. Work related with performance prediction of message-oriented middleware and performance analysis using statistical inferencing is summarized in Section 3. In Section 4, we demonstrate how the performance of message-oriented middleware can be captured using a combination of systematic benchmarking and statistical inference. We discuss our results in Section 5. Finally, Section 6 concludes the paper.

2   Overview

In this section we describe our approach focusing on performance analyses of message-oriented middleware (MOM) platforms. The influence of general configurations and patterns on a MOM's performance (delivery time, throughput, and resource utilization) are well understood [11,25]. However, the exact quantification of these influences is still cumbersome and has to be done for each implementation and each execution environment. In the case of MOM, the implementation is known to have a large impact on the overall performance [25]. Some implementations scale better with a larger number of processors or make better use of the operating system's I/O features. Capturing such low-level details in a generic performance model is impossible. Even if accurate performance models of a MOM are available, they have to be kept up to date and adjusted for new execution environments. Slight changes in the configuration can already affect the overall performance [11,25,16]. To consider such effects in a priori predictions, software architects need an approach to create accurate performance models for their middleware platform, even if the actual implementation is unknown. The performance models have to be parameterized and thus reflect the influence of the system's usage (input parameters, system state, arrival rate) on timing behavior, throughput, and resource utilization.

In our approach, we use systematic measurements and statistical inference to capture the performance of a MOM platform. We abstract from internals of the MOM implementation and identify functional dependencies between input parameters (message size, style of communication) and the observed performance. The resulting models are woven into the software architectural model. The combination of model-driven approaches and measurement-based model inference allows software architects to evaluate the effect of different middleware platforms on the performance of the overall system. Figure 1 illustrates the overall process of combining parametric performance completions with statistical model inference.

The process in Figure 1 is a specialization of the performance completion instantiation by the software architect [11, Figure 6]. We assume that the completion has already been designed and performance-relevant parameters are known. In the following, we describe the steps of the process in more detail.

Benchmarking (Data Collection). In the first step, we measure the influence of performance-relevant parameters for the middleware platform in its target execution

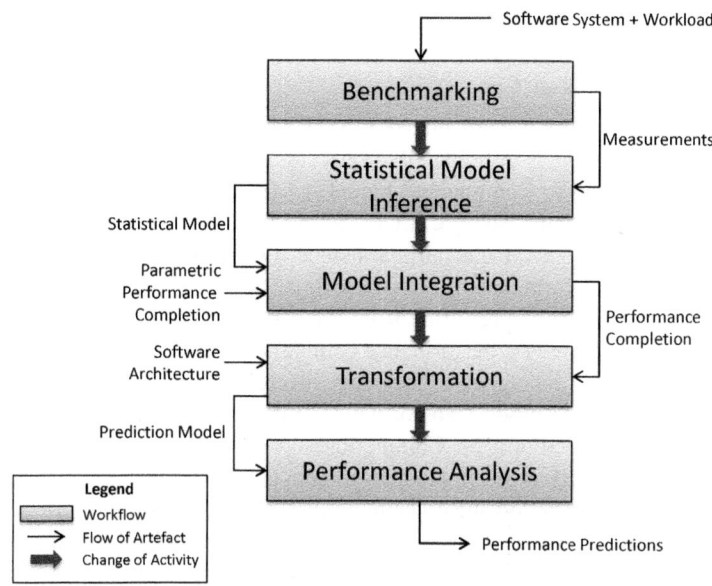

Fig. 1. Statistical Inference of Software Performance Models for Parametric Performance Completions

environment. A standard industry benchmark (cf. Section 4.3) quantifies the delivery time of messages, the MOM's throughput, and the utilization of resources. To capture the influence of parameters, the benchmark is executed several times with different configurations (cf. Section 4.1). In our experiments, we focus on the influence of arrival rates, messages sizes, and persistence of messages (messages are stored on hard disk until they are delivered).

Model Inference (Data Aggregation). The collected data is used to infer (parameters of) a prediction model. In Section 4.3, we use statistical inference techniques [13], more specifically Multivariate Adaptive Regression Splines (MARS) [10] and genetic optimization, to derive the influence of a MOM's usage on its performance.

Other inference techniques, such as [21,23,19], can be used to estimate parameters of queueing networks if the (major) resources and the structure of the system under study are known. However, these approaches are bound to the assumptions of the underlying queueing model, such as FCFS or PS scheduling, which may not hold in reality. Furthermore, they cannot (directly) predict the effect of input parameters (such as message size) on performance.

Statistical inference of performance metrics does not require specific knowledge on the internal structure of the system under study. However, statistical inference can require assumptions on the kind of functional dependency of input (independent) and output (dependent) variables. The inference approaches mainly differ in their degree of model assumptions. For example, linear regression makes rather strong assumptions on the model underlying the observations (they are linear) while the nearest neighbor estimator makes no assumptions at all. Most other statistical estimators lie between both extremes. Methods with stronger assumptions, in general, need less data to provide reliable estimates, if the assumptions are correct. Methods with less assumptions are more flexible, but require more data.

Model Integration. The models inferred in the previous step are integrated into software performance models to predict their effect on the overall performance of the system. We use the Palladio Component Model (PCM) [6] in combination with parametric performance completions [11] to evaluate the performance of the system under study. The PCM is well suited for our purposes since it captures the effect of input parameters on software performance. Stochastic expressions of the PCM can be used to directly include the functions resulting from the statistical analysis into the middleware components of a parametric performance completion. Performance completions allow software architects to annotate a software architectural model. The annotated elements are refined by model-to-model transformations that inject low-level performance influences into the architecture [15]. Completions consist of an architecture-specific part that is newly generated for each annotation (adapter components) and an architecture-independent part that models the consumption of resources (middleware components). Completions are parametric with respect to resource demands of the middleware. The demands have to be determined for each middleware implementation and for each execution environment.

Transformation. Finally, model-to-model transformations integrate the completion into architectural models [15]. The performance of the overall system can be determined using analytical models (such as queueing networks or stochastic Petri nets) or simulations.

In this paper, we focus on the first two steps (Benchmarking and Statistical Model Inference). A description of the remaining steps can be found in [11,15].

3   Related Work

Current software performance engineering approaches can be divided in (i) early-cycle predictive model-based approaches (surveyed in [3] and [18]), (ii) late-cycle measurement-based approaches (e.g. [1,2,4]), and (iii) combinations of measurement-based and model-based approaches (e.g. [8,19] [29]). Late-cycle measurement-based approaches as well as the approaches that combine model-based and measurement-based performance engineering mainly rely on statistical inferencing techniques to derive performance predictions based on measurement data.

Zheng et al. [30] apply Kalman Filter estimators to track parameters that cannot be measured directly. To estimate the hidden parameters, they use the difference between measured and predicted performance as well as knowledge about the dynamics of the performance model. In [23] and [19], statistical inferencing is used for estimating service demands of parameterized performance models. Pacifici et al. [23] analyze multiple kinds of web traffic using CPU utilization and throughput measurements. They formulate and solve the problem using linear regressions. In [19], Kraft et al. apply a linear regression method and the maximum likelihood technique for estimating the service demands of requests. The considered system is an ERP application of SAP Business Suite with a workload of sales and distribution operations.

Kumar et al. [21] and Sharma et al. [26] additionally take workload characteristics into account. In [21], the authors derive a mathematical function that represents service times and CPU overheads as functions of the total arriving workload. Thereby, the functional representation differs depending on the nature of the system under test. The work focuses on transaction-based, distributed software systems. Sharma et al. [26] use statistical inferencing to identify workload categories in internet services. Using coarse grained measurements of system resources (e.g. total CPU usage, overall request rate), their method can infer various characteristics of the workload (e.g. the number of different request categories and the resource demand of each category). They apply a machine learning technique called independent component analysis (ICA) to solve the underlying blind source separation problem. The feasibility of their approach is validated using an e-commerce benchmark application.

Other researchers focus on measurement-based and/or analytical performance models for middleware platforms. Liu et al. [22] build a queuing network model whose input values are computed based on measurements. The goal of the queuing network model is to derive performance metrics (e.g. response time and throughput) for J2EE applications. The approach applied by Denaro et al. [9] completely relies on measurements. The authors estimate the performance of a software system by measurements of application specific test cases. However, both approaches simplify the behavior of an application, and thus, neglect its influence on performance. Recently, Kounev and Sachs [17] surveyed techniques for benchmarking and performance modeling of event-based systems. They reviewed several techniques for (i) modeling message-oriented middleware systems and (ii) predicting their performance under load considering both analytical and simulation-based approaches.

4   Capturing the Performance of Message-Oriented Middleware with Statistical Inference

In the following, we demonstrate how the performance of Message-oriented Middleware (MOM) can be captured using statistical inference. For this purpose, we first introduce our method for gathering the required performance data (Section 4.1) as well as the tools and techniques to derive statistical models from measurements (Section 4.2). The application of these methods to message-oriented systems follows in Section 4.3. The resulting models reflect the influence of message size, arrival rate, and configurations on delivery times, resource utilization, and throughput. Finally, we compare our predictions to measurements that are not part of the training set (Section 4.4).

4.1   Measurement Method

In order to apply statistical inferencing to the performance of MOM, we first need to measure the influence of different parameters (e.g., message size and persistence) on its performance. The strategy of sampling the effect of different parameter combinations on performance is critical, since it has to be detailed enough to achieve accurate predictions but must also be kept feasible at the same time (i.e., measurements must not last too long).

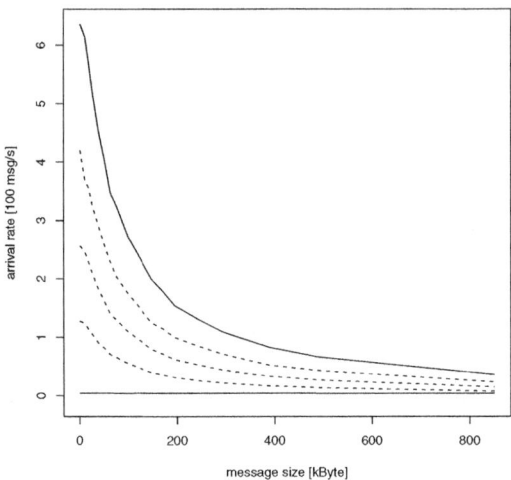

Fig. 2. Measurement strategy

For this reason, we separate the measurements into three phases. First, we determine the maximal throughput of the system for each message size $m \in M$. While a high throughput can be achieved for small messages, the throughput decreases significantly for larger messages. In Figure 2, the upper solid line illustrates the dependency of the maximal throughput and the size of a message. In queuing theory, the throughput (X) can be computed from the resource utilization (U) and the service demand (D) by $X = U/D$. If we assume that the resource is fully utilized ($U = 1$), we can compute the maximal throughput $X_{max} = 1/D$. In a flow balanced system, the arrival rate (λ) is equal to the throughput of the system. Thus, the maximal arrival rate which can be handled by the system is $\lambda_{max} = X_{max}$. To determine the maximal arrival rate, we increase the load of the system until $U \approx 1$ and still $\lambda \approx X$, i.e., the system can still handle all incoming messages. We focus our measurements on arrival rates between 0 and λ_{max},i.e, $0 < \lambda \leq \lambda_{max}$. The performance measurements for λ_{max} represent the worst case performance of the system if it is still able to process all messages.

In the second phase, we measure the influence of individual parameters without resource contention. For example, we measure the effect of different message sizes on the delivery time when only one message is processed at a time. These measurements provide the baseline of our curve. They represent the best achievable performance for the system under study. In Figure 2, the solid line at the bottom depicts the baseline for a MOM with persistent message delivery (i.e., messages are stored on hard disk until they are delivered).

In the final phase, we sample the performance of the system under study between the best case and the worst case performance. For this purpose, we separate the arrival rate between the best and the worst case performance into N equidistant steps. For each message size $v \in V$, we measure the performance of the MOM for arrival rates of $\lambda_i = \lambda_{max} * i/N$ for $i \in \{1, \ldots, N-1\}$. The dashed lines in Figure 2 show the relative measurements for $N = 4$ steps.

4.2   Statistical Model Inference

Statistical inferencing is the process of drawing conclusions by applying statistics to observations or hypotheses based on quantitative data. The goal is to determine the relationship between input and output parameters observed at some system (sometimes also called independent and dependent variables). In this paper, we use *Multivariate Adaptive Regression Splines* (MARS) and genetic optimization to estimate the dependency between different system characteristics (configuration and usage) and performance metrics of interest.

Multivariate Adaptive Regression Splines (MARS). MARS [10] is a statistical method for flexible regression modeling of multidimensional data which has already been successfully employed in software performance prediction [8]. MARS is a non-parametric regression technique which requires no prior assumption as to the form of the data. The input data may be contaminated with noise or the system under study may be responding to additional hidden inputs that are neither measured or controlled. The goal is to obtain a useful approximation to each function using a set of training data. Therefore, the method fits functions creating rectangular patches where each patch is a product of linear functions (one in each dimension). MARS builds models of the form $f(x) = \sum_{i=1}^{k} c_i B_i(x)$, the model is a weighted sum of basis functions $B_i(x)$, where each c_i is a constant coefficient [10]. MARS uses expansions in piecewise linear basis functions of the form $[x - t]_+$ and $[t - x]_+$. The $+$ means positive part, so that

$$[x - t]_+ = \begin{cases} x - t \text{ , if } x > t \\ 0 \text{ , otherwise} \end{cases} \quad \text{and} \quad [t - x]_+ = \begin{cases} t - x \text{ , if } x < t \\ 0 \text{ , otherwise} \end{cases}$$

The model-building strategy is similar to stepwise linear regression, except that the basis functions are used instead of the original inputs. An independent variable translates into a series of linear segments joint together at points called knots [8]. Each segment uses a piecewise linear basis function which is constructed around a knot at the value t. The strength of MARS is that it selects the knot locations dynamically in order to optimize the goodness of fit. The coefficients c_i are estimated by minimizing the residual sum-of-squares using standard linear regression. The residual sum of squares is given by $RSS = \sum_{i=1}^{N} (\widehat{y_i} - \overline{y})^2$, where $\overline{y} = \frac{1}{N} \sum \widehat{y_i}$, where N is the number of cases in the data set and $\widehat{y_i}$ is the predicted value.

Genetic Optimization (GO). If the functional dependency between multiple parameters is known, i.e., a valid hypothesis exists, then either non-linear regression or GO can be used to fit the function against measured data. Non-linear regressions allow various types of functional relationships (such as exponential, logarithmic, or Gaussian functions). Non-linear regression problems are solved by a series of iterative approximations. Based on an initial estimate of the value of each parameter, the non-linear regression method adjusts these values iteratively to improve the fit of the curve to the data. To determine the best-fitting parameters numerical optimization algorithms (such as Gauss-Newton or Levenberg-Marquardt) can be applied.

Another way of identifying a good-fitting curve for a non-linear problem is the use of GOs. In [14] the author describes the basic principals of GOs. GOs simulate processes of biological organisms that are essential to evolution. They combine two techniques at the same time in an optimal way: (i) exploration which is used to investigate new areas in the search space, and (ii) exploitation which uses knowledge found at points previously visited to help finding better points [5]. Compared to the non-linear regression techniques GO is more robust, but requires more time. In our case, the basis of the GO is an error function which has to be minimized. Errors represent the difference between the observations and the model's predictions. It must be taken into account that the definition of the error metric can influence the accuracy of fitting. For example, if error is expressed as absolute measure, the approximation is inaccurate for small values at large scattering. If error is expressed as relative measure, small values are approximated better while large values can show stronger deviations.

We use mean squared error (MSE) and relative mean squared error (RMSE) to measure the difference between predicted and observed value. The MSE is given by $MSE = \frac{1}{N} \sum_{i=1}^{N} (\widehat{y_i} - y_i)^2$ and the RMSE is given by $RMSE = \frac{1}{N} \sum_{i=1}^{N} (\frac{\widehat{y_i} - y_i}{y_i})^2$. In both cases N is the number of cases in the data set, y is defined as observed value, $\widehat{y_i}$ as the predicted value.

In the following section, we apply the methods for statistical model inference presented here to derive a performance model for message-oriented systems.

4.3   Analyzing Message-Oriented Systems

In message-oriented systems, components communicate by exchanging messages using a message-oriented middleware. Such a loose coupling of communicating parties has several important advantages: i) message producers and consumers do not need to be aware of each other, ii) they do not need to be active at the same time to exchange information, iii) they are not blocked when sending or receiving messages. Most MOM platforms offer two types of communication patterns: (a) Point-to-Point (P2P), where each message is consumed by exactly one message receiver and (b) Publish/Subscribe, where each message can be received by multiple receivers [28]. A discussion of messaging patterns influencing the software performance is provided in [11].

MOM Benchmarks: SPECjms2007 and jms2009-PS. *SPECjms2007* is the first industry standard benchmark for Java Message Services (JMS). It was developed by the Standard Performance Evaluation Corporation (SPEC) under the leadership of TU Darmstadt. The underlying application scenario models a supermarket's supply chain where RFID technology is used to track the flow of goods between different parties. Seven interactions such as order management are modeled in detail to stress different aspects of MOM performance.

jms2009-PS [24] is built on top of the SPECjms2007 framework and SPECjms2007 workload [25] using pub/sub communication for most interactions. Both benchmarks are focused on the influence of the MOM's implementation and configuration. The benchmarks minimize the impact of other components and services that are typically used in the chosen application scenario. For example, the database used to store business data and manage the application state could easily become the limiting factor and thus is not represented in the benchmark. This design allows us to focus our evaluation on the influences of MOM without disturbances.

Benchmark Application. For our experiments, we selected *Interaction 4: Supermarket (SM) Inventory Management*. This interaction exercises P2P messaging inside the SMs. The interaction is triggered when goods leave the warehouse of a SM (e.g., to refill a shelf). Goods are registered by RFID readers and the local warehouse application is notified so that inventory can be updated. The size of such messages varies from very small (a single good) to very large (pallets). Therefore they can be used to test JMS performance for all message sizes.

Experimental Environment. We statistically inferred a performance model for Active MQ 5.3 running on a IBM x3850 Server with a 2-Core Intel Xeon 3.5 GHz, a RAID 10 with 6 SAS hard drives and 16 GByte of RAM running under Debian Linux 2.6.26. During the measurements, all satellites where hosted on a Windows Server 2003 System with 16 GByte of RAM and two 4-Core Intel Xeon 2.33 GHz. The utilization of the host for the satellites never exceeded 20%. The benchmark was executed 288 times. Each run lasted about 6 minutes leading to a total measurement time of approximately 31 hours. During each run, the inventory management send between 1800 and 216000 messages to the supermarket server. The actual number depends on the configured arrival rate of messages. For each run, we measured the utilization of CPUs and hard disk, network traffic and throughput as well as the delivery time of messages. In the following, we analyze the measurements collected by the jms2009-PS benchmark using the statistical inferencing techniques presented in Section 4.2.

Analysis. We determine the functional dependency of performance metrics on the MOM's usage applying MARS and genetic optimization. For the analyses, the actual arrival rate and message size can be computed based on the benchmark's configuration. In case of interaction 4 "'Supermarket Inventory Management'", the size of a message v (in kilobyte) is given by the linear equation $v = m_1 * x + b$ [25], where $m_1 = 0.0970$ and $b = 0.5137$. Furthermore, the total arrival rate of messages ξ_4 per second is a multiple of the arrival rate for each supermarket (λ_4): $\xi_4 = \lambda_4 * |\Psi_{SM}|$, where $\Psi_{SM} = \{SM_1, SM_2, \ldots, SM_{|\Psi_{SM}|}\}$ is the set of all supermarkets. Since we only consider flow-balanced scenarios, the number of messages sent and received are equal. Furthermore, no other messages are sent through the channels of interaction 4.

In the first measurement phase, we determine the maximal throughput for persistent and non-persistent message delivery. The performance metrics collected in this setting represent the worst case performance of the MOM. The message size lies between 1 and 850 kBytes while the maximal throughput ranges from 6 to 900 messages per second. The maximal throughput decreases exponentially with an increasing message size for persistent and non-persistent delivery.

In the second phase, we analyze the influence of the message size without contention. The total arrival rate is set to 0.5 messages per second for this purpose. The results represent the best achievable performance for each message size. The mean delivery time of the messages ranges from less than a millisecond to approx. 85 ms. Here, we observed an almost linear growth of delivery time for increasing message sizes.

In the final phase, we analyze the intermediate performance between the best case and worst case observed. Figure 3 shows the utilization of the MOM's host machine as a function of message size and arrival rate. Figure 3(a) suggests that, for a fixed message size, the dependency is almost linear. However, the gradient increases significantly for

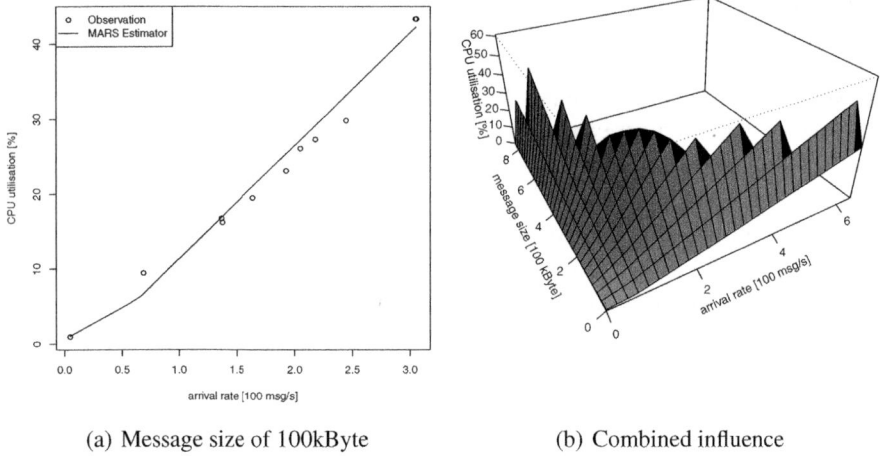

(a) Message size of 100kByte   (b) Combined influence

Fig. 3. CPU utilization as a function of message size and arrival rate

larger messages (cf. Figure 3(b)). In our measurements, the CPU utilization never exceeded 50%. This observation is unexpected, especially for large messages. However, the physical resources were not the limiting factor in our experiments, but in the implementation of the MOM. Active MQ 5.3 uses only a single thread to process its I/O. This thread can become the bottleneck in multiprocessing environments. Statistically inferred models can cover this effect without knowledge about the internal cause.

So far, MARS provided good approximations of the measurements. However, it fails to accurately reflect the effect of arrival rates and messages sizes on delivery times. Figure 4(a) shows the averages of the measured delivery time (circles) compared to predictions of MARS (dashed line). In this case, regression splines do not capture the

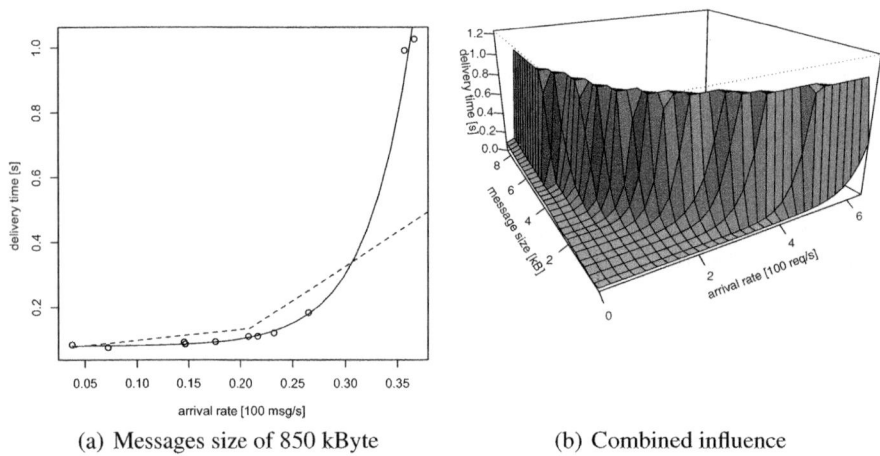

(a) Messages size of 850 kByte   (b) Combined influence

Fig. 4. Functional dependency of delivery times on arrival rate and message size

steep increase in delivery times for an arrival rate of 35 msg/s (with messages of 850 kByte). Exponential distributions, which are fitted to the measurements using genetic optimization (cf. Section 4.2), provide much better results. In Figure 4(a), the solid line depicts an exponential function fitted to the delivery time of messages with a size of 850 kByte. For an arrival λ of messages with 850 kByte, the exponential function

$$f_{850}^{dt}(\lambda) = \exp(24.692 * (\lambda - 0.412)) + 0.079$$

accurately reflects the changes of the delivery time in dependence of the arrival rate of messages. The relative mean squared error (RMSE) of measurements and predictions is 0.061 compared to 3.47 for MARS. Figure 4(b) illustrates the result of the genetic optimization for different message sizes and different arrival rates. For each message size the exponential function is determined separately. The resulting terms are combined by linear interpolation. Let v be the size of the message whose delivery time is to be determined and m and n message sizes with $n \leq v < m$ that are close to v and for which $f_n^{dt}(\lambda)$ and $f_m^{dt}(\lambda)$ are known, then:

$$f^{dt}(v, \lambda) = f_n^{dt}(\lambda) + \frac{f_m^{dt}(\lambda) - f_n^{dt}(\lambda)}{m - n} (v - n).$$

This function reduces the sum of the relative mean squared error (RMSE) from 341.4 (MARS) to 10.7. The additional knowledge about the type of the function significantly decreases the error of our statistical estimator. However, at this point, it is still unclear whether linear interpolation is appropriate to estimate the delivery time for message sizes whose exponential functions have not been approximated explicitly. In the following section, we address this question by comparing measurements for message sizes and arrival rates that are not part of the training set to the predictions of the statistical models.

4.4   Evaluation of the Statistical Models

In order to validate the prediction model for MOM developed in Section 4.3, we compare the predicted delivery times and resource utilization to observations that are not part of the training set. The results indicate whether the approach introduced in the paper yields performance models with the desired prediction accuracy. More specifically, we address the following questions: i) "Is the training set appropriate for statistical inferencing?" and ii) "Are the chosen statistical methods for model inference sufficient to accurately reflect the systems performance?". To answer both questions, we set up a series of experiments where the arrival rate λ is 200 messages per second and the message size is varied between 0.6 kByte and 165.4 kByte in steps of 9.7 kByte. The experiments have been repeated three times.

   Figure 5 illustrates the results of the experiments as well as the corresponding predictions for delivery time (Figure 5(a)) and resource utilizations (Figure 5(b)–5(d)). In general, predictions and observations largely overlap. The interpolation used to estimate the delivery time captures the influence of messages sizes accurately. The relative mean squared error (RMSE) for predicted delivery times is 0.10. The partly unsteady shape of the prediction curve is a consequence of the interpolation. As a variant of the nearest

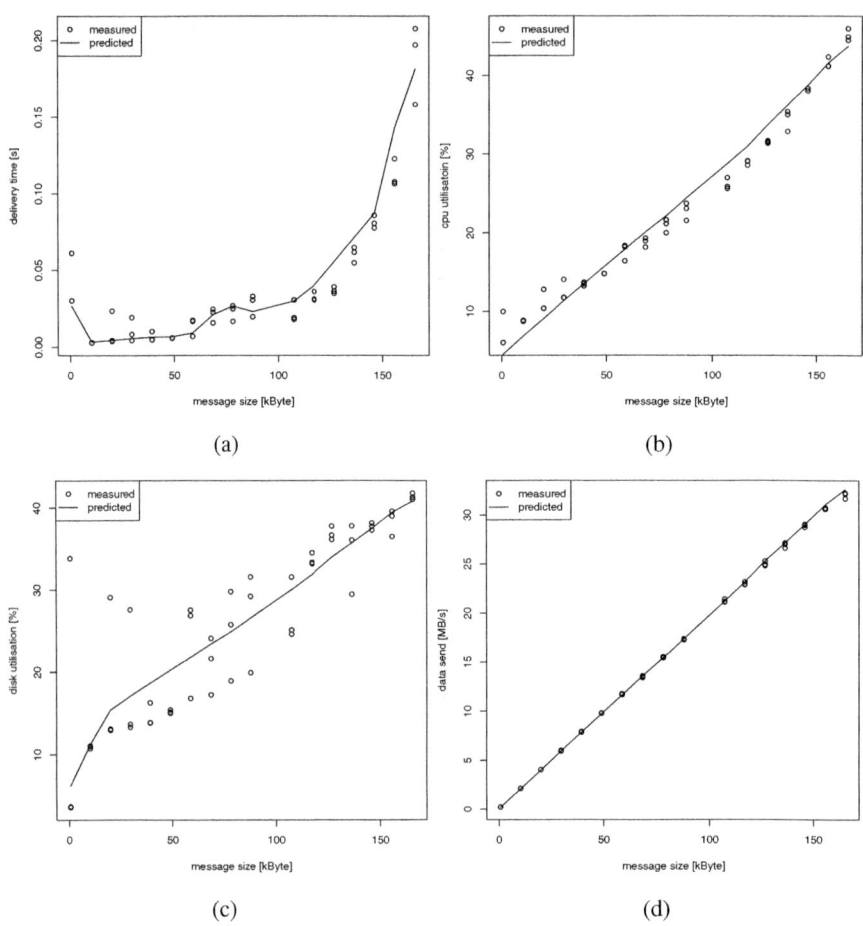

Fig. 5. Evaluation results

neighbor estimator, it is quite sensitive to deviations in the training set and passes them down to the predictions. Furthermore, the almost linear growth of the utilization of all resources is accurately reflected in the corresponding MARS functions. The measured utilization of the hard disk shows a much larger variance than the utilization of other resources. This effect occurs because after each run the files used by Active MQ to store the messages are deleted. The deletion and recreation affects the fragmentation of the files which in turn can influence the disk utilization by a factor of three.

To answer the questions posed in the beginning, the training set is appropriate to capture the performance of the system under study. Furthermore, the chosen statistical inferencing techniques were able to extract accurate performance models from the training data. However, the interpolation for different message sizes might become instable if the training data has a high variance. In the following, we discuss the benefits and drawbacks of the approach for statistical model inferencing presented in this paper.

5   Discussion

The evaluation in the previous section demonstrates the prediction accuracy of performance models inferred using the approach proposed in this paper. For such models, no knowledge about the internals of the system under study is needed. In the case of Active MQ 5.3, its internal I/O thread became the limiting factor in our experiments while no physical resource was fully utilized. Modeling such behavior with queueing networks is challenging and requires extended queueing networks such as Queueing Petri Nets. The method for statistical inferencing proposed in this paper is based on functional dependencies only and thus allows to capture such effects without drilling down into the details of the middleware's implementation. However, observations like for Active MQ 5.3 provide valuable feedback for middleware developers, but are of minor interest for the application developers. They are mainly interested in how such internal bottlenecks will influence the performance of the overall system.

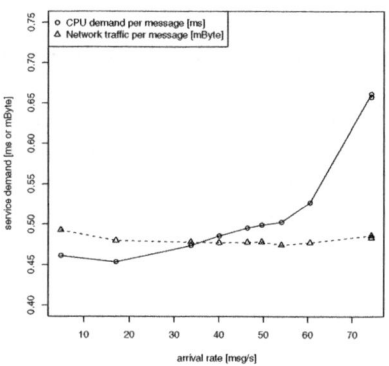

Fig. 6. Load dependent resource demand

Load dependent resource demands are typically problematic in software performance prediction. Figure 6 shows the resource demand of a single message delivery for the network (in megabyte) and the CPU (in milliseconds). The data send over the network per message stays constant, independent of the arrival rate. By contrast, the resource demand for the CPU increases by 44% from 0.45 ms to 0.65 ms. The additional demand for processing time is caused by increasing I/O waits for a larger number of messages. Reflecting such a behaviour in queueing networks requires advanced inferencing techniques. By contrast, it plays a minor role for statistically inferred models proposed in this paper.

The drawback of such measurement-based models is the large amount of measurements necessary for their derivation. To derive the performance model for Active MQ 5.3, we conducted 288 benchmark runs that lasted approximately 31 hours. In this scenario, the measurements where fully automated and thus still feasible. However, as soon as the number of parameters that can be varied increases, the number of measurements needed increases rapidly. One approach to reduce the number of measurements is to add mare assumptions about the data dependencies to the inferencing technique. For example, given the exponential relationship of arrival rate and delivery time, only a very few measurements may be sufficient to characterize the function. An extensive discussion on the challenges of statistical inference for software performance models can be found in [12].

6 Conclusions

In this paper, we proposed statistical inferencing of performance models based on measurements only. Our approach focuses on the observable data and does not consider the structure of the system. We applied our approach to model the performance of Active MQ 5.3. The performance metrics considered include the delivery time of messages, throughput, and utilization of different resources. We used MARS as well as genetic optimization to infer their dependency on message size and arrival rates. The comparison of predictions and measurements demonstrated that the model can accurately predict the performance outside the original training set.

The method allows software architects to create performance models for middleware platforms without knowing or understanding all performance relevant internals. The models remain on high level of abstraction but still provide enough information for accurate performance analyses. Software architects can include a wide range of different implementations for the same middleware standard in their performance prediction without additional modeling effort. Having a simple means to include the performance influence of complex software systems into prediction models is a further, important step towards the application of software performance engineering in practice.

Based on the results presented in this paper, we plan the following steps. First, we need to reduce the number of measurements necessary to create performance models. This might be achieved by adding assumptions about the functional dependencies between input and output variables to the model. Furthermore, the results for one execution environment might be transferable to other environments with a significantly lower number of measurements. Second, we plan to apply our approach to other middleware platforms including common application servers. Finally, we will fully integrate the resulting models into software performance engineering approaches (namely the Palladio Component Model) to allow a direct usage of the models for the performance analysis of enterprise applications.

References

1. Arlitt, M., Krishnamurthy, D., Rolia, J.: Characterizing the scalability of a large web-based shopping system. ACM Trans. on Internet Technology (TOIT), 44–69 (2001)
2. Avritzer, A., Kondek, J., Liu, D., Weyuker, E.J.: Software performance testing based on workload characterization. In: WOSP, pp. 17–24 (2002)
3. Balsamo, S., Di Marco, A., Inverardi, P., Simeoni, M.: Model-Based Performance Prediction in Software Development: A Survey. IEEE Trans. on Software Engineering, 295–310 (2004)
4. Barber, S.: Creating effective load models for performance testing with incomplete empirical data. In: WSE, pp. 51–59 (2004)
5. Beasley, D., Bull, D.R., Martin, R.R.: An overview of genetic algorithms: Part 1, fundamentals (1993)
6. Becker, S., Koziolek, H., Reussner, R.: The Palladio component model for model-driven performance prediction. Journal of Systems and Software, 3–22 (2009)

7. Brosig, F., Kounev, S., Krogmann, K.: Automated Extraction of Palladio Component Models from Running Enterprise Java Applications. In: ROSSA (2009)
8. Courtois, M., Woodside, M.: Using regression splines for software performance analysis and software characterization. In: WOSP, pp. 105–114 (2000)
9. Denaro, G., Polini, A., Emmerich, W.: Early performance testing of distributed software applications. SIGSOFT Software Engineering Notes, 94–103 (2004)
10. Friedman, J.H.: Multivariate adaptive regression splines. Annals of Statistics, 1–141 (1991)
11. Happe, J., Becker, S., Rathfelder, C., Friedrich, H., Reussner, R.H.: Parametric Performance Completions for Model-Driven Performance Prediction. Performance Evaluation (2009)
12. Happe, J., Li, H., Theilmann, W.: Black-box Performance Models: Prediction based on Observation. In: QUASOSS, pp. 19–24 (2009)
13. Hastie, T., Tibshirani, R., Friedman, J.: The Elements of Statistical Learning: Data mining, Inference and Prediction. Springer Series in Statistics (2009)
14. Holland, J.H.: Adaptation in Natural and Artificial Systems. University of Michigan Press, Ann Arbor (1975)
15. Kapova, L., Goldschmidt, T.: Automated feature model-based generation of refinement transformations. In: SEAA-EUROMICRO, pp. 141–148 (2009)
16. Kapova, L., Zimmerova, B., Martens, A., Happe, J., Reussner, R.H.: State dependence in performance evaluation of component-based software systems. In: WOSP/SIPEW (2010)
17. Kounev, S., Sachs, K.: Benchmarking and performance modeling of event-based systems. IT - Information Technology, 262–269 (2009)
18. Koziolek, H.: Performance evaluation of component-based software systems: A survey. Performance Evaluation (2009)
19. Kraft, S., Pacheco-Sanchez, S., Casale, G., Dawson, S.: Estimating service resource consumption from response time measurements. In: Valuetools (2006)
20. Krogmann, K., Kuperberg, M., Reussner, R.: Using Genetic Search for Reverse Engineering of Parametric Behaviour Models for Performance Prediction. IEEE Trans. on Software Engineering (2010)
21. Kumar, D., Zhang, L., Tantawi, A.: Enhanced inferencing: Estimation of a workload dependent performance model. In: Valuetools (2009)
22. Liu, Y., Fekete, A., Gorton, I.: Design-level performance prediction of component-based applications. IEEE Trans. Software Eng. 31(11), 928–941 (2005)
23. Pacifici, G., Segmuller, W., Spreitzer, M., Tantawi, A.: Dynamic estimation of cpu demand of web traffic. In: Valuetools, p. 26 (2006)
24. Sachs, K., Appel, S., Kounev, S., Buchmann, A.: Benchmarking publish/subscribe-based messaging systems. In: DASFAA Workshops: Benchmar'X10 (2010)
25. Sachs, K., Kounev, S., Bacon, J., Buchmann, A.: Performance evaluation of message-oriented middleware using the SPECjms 2007 benchmark. Performance Evaluation (2009)
26. Sharma, A., Bhagwan, R., Choudhury, M., Golubchik, L., Govindan, R., Voelker, G.M.: Automatic request categorization in internet services (2008)
27. Smith, C.U.: Performance Engineering of Software Systems. Addison-Wesley, USA (1990)
28. Sun Microsystems, Inc. Java Message Service (JMS) Specification - Version 1.1 (2002)
29. Woodside, M., Franks, G., Petriu, D.C.: The Future of Software Performance Engineering. In: ICSE, pp. 171–187 (2007)
30. Zheng, T., Woodside, C.M., Litoiu, M.: Performance model estimation and tracking using optimal filters. IEEE Trans. Software Engineering, 391–406 (2008)

Parameterized Reliability Prediction for Component-Based Software Architectures

Franz Brosch[1], Heiko Koziolek[2], Barbora Buhnova[3], and Ralf Reussner[1]

[1] FZI Karlsruhe, Haid-und-Neu-Str. 10-14, 76131 Karlsruhe, Germany
[2] ABB Corporate Research, Wallstadter Str. 59, 68526 Ladenburg, Germany
[3] Masaryk University, Botanicka 68a, 60200 Brno, Czech Republic
{brosch,reussner}@fzi.de, heiko.koziolek@de.abb.com, buhnova@fi.muni.cz

Abstract. Critical properties of software systems, such as reliability, should be considered early in the development, when they can govern crucial architectural design decisions. A number of design-time reliability-analysis methods has been developed to support this task. However, the methods are often based on very low-level formalisms, and the connection to different architectural aspects (e.g., the system usage profile) is either hidden in the constructs of a formal model (e.g., transition probabilities of a Markov chain), or even neglected (e.g., resource availability). This strongly limits the applicability of the methods to effectively support architectural design. Our approach, based on the Palladio Component Model (PCM), integrates the reliability-relevant architectural aspects in a highly parameterized UML-like model, which allows for transparent evaluation of architectural design options. It covers the propagation of the system usage profile throughout the architecture, and the impact of the execution environment, which are neglected in most of the existing approaches. Before analysis, the model is automatically transformed into a formal Markov model in order to support effective analytical techniques to be employed. The approach has been validated against a reliability simulation of a distributed Business Reporting System.

1 Introduction

Software reliability is defined as the probability of failure-free operation of a software system for a specified period of time in a specified environment [1]. In practice, developers often ensure high software reliability only through software testing during late development stages. Opposed to this, architecture-based software reliability analysis ([2,3,4]) aims at improving reliability of component-based software architectures already during early development stages. This helps software architects to determine the software components mostly affecting system reliability, to study the sensitivity of the system reliability to component reliabilities, and to support decisions between different design alternatives.

To enable architecture-based software reliability analyses, reliability specifications of individual software components are required. Ideally, they are created by the component vendors. However, it is hard for a component vendor to specify a software component's reliability, because it depends not only on the

G.T. Heinemann, J. Kofron, and F. Plasil (Eds.): QoSA 2010, LNCS 6093, pp. 36–51, 2010.

component implementation, but also on factors outside the vendor's control. Besides its implementation, a software component's reliability depends on (i) its usage profile [5] (e.g., how often the component is called, which parameters are used), (ii) the reliability of external services [6] (e.g., how reliable the component's required services are), and (iii) the reliability of the execution environment [1] (e.g., how reliable the underlying middleware/hardware is). Existing reliability prediction methods, typically Markov-chain based, either do not cover all these aspects (mainly neglecting the execution environment reliability), or hard-code their influence into the model (transition probabilities), which reduces the reusability of the model in assessing architectural design alternatives.

We introduce a novel approach that takes all the above mentioned factors into account. We extend the work presented in [6] with the propagation of the usage profile throughout a component-based software architecture, as well as the availability of the underlying hardware resources. We use the Palladio Component Model (PCM) [7] as a design-oriented modelling language for component-based software architectures, and extend the PCM with capabilities for reliability prediction. Besides the inclusion of multiple influence factors to component reliability, our approach bears the advantage of providing a modelling language closely aligned with software architecture concepts (instead of Markov chains, which are then generated automatically).

Using the PCM, multiple developer roles (e.g., component developer, domain expert, etc.) can independently contribute their parts to the architectural model thus reducing the complexity of the overall task. Through parameterisation, software component reliability specifications are reusable with respect to varying system usage profiles, external services, and hardware resource allocations. Software architects can conduct reliability predictions using automatic methods.

The contributions of this paper are (i) a highly parameterized reliability model including all architectural aspects explicitly, (ii) a novel method of propagating hardware-level availability to the system-level reliability based on the real usage of the hardware, and (iii) a developer-friendly support of model creation in a UML-like notation with automatic transformation to Markov chains. The approach is validated on a case study of a distributed business reporting system. The whole approach is implemented as an Eclipse-based tool [8], supporting not only the modelling process and reliability analysis, but also the reliability simulation and sensitivity analysis, which aim to further facilitate the architecture design.

This paper is organised as follows: Section 2 surveys related work. Section 3 describes the models used in our approach and focuses on the PCM reliability extensions. Section 4 explains how to predict the reliability of a PCM instance, which includes solving parameter dependencies, generating a Markov model, and solving the Markov model. Section 5 documents the case study before Section 6 concludes the paper.

2   Related Work

Seminal work in the area of software reliability engineering [1] focussed on system tests and reliability growth models treating systems as black boxes. Recently, several architecture-based reliability analysis approaches have been proposed [2,3,4] treating systems as a composition of software components. In the following, we examine these approaches regarding their modelling of the influence factors on component reliability, namely usage profile, and execution environment.

To model the influence of the usage profile on system reliability, the propagation of inputs from the user to the components and from components to other components (i.e., external calls) have to be modelled. Goseva et al. [2] state that most approaches rely on estimations of transition probabilities between software components. Cheung [5] states that the transition probabilities could be obtained by assembling and deploying the components and executing the expected usage profile against them. However, this requires software architects to set up the whole system during architecture design, which is often neither desired nor possible.

Recent approaches by Wang et al. [9] and Sharma et al. [10] extend Cheung's work to support different architectural styles and combined performance and reliability analysis. However, they rely on testing data or the software architecture's intuition to determine the transition probabilities. Reussner et al. [6] assume fixed transition probabilities between components, therefore their models cannot be reused if the system-level usage profile changes. Cheung et al. [11] focus on the reliability of individual components and do not include calls to other components.

Several approaches have been proposed including properties of the execution environment into software reliability models. Sharma et al. [12] provide a software performability model incorporating hardware availability and different states of hardware resources, but disregard the usage profile propagation and component dependencies. Furthermore, the approach calculates the throughput of successful requests in presence of hardware failures, but not the system reliability. The same holds for the approaches of Trivedi et al. [13] and Vilkomir et al. [14], who design complex availability models of the execution environment, but do not link it to the software level to quantify the overall system reliability.

Popic et al. [15] take failure probabilities of network connections into account, but not the failure probabilities of other hardware resources. Sato and Trivedi [16] combine a system model (of interacting system services) with a resource availability model. However, they do not include pure software failures (not triggered by execution environment), assume fixed transition probabilities among services, and do not model usage profile dependencies of services. Yacoub et al. [17] include communication link reliabilities in their approach but neglect hardware availability.

We described a preliminary work to the approach in this paper, which was not related to the PCM and did not consider hardware availability, in [18].

3   Modelling Reliability with the PCM

To provide the reader with a quick introduction to the modelling capabilities of the PCM we first discuss a simple example (Section 3.1), then describe the modelling capabilities more in detail structured according to the involved developer roles (Section 3.2), and finally introduce our extension to the PCM to allow for reliability analysis (Section 3.3).

3.1   Example

Figure 1 shows a condensed example of a PCM instance. It is composed out of four kinds of models delivered independently by four different developer roles.

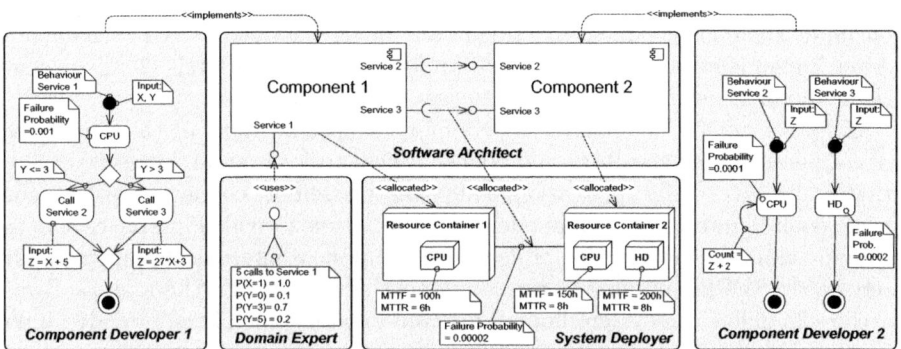

Fig. 1. PCM Example

Component developers provide abstract behavioural specifications of component services. They can annotate internal computations of a service with failure probabilities. Additionally, they can annotate external calls as well as control flow constructs with parameter dependencies. The latter allow the model to be adjusted for different system-level usage profiles. *Software architects* compose the component specifications into an architectural model. *System deployers* model the resource environment (e.g., CPUs, network links) annotated with failure properties and allocate the components in the architectural model to the resources. Finally, *domain experts* specify the system-level usage model in terms of stochastic call frequencies and input parameter values, which then can be automatically propagated through the whole model. Once the whole model is specified, it can be transformed into a Markov model to conduct reliability predictions (cf. Section 4).

3.2   Modelling Software and Hardware with the PCM

In this section, we informally describe the features of the PCM meta-model and then focus on our extensions for reliability prediction. The division of work targeted by component-based software engineering (CBSE) is enforced by the PCM, which structures the modelling task to different languages reflecting the responsibilities of the discussed developer roles.

Using the PCM, *component developers* are responsible for the specification of components, interfaces, and data types. Components can be assembled into composite components making the PCM a hierarchical component model. For each provided service of a component, component developers can supply a so-called service effect specification (SEFF), which abstractly models the usage of required services by the provided service (i.e., external calls), and the consumption of resources during component-internal processing (i.e., internal actions). SEFFs may include probabilistic or value-guarded branches, loops, and forks to model the control flow of the component service. To specify parameter dependencies on control flow constructs, we have developed a so-called stochastic expression language [19], which enables modelling arithmetic or boolean operations on input parameter values. At design time developers model SEFFs manually. After implementation developers can apply static code analysis [20] or execute the component against different test cases to derive SEFFs.

Software architects retrieve the component specifications of the component developers from a repository and connect them to form an architectural model that realises a specific application. They create assembly connectors, which connect required interfaces of components to compatible provided interfaces of other components. They ideally do not deal with component internals, but instead fully rely on the SEFFs supplied by the component developers. Furthermore, software architects define the system boundaries and expose some of the provided interfaces to be accessible by users.

System deployers are responsible for modelling the resource environment, which is a set of resource containers (i.e., computing nodes) connected via network links. Each resource container may include a number of modelled hardware resources (e.g., CPU, hard disk, memory, etc.). Resources have attributes, such as processing rates or scheduling policies. System deployers specify concrete resources, while component SEFFs only refer to abstract resource types. When specifying the allocation of components to resource containers, the resource demands can be directed to concrete resources. This method allows to easily exchange the resource environment in the model without the need to adapt the component specifications.

Domain experts specify the usage model, which involves the number and order of calls to component services at the system boundaries. The model can contain control flow constructs (e.g., branches, loops). For each called service, the domain experts also characterise its input parameter values. They can use the stochastic expression language to model a parameter taking different values with specific probabilities. Once the usage model is connected to the system model by the software architect, tools can propagate the parameter values through the parameterised expressions specified by component developers. Because of the parameterisation, the usage model can easily be changed at the system boundaries and the effect on the component specifications can be recalculated.

3.3 PCM Extensions for Modelling Reliability

In this paper, we incorporate the notion of *software failures*, *communication link failures*, and *unavailable hardware* into the PCM and extend its meta model accordingly. The following paragraphs briefly describe the rationale behind our approach.

Software failures occur during service execution due to faults in the implementation. A PCM *internal action* from a SEFF abstracts component-internal processing and can be annotated with a *failure probability*, describing the probability that the internal action fails while being executed. We assume that any failure of an internal action leads to a system failure. To estimate the failure probabilities component developers can use software reliability growth models [1], statistical testing [2], or code coverage metrics on their components. Our approach relies on these proven approaches to determine the failure probabilities. We will show in Section 5 on how to deal with uncertain failure probabilities using a sensitivity analysis.

Communication link failures include loss or damage of messages during transport, which results in service failure. Though transport protocols like TCP include mechanisms for fault tolerance (e.g., acknowledgement of message transport and repeated message sending), failures can still occur due to overload, physical damage of the transmission link, or other reasons. As such failures are generally unpredictable from the point of view of the system deployer, we treat them like software failures and annotate communication links with a failure probability in the PCM model. System deployers can define these failure probabilities either from experience with similar systems or by running tests on the target network.

Unavailable hardware causes a service execution to fail. Hardware resource breakdowns mainly result from wear out effects. Typically, a broken-down resource (e.g., a CPU, memory, or storage device) is eventually repaired or replaced by a functionally equivalent new resource. In the PCM, we annotate hardware resources with their *Mean Time To Failure* (MTTF) and *Mean Time To Repair* (MTTR). System deployers have to specify these values. Hardware vendors often provide MTTF values in specification documents. System deployers can refine these values on experience [21]. MTTR values can depend on hardware support contracts. For example, IT administration could warrant replacing failed hardware resources within one working day.

While we are aware that there are other reasons for failure (e.g., incompatibilities between components), we focus on the three failure classes described above, which in many cases have significant impact on overall system reliability. We will target further failure classes as future work.

4   Predicting Reliability with the PCM

Once a full PCM instance is specified by combining the different models described in the former section, we can predict its reliability in terms of the *probability of failure on demand* (POFOD) for a given usage model. The prediction process requires solving parameter dependencies (Section 4.1), determining probabilities of physical system states (Section 4.2), and generating and solving Markov chains (Section 4.3).

4.1   Solving Parameter Dependencies

Once the domain expert has specified input parameters in the usage model and the software architect has assembled an architectural model, a tool can propagate the parameter values of the usage model through the architectural model to solve the parameter dependencies on branch probabilities and loop counts.

The algorithm behind the tool [18] requires to separate the input domain of a component service into a finite number of equivalence classes and to provide a probability for each class. The equivalence classes can be derived using techniques from partition testing [22]. The probabilities for input classes of components directly accessed by users (i.e., the system-level usage profile) have to be estimated by domain experts. After running the algorithm, all parameter dependencies are resolved and all SEFFs contain calculated branch probabilities and loop iteration counts, which can later be used for the construction of Markov chains. We have documented the model traversal algorithm for resolving the parameter dependencies formally in [19].

Consider the example in Fig. 1. The domain expert (lower left) has specified that the parameter X for calling Service 1 will always have the value 1, while the parameter Y will take the value 0 with a probability of 10 percent, 3 with a probability of 70 percent, and 5 with a probability of 20 percent. Our tool uses the values for Y to derive the branch probabilities in the SEFFs of Component Developer 1 from the parameter dependencies $Y \leq 3$ and $Y > 30$ to 0.8 and 0.2 respectively. Furthermore, it uses the value for X ($= 1$) to resolve the value for Z in the SEFF to $6 = 1 + 5$ for the call to Service 2 and to $30 = 27 * 1 + 3$ for the call to Service 3. In the SEFF for Service 2 (Component Developer 2), the current value for Z ($= 6$) can be used to resolve the parameter dependency on the loop count, which is determined to be 8 according to the calculated input parameter values.

4.2   Determining Probabilities of Physical System States

After solving the parameter dependencies, our approach generates Markov chains for all possible cases of hardware resource availability. We call each of these cases a *physical system state* and calculate their occurrence probabilities from the MTTF/MTTR values specified in a PCM instance. Let $R = \{r_1, r_2, .., r_n\}$ be the set of resources in the system. Each resource r_i is characterized by its $MTTF_i$ and $MTTR_i$ and has two possible states OK and NA (not available). Let $s(r_i)$ be the current state of resource r_i. Then, we have:

$$P(s(r_i) = OK) = \frac{MTTF_i}{MTTF_i + MTTR_i}$$

$$P(s(r_i) = NA) = \frac{MTTR_i}{MTTF_i + MTTR_i}$$

This calculation of the resource availabilities can be refined using continuous time Markov chains (CTMC), also see [12]. Let S be the set of possible physical system states, that is, $S = \{s_1, s_2, .., s_m\}$, where each $s_j \in S$ is a combination of states of all n resources:

$$s_j = (s_j(r_1), s_j(r_2), .., s_j(r_n)) \in \{OK, NA\}^n$$

As each resource has 2 possible states, there are 2^n possible physical system states, that is, $m = 2^n$. At an arbitrary point in time during system execution, let $P(s_j)$ be the probability that the system is in state s_j. Assuming independent resource failures, the probability of each state is the product of the individual resource-state probabilities:

$$\forall j \in \{1, .., m\} : P(s_j) = \prod_{i=1}^{n} P(s(r_i) = s_j(r_i))$$

Considering the example from Figure 1, there are three hardware resources included in the model (two CPUs and one HD), leading to $2^3 = 8$ possible physical system states, whose probabilities are listed in Table 1. The state probabilities are used for calculation of overall system reliability (see Section 4.3).

Table 1. Physical System State Probabilities for the Example PCM Instance

		State 1	State 2	State 3	State 4	State 5	State 6	State 7	State 8
Resource Status	CPU1	NA	NA	NA	NA	OK	OK	OK	OK
	CPU2	NA	NA	OK	OK	NA	NA	OK	OK
	HD	NA	OK	NA	OK	NA	OK	NA	OK
	Probability	0,000110	0,002756	0,002067	0,051671	0,001837	0,045930	0,034447	0,861182

4.3 Generating and Solving Markov Chains

For each physical system state determined above, our tool generates a separate absorbing discrete-time Markov chain (DTMC). The chain represents all possible service execution paths, together with their probabilities, under the specific physical system state. Thus, the state (availability of hardware resources) is fixed along a system service execution, which better reflects the fact that resource failure and repair times are orders of magnitude longer than the duration of a single service. Note that this means that resources are not expected to fail or be repaired during service execution. However, this inaccuracy is negligible, which is confirmed also by the validation (see Section 5).

The DTMC is based on a combination of all SEFFs in a PCM instance triggered by the usage model. It contains a state for each action of each SEFF. Three additional states represent execution start, success, and failure. The DTMC transitions denote all possible execution paths and their probabilities.

Figure 2 illustrates the DTMC generated for the example from Figure 1, assuming that the system is in a state where both CPUs are ok, but the HD is unavailable. The execution starts with a call to Service 1, followed by an internal action requiring the first CPU. Afterwards, either Service 2 or 3 are called over the network, which then use the second CPU and the HD respectively.

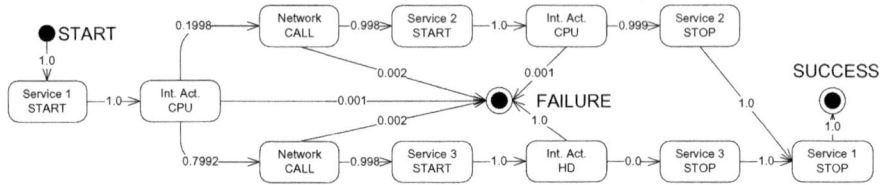

Fig. 2. Discrete-time Markov Chain

Markov states originating from internal actions and network calls have a transition to the failure state. For internal actions the transition can be triggered by either software failure (with given failure probability) or by unavailability of required hardware. Depending on the physical system state represented by the Markov chain, the failure probability of the internal action is either equal to the specified failure probability or equal to 1.0 if the required resource is unavailable. In the example, the internal action of Service 3 requires the unavailable HD and thus fails with probability 1.0. For network calls, the transition probability to the failure state is the failure probability of the communication link. In the example, each of the calls to Services 2 and 3 involves the communication link between Resource Container 1 and 2.

For each physical system state s_j, we denote $P(SUCCESS|s_j)$ as the probability of success on condition that the system is in state s_j. We calculate $P(SUCCESS|s_j)$ as the probability to reach the success state (from the start state) in the corresponding DTMC. In the example, we have $P(SUCCESS|s_j) = 0.1992$. Having determined the state-specific success probabilities, the overall probability of success can be calculated as a weighted sum over all individual results:

$$P(SUCCESS) = \sum_{j=1}^{m}(P(SUCCESS|s_j) \times P(s_j))$$

In our example, we have $P(SUCCESS) = 0.8881$.

5   Case Study Evaluation

The goal of the case study evaluation described in this section is (i) to assess the validity of our prediction results, (ii) to demonstrate the new prediction capabilities with sensitivity analyses, and (iii) to assess the scalability of our approach.

We have applied our modelling and prediction approach on the PCM instance of a distributed, component-based system (Section 5.1). To reach (i), we have predicted its reliability and compared the results to data monitored during a reliability simulation (Section 5.2). To reach (ii), we ran several prediction series, where we analysed the impact of usage profile and hardware changes on system reliability (Section 5.3). To reach (iii), we investigated the execution time for predictions based on different model sizes (Section 5.4).

5.1   Model of a Business Reporting System

Fig. 3 illustrates some parts of the so-called Business Reporting System (BRS), which is the basis for our case study evaluation (the PCM instance for the BRS can be downloaded at [8]). The model is based on an industrial system [23], which generates management reports from business data collected in a database.

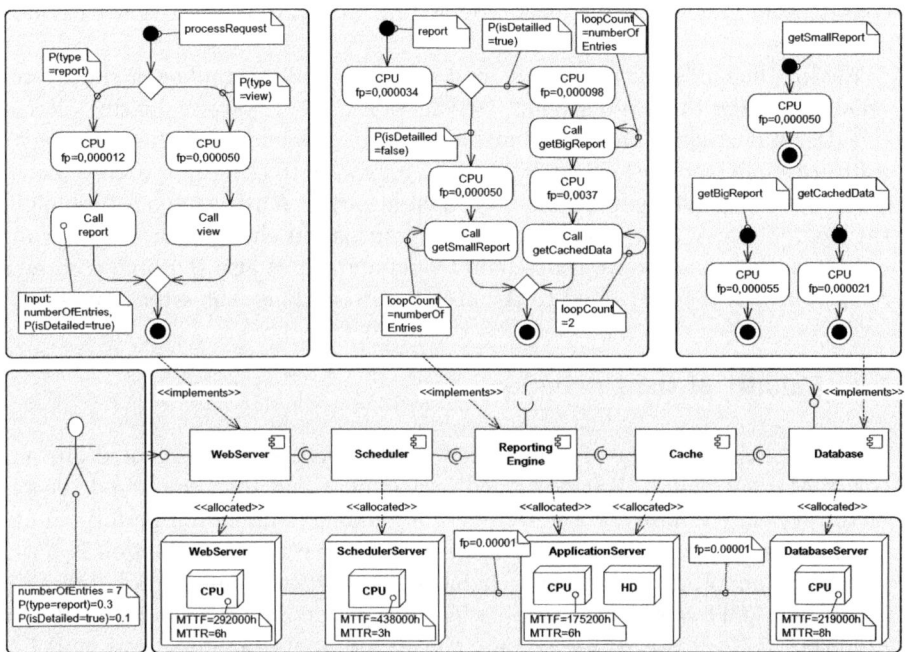

Fig. 3. PCM Instance of the Business Reporting System (Overview)

Users can query the system via web browsers. They can simply view the currently collected data or generate different kinds of reports (coarse or detailed) for a configurable number of database entries. The usage model provided by the domain expert (left hand side of Fig. 3) shows that a user requests a report in 30 percent of the cases, from which 10 percent are detailed reports. An average user requests reports for 7 database entries.

On a high abstraction level, the system consists of five independent software components running on four servers. The web server propagates user requests to a scheduler component, which dispatches them to possibly multiple application servers. The application servers host a reporting engine component, which either directly accesses the database or queries a cache component.

As failure data was not available for the system, we estimated the failure rates of the software components and hardware devices. Determining failure probabilities for software components is beyond the scope of this paper (cf. [1]). However, to make our model as realistic as possible, we used empirical data as a basis for failure rates estimation. Goseva et al. [24] reported on failure probabilities for software components in a large-scale software system, which were derived from a bug tracking system. We aligned the failure probabilities of the internal actions in the BRS with these failure probabilities. Schroeder et al. [21] analysed the actual failure rates of hardware components of several large systems over the course of several years. Their data provided a basis for estimating the MTTF and MTTR numbers of our case study model, which are considerably lower than the ones provided by hardware vendors in specification documents.

Having the model of the system, we can use our analysis tool to predict system reliability under the given settings (see Section 5.2), or start evaluating alternative design decisions. These may include changing the usage profile, topology of software components, their deployment to hardware resources, or even replacing the components (changing their implementation) or hardware nodes (changing their parameters). Any of these local and transparent changes may significantly influence the generated Markov-chain model and hence also the predicted reliability, which is then reported to the architect to evaluate the alternatives.

5.2   Validity of the Predictions

To validate the accuracy of our prediction approach, we first executed our analytical Markov chain solver described in Section 4 and then compared the predicted system reliability to the results of a reliability simulation performed over the PCM instance of the BRS. Notice that the goal of our validation is not to justify the annotations used for reliability, like software failure probabilities or hardware MTTF / MTTR values, which are commonly used and described in literature [2,12]. Instead, we validate that if all inputs (architectural model including reliability annotations) are accurately provided, our method produces an accurate result (system reliability prediction).

For simulation purposes, we have implemented a tool based on the SSJ framework [25]. The tool uses model transformations implemented with the OAW framework to generate Java code from the PCM instance under study. During a simulation run, a generated SSJ load driver creates requests to the code according to the usage model specified as a part of the PCM model. Software failures, communication link failures, and the effects of unavailable hardware are included into the simulation to assess system reliability.

To simulate a software failure, an exception may be raised during execution of an internal action. A random number is generated according to the given failure probability, and decides about success or failure of the internal action. Communication link failures are handled in the same way. Furthermore, the simulation includes the notion of hardware resources and their failure behaviour. It uses the given MTTF/MTTR values as mean values of an exponential distribution and draws samples from the distribution to determine actual resource failure and repair times. Whenever an internal action requires a currently unavailable hardware resource, it fails with an exception. Taking all possible sources of failure into account, the simulation determines system reliability as the ratio of successful service executions to the overall execution count.

Compared to our analysis tools, simulation takes longer, but is more realistic and therefore can be used for validation. Values of variables in the control flow are preserved within their scope, as opposed to analysis, where each access to a variable requires drawing a sample from its probability distribution (cf. [19]). Resources may fail and be repaired anytime, not only between service executions. Resource states are observed over (simulated) time, leading to more realistic failure behaviour of subsequent service executions.

Regarding the case study, our analysis tools predicted the probability of successful service execution as 0.9960837 for the usage model of the BRS sketched in Fig. 3. Because the model involves 5 resources, 32 $(= 2^5)$ different Markov chains were generated to include all possible physical system states. Each generated Markov chain consisted out of 6 372 states and 6 870 transitions, because our approach involves unrolling the loops of the service effect specifications according to the specified usage profile and incorporating hardware resources. Solving the parameter dependencies, generating the different chains, and computing their absorption probabilities took less than 1 second on an Intel Core 2 Duo with 2.6 GHz and 2 GB of RAM.

To validate this result, we applied the simulation tool on the BRS PCM instance and simulated its execution for 1 year (i.e., 31 536 000 seconds of simulation time). The usage model described above was executed 168 526 times during the simulation run taking roughly 190 simulated seconds per execution. We recorded 562 internal action failures, 75 communication link resource failures and 26 resource failures during the simulation run. The simulation ran for 657 seconds (real time) and produced more than 800 MB of measured data. The success probability predicted by the simulation tool was 0.9960658, which deviates from the analytical result by approximately 0.00179 percent.

The high number of resource failures during simulation stems from the fact that we divided all given MTTF/MTTR values in the model by a constant factor. This measure allowed us to observe a statistical relevant number of over 20 resource failures during simulation, while leaving probabilities of physical system states (see Section 4.2) and the calculated system reliability unchanged.

Considering validation results, we deem the analytical method and tool implementation sufficiently accurate for the model described in this paper.

5.3   Sensitivity Analyses

To further analyse the system reliability of the BRS, we conducted several sensitivity analyses involving changing failure probabilities and usage probabilities

Fig. 4 shows the impact of different failure probabilities of component internal actions to the system reliability. The failure probabilities of the actions 'acceptView', 'prepareSmallReport', and 'getBigReport' have been varied around $fp = 0.00005$. The slopes of the curves indicate that the system reliability of the BRS under the given usage model is most sensitive to the action 'acceptView' of the web server component. This information is valuable for the software

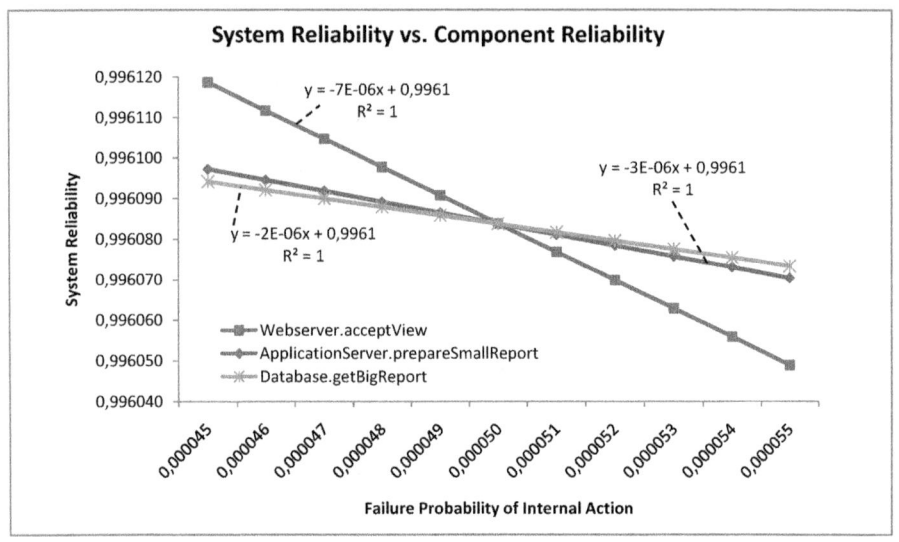

Fig. 4. Sensitivity to Failure Probabilities

architect, who can decide to put more testing effort into the web server component, to exchange the component with another component from a third party vendor, or to run the web server component redundantly.

Our parameterised behavioural descriptions allow to easily change the system-level usage model and investigate the impact on the system reliability. The parameter values are propagated through the architecture and can influence branch probabilities and loop iteration numbers. Former approaches require to change these inner component annotations manually, which is laborious and may be even hard to determine due to complex control and data flow in a large system. Fig. 5 shows the impact of different usage probabilities on system reliability. The figure suggests that the model is more sensitive to the portion of detailed reports required by the user. The impact of having more users requesting view queries is less pronounced as indicated by the lower slope of the curve.

5.4 Scalability

The scalability of our approach requires special attention. The method for incorporating hardware reliability described in Section 4 increases the number of Markov chains to be solved exponentially in relation to the number of resources in the model. To examine the impact of this relation to the practicability of our approach, we analysed a number of simple PCM instances with a growing number of resources and recorded the execution time for our prediction tool.

We found that we can analyse models with up to approximately 20 resources within one hour. This involves generating and solving more than 1 000 000 Markov chains. We believe that the number of 20 different resources is sufficient for a

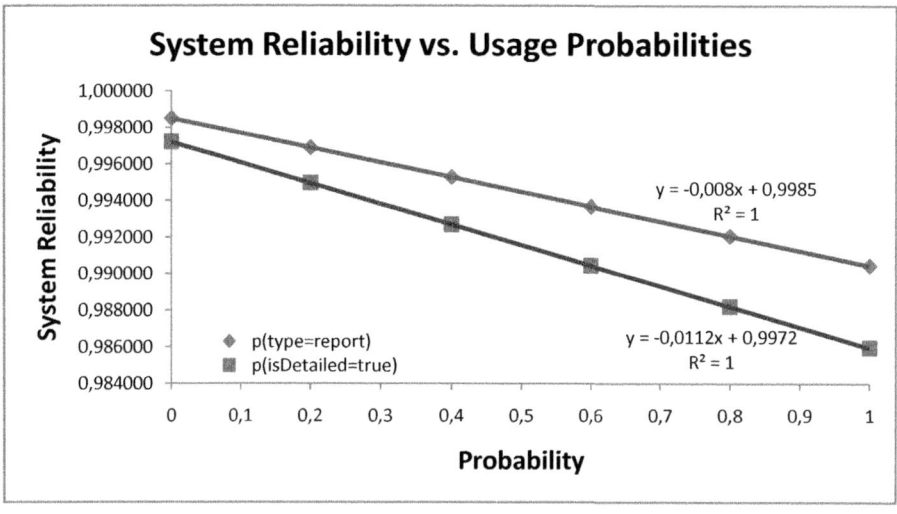

Fig. 5. Usage Profile Change 1: Usage Probabilities

large number of realistic systems. Larger models need to be analysed partially or resources have to be grouped. It is also possible to assume some resources in a large model as always available, which then decreases the effort for the predictions. Other techniques, like the possibilities for distributed analysis and multi-core processors, or employment of more efficient Markov model solution techniques,are meant for future research.

6   Conclusions

We presented an approach for reliability analysis of component-based software architectures. The approach allows for calculation of the probability of successful service execution. Compared to other architecture-based software reliability methods, our approach takes into account more influence factors, such as the hardware and usage profile. The usage profile on the system level is automatically propagated to determine the individual usage profiles of all involved software components. We have used an absorbing discrete-time Markov chain as analysis model. It represents all possible execution paths through the architecture, together with their probabilities.

The extensive parameterization of our model allows for sensitivity analysis in a straightforward way. In our case study, we examined the sensitivity of system reliability to individual failure probabilities, variations in the system-level usage profile, and changing hardware availability due to wear out effects. Furthermore, we implemented a reliability simulation to validate our results. In the case study, simulation results differed less than 0.002 percent from the analytical solution.

We will extend and further validate our approach in future work. We plan to include fault tolerance mechanisms, error propagation, concurrency modelling, and probabilistic dependencies between individual software and hardware failures. Furthermore, we want to include the reliability of middleware, virtual machines, and operating systems into our approach. With these extensions, we aim to further increase the accurateness of our approach and support analysis for a larger class of systems.

Acknowledgments. This work was supported by the European Commission as part of the EU-projects SLA@SOI (grant No. FP7-216556) and Q-ImPrESS (grant No. FP7-215013), as well as the German Federal Ministry of Education and Research (grant No. 01BS0822).

References

1. Musa, J.D., Iannino, A., Okumoto, K.: Software reliability: measurement, prediction, application. McGraw-Hill, Inc., New York (1987)
2. Goseva-Popstojanova, K., Trivedi, K.S.: Architecture-based approach to reliability assessment of software systems. Performance Evaluation 45(2-3), 179–204 (2001)
3. Gokhale, S.S.: Architecture-based software reliability analysis: Overview and limitations. IEEE Trans. on Dependable and Secure Computing 4(1), 32–40 (2007)
4. Immonen, A., Niemelä, E.: Survey of reliability and availability prediction methods from the viewpoint of software architecture. Journal on Softw. Syst. Model. 7(1), 49–65 (2008)
5. Cheung, R.C.: A user-oriented software reliability model. IEEE Trans. Softw. Eng. 6(2), 118–125 (1980)
6. Reussner, R.H., Schmidt, H.W., Poernomo, I.H.: Reliability prediction for component-based software architectures. Journal of Systems and Software 66(3), 241–252 (2003)
7. Becker, S., Koziolek, H., Reussner, R.: The Palladio Component Model for Model-Driven Performance Prediction. Journal of Systems and Software 82(1), 3–22 (2009)
8. PCM: Palladio Component Model (January 2010), www.palladio-approach.net (Last retrieved 2010-15-01)
9. Wang, W.L., Pan, D., Chen, M.H.: Architecture-based software reliability modeling. Journal of Systems and Software 79(1), 132–146 (2006)
10. Sharma, V., Trivedi, K.: Quantifying software performance, reliability and security: An architecture-based approach. Journal of Systems and Software 80, 493–509 (2007)
11. Cheung, L., Roshandel, R., Medvidovic, N., Golubchik, L.: Early prediction of software component reliability. In: Proc. 30th Int. Conf. on Software Engineering (ICSE 2008), pp. 111–120. ACM, New York (2008)
12. Sharma, V.S., Trivedi, K.S.: Reliability and performance of component based software systems with restarts, retries, reboots and repairs. In: Proc. 17th Int. Symp. on Software Reliability Engineering (ISSRE 2006), pp. 299–310. IEEE Computer Society Press, Los Alamitos (2006)
13. Trivedi, K., Wang, D., Hunt, D.J., Rindos, A., Smith, W.E., Vashaw, B.: Availability modeling of SIP protocol on IBM WebSphere. In: Proc. 14th IEEE Int. Symp. on Dependable Computing (PRDC 2008), pp. 323–330. IEEE Computer Society Press, Los Alamitos (2008)

14. Vilkomir, S.A., Parnas, D.L., Mendiratta, V.B., Murphy, E.: Availability evaluation of hardware/software systems with several recovery procedures. In: Proc. 29th Int. Computer Software and Applications Conference (COMPSAC 2005), pp. 473–478. IEEE Computer Society Press, Los Alamitos (2005)
15. Popic, P., Desovski, D., Abdelmoez, W., Cukic, B.: Error propagation in the reliability analysis of component based systems. In: Proc. 16th IEEE Int. Symp. on Software Reliability Engineering (ISSRE 2005), pp. 53–62. IEEE Computer Society, Washington (2005)
16. Sato, N., Trivedi, K.S.: Accurate and efficient stochastic reliability analysis of composite services using their compact markov reward model representations. In: Proc. IEEE Int. Conf. on Services Computing (SCC 2007), pp. 114–121. IEEE Computer Society, Los Alamitos (2007)
17. Yacoub, S.M., Cukic, B., Ammar, H.H.: A scenario-based reliability analysis approach for component-based software. IEEE Transactions on Reliability 53(4), 465–480 (2004)
18. Koziolek, H., Brosch, F.: Parameter dependencies for component reliability specifications. In: Proc. 6th Int. Workshop on Formal Engineering Approaches to Software Components and Architecture (FESCA 2009). ENTCS. Elsevier, Amsterdam (2009) (to appear)
19. Koziolek, H.: Parameter Dependencies for Reusable Performance Specifications of Software Components. PhD thesis, Department of Computing Science, University of Oldenburg, Germany (March 2008)
20. Kappler, T., Koziolek, H., Krogmann, K., Reussner, R.: Towards Automatic Construction of Reusable Prediction Models for Component-Based Performance Engineering. In: Proc. Software Engineering 2008 (SE 2008). LNI, vol. 121, February 2008. pp. 140–154. GI (2008)
21. Schroeder, B., Gibson, G.A.: Disk failures in the real word: What does an mttf of 1,000,000 hours mean to you? In: Proc. 5th USENIX Conference on File and Storage Technologies, FAST 2007 (2007)
22. Hamlet, D.: Tools and experiments supporting a testing-based theory of component composition. ACM Transaction on Software Engineering Methodology 18(3), 1–41 (2009)
23. Wu, X., Woodside, M.: Performance modeling from software components. In: Proc. 4th International Workshop on Software and Performance (WOSP 2004), vol. 29, pp. 290–301 (2004)
24. Goseva-Popstojanova, K., Hamill, M., Perugupalli, R.: Large empirical case study of architecture–based software reliability. In: Proc. 16th IEEE Int. Symp. on Software Reliability Engineering, ISSRE 2005 (2005)
25. SSJ: Stochastic Simulation in Java (January 2010), http://www.iro.umontreal.ca/~simardr/ssj/indexe.html (Last retrieved 2010-01-15)

Architecture-Driven Reliability and Energy Optimization for Complex Embedded Systems

Indika Meedeniya[1], Barbora Buhnova[2], Aldeida Aleti[1], and Lars Grunske[1]

[1] Faculty of ICT, Swinburne University of Technology
Hawthorn, VIC 3122, Australia
{imeedeniya,aaleti,lgrunske}@swin.edu.au
[2] Faculty of Informatics, Masaryk University
60200 Brno, Czech Republic
buhnova@fi.muni.cz

Abstract. The use of redundant computational nodes is a widely used design tactic to improve the reliability of complex embedded systems. However, this redundancy allocation has also an effect on other quality attributes, including energy consumption, as each of the redundant computational nodes requires additional energy. As a result, the two quality objectives are conflicting. The approach presented in this paper applies a multi-objective optimization strategy to find optimal redundancy levels for different architectural elements. It is implemented in the ArcheOpterix tool and illustrated on a realistic case study from the automotive domain.

1 Introduction

Motivation. Reliability is one of the key quality attributes of complex embedded systems [1]. To increase reliability, replication of computational nodes (so-called *redundancy allocation*) is used, which however introduces additional life-cycle costs for manufacturing and usage of the system. One more drawback of introducing redundancy is that the system requires more energy to support the additional computational nodes. In most embedded systems, reducing energy consumption is an important design objective, because these systems must support their operation from a limited battery that is hard to recharge (e.g., in deep-sea or outer-space missions) or at least uncomfortable to be recharged very often (e.g., in mobile phones or electric cars). This is further stressed in systems requiring the minimal size of the battery (e.g., in nano-devices).

State of the art. Research in both reliability and energy consumption for embedded systems is already well established. These two quality attributes are however rarely used in trade-off studies. Energy consumption is typically put in connection with performance [2,3]. Reliability (when resolved using redundancy allocation) is typically put in connection with production costs [4,5,6]. The approaches balancing both reliability and energy consumption do not deal with architecture-level optimization, and are often strongly driven by energy consumption rather

G.T. Heinemann, J. Kofron, and F. Plasil (Eds.): QoSA 2010, LNCS 6093, pp. 52–67, 2010.

then reliability. Such approaches typically examine low-level decision such as voltage reduction [7,8] or channel coding techniques [9] to improve energy consumption without threatening reliability. Such techniques can be however hardly employed to maximize reliability and minimize energy consumption at the same time, since they have only a minor impact on reliability.

Aim of the paper. In this paper we aim to apply a trade-off analysis between reliability and energy consumption at an architectural level, and employ the technique of *redundancy allocation*, which has a significant effect on both the discussed quality attributes – reliability and energy consumption. To achieve this aim, we identify the main reliability- and energy-relevant attributes of distributed embedded systems with respect to the redundancy allocation problem. We formalize the system model in terms of an annotated Markov Reward Model, formulate the optimization problem, and design an algorithm to resolve it. The whole approach is implemented within the ArcheOpterix framework [10], and illustrated on a realistic case study from the automotive domain.

Contribution of the paper. There are three main contributions of the paper: (i) architecture-level technique to optimize reliability and energy consumption, (ii) a novel formalization of the problem and its solution, based on the expected number of visits of individual subsystems and links in between, and (iii) employment of a meta-heuristic optimization algorithm, which reduces the likelihood to get stuck in local optima as the greedy algorithms used by related approaches.

Outline of the paper. The paper is structured as follows. After discussion of related work in Section 2, we summarize the essential definitions in Section 3 and present system model and its formalization in Section 4. Based on the model, Section 5 describes our technique of quantifying the quality of a single architectural alternative, from both a reliability and an energy-consumption point of view, and Section 6 designs an optimization algorithm to find the set of near-optimal candidates. Finally, Section 7 discusses our tool support, Section 8 illustrates the approach on a case study, and Section 9 concludes the paper.

2   Related Work

Estimation and optimization of the energy consumption of embedded systems has been the focus of many research groups. The application of energy optimization is evident in design, implementation and runtime [11]. Energy-aware compilation [12] and software design [13,14,15] has been addressed to achieve energy advantage independent from the hardware-level optimization. Apart from the limited optimizations in different parts of systems, a system-level energy consumption optimization has been proposed by Benini et al. [11]. Energy-efficient runtime adaptation of embedded systems has also been a primary approach, which can be broadly categorized as predictive, adaptive and stochastic control [2]. A key commonality of the approaches is that they use greedy heuristics for the optimization and focus on the balance of energy consumption and performance.

A number of formal models have been adopted in the context of embedded-systems energy consumption estimation. *Continuous Time Markov Chains (CTMC)* have been widely used including the work of Qiu et al. [16]. Vijayakrishnan et al. [17] proposed to use the more powerful model of *Generalized Stochastic Petri Nets (GSPN)*. The use of *Markov Reward Models (MRM)* has gained visibility [18,19] due to their power of modeling and expressiveness in the domain of energy consumption. Cloth et al. [20] presented the efficient use of MRMs in energy-consumption modeling for embedded systems.

On the reliability side, there is a considerable amount of approaches that address the *Redundancy Allocation Problem (RAP)* [4] at the system architecture design level. Coit et al. [4] introduced an approach solving RAP defined as the use of functionally similar (but not necessarily identical) components in a way that if one component fails, the redundant part performs required functionality without a system failure. They have visualized the problem as the minimization of cost incurred for the redundancy allocation while satisfying a user defined system reliability level. In [4], *Genetic Algorithms (GA)* have been proposed for the optimization of component redundancy allocation, and *Neural networks (NN)* techniques have also been integrated in [21]. Kulturel-Konak et al. [5] has presented *Tabu Search* as the design space exploration strategy. The RAP has been adapted to *Ant Colony Optimization (ACO)* by Liang et al. [22]. Significant similarity of all the approaches is the view on RAP as cost minimization problem while satisfying the predefined reliability constraints. Grunske [23] addressed RAP by integrating multi-objective optimization of the reliability and weight.

Finally, the trade-off with respect to energy consumption and reliability has been the focus of a few research contributions. Negative implications on the reliability has been investigated due to energy optimization methods such as voltage reduction [7,8] and channel coding techniques in the communication [9], which are however not connected to RAP. The work of Zhang et al. [24] on finding trade-offs of energy, reliability, and performance in redundant cache line allocation can be viewed as conceptually close to RAP context. Similarly, Perillo et al. [25] have presented an approach of finding the optimal energy management with redundant sensors. However, both these contributions observe only the static (hardware) architecture of the system, without taking the system execution and its control flow (software layer) into account. This allows them to disregard from the execution transfer among system components (which is crucial in software architectures), and to employ simple additive models.

In contrast to the above mentioned approaches, this paper describes a novel *architecture-level* approach of finding the *optimal redundancy levels* of system components (integrating both *software* and *hardware*) with respect to system *reliability* and *energy consumption*.

3   Preliminaries

This section outlines the definitions and preliminary formalizations used in the rest of the paper.

Definition 1. *A* Discrete Time Markov Chain (DTMC) *is a tuple* (S, P) *where* S *is a finite set of states, and* $P : S \times S \to [0, 1]$ *is a transition probability matrix.*

A DTMC is called absorbing when at least one of its states has no outgoing transition [18]. Such states are called absorbing states.

Definition 2. *A labeled discrete time* Markov Reward Model (MRM) *is a triple* $\mathcal{M} = ((S, P), \rho, \tau)$ *where* (S, P) *is an underlying DTMC,* $\rho : S \to \mathbb{R}_{\geq 0}$ *is a state reward structure and* $\tau : S \times S \to \mathbb{R}_{\geq 0}$ *is an impulse reward structure satisfying* $\forall s \in S : \tau(s, s) = 0.$

A path of an absorbing DTMC is a finite sequence $\sigma = s_0 s_1 s_2 ... s_n$ of states, where s_n is an absorbing state. Let $X_\sigma(s)$ denote the number of visits of state s in path σ. Similarly, let $XT_\sigma(s, s')$ represent the number of occurrences of transition (s, s') in σ. Then we can calculate the *accumulated reward of* σ as:

$$R_\sigma = \sum_{s \in S} (X_\sigma(s) \cdot \rho(s)) + \sum_{(s,s') \in (S \times S)} (XT_\sigma(s, s') \cdot \tau(s, s')) \qquad (1)$$

Having the expected number of visits of each state($E[X(s)]$) and transition ($E[XT(s, s')]$), the expected value of the *accumulated reward in all paths* can be computed as:

$$E[R] = \sum_{s \in S} (E[X(s)] \cdot \rho(s)) + \sum_{(s,s') \in (S \times S)} (E[XT(s, s')] \cdot \tau(s, s')) \qquad (2)$$

In this paper, we use the method introduced by Kubat [26] to compute the expected number of visits of a state/transition and the above relationship in estimating the energy consumption, as described in Section 5.1.

4   System Model

In our approach, we target event-triggered embedded systems that are structured into interacting components (system elements), called special purpose microprocessors (MPs). The MPs are self-contained micro-computers along with the software, dedicated to fulfill a specific functionality. They have only one entry and exit point, and behave the same for each execution (visit of the MP by system control flow). For example, in an autonomous weather data gathering robot, these MPs are responsible for activities such as reading inputs from sensors and calculating the relative humidity of the environment. As the MPs need to communicate with each other during the operation, they are connected via communication channels forming a distributed architecture.

Inter-component communication is modeled as an execution transfer from one component to another. In the redundancy allocation domain, systems are modelled as *Series-Parallel (S-P)* systems [4,5,22,23], with logical constructs for both serial and parallel execution. In the embedded systems domain, the models can be viewed as overlapped sets of S-P models (for individual system-level services[1]), because the execution can start in different components (triggering the services). The execution finishes in the components with no continuation of the execution transfer. The existence of such components is implied by the nature of services, which represent finite scenarios of system execution.

For the redundancy allocation, we use the *hot spare* design topology with *N-Modular Redundancy (NMR)* extension [27]. In hot sparing, each component in the system has a number of replicas (possibly zero), all of which are active at the same time, mimicking the execution of the original component. With the NMR extension the system employs a decision mechanism in the form of majority voting, applied on entry to a component (if multiple replicas deliver their results to the entry gate). See Figure 1 that illustrates the concept. By merging the hot spare and NMR, the system can be configured to tolerate fail-stop, crash, commission and value failures. In this configuration, each component with its parallel replicas is considered as a single unit called *subsystem*.

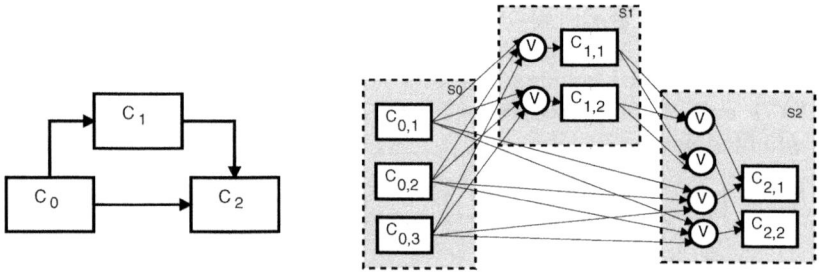

Fig. 1. Component-interaction model, without and with redundancies

4.1   Formalization of the Model

Let $C = \{c_1, c_2, ..., c_n\}$, $n \in \mathbb{N}$, denote the set of all components (before replication), and $\mathcal{I} = \{1, 2, ..., n\}$ the index set for components in C. The assignment of the redundancy level for all components is denoted a, and the set of all possible a is denoted $A = \{a \mid a : C \to N\}$, where $N = \{n \mid 0 \leq n \leq max, n \in \mathbb{N}_0\}$ delimits the redundancy level of a component[2]. Note that, since C and N are finite, A is also finite. A component c_i together with its redundancies form a subsystem S_i, which can be uniquely determined by c_i (what we do along the formalization).

Underlying DTMC model. The interaction among components without replication (Figure 1 on the left) can be formalized in terms of an absorbing DTMC, where nodes represent system components $c_i \in C$, and transitions the transfer of

---

[1] In embedded systems, a *service* is understood as a system-level functionality employing possibly many components.

[2] The original component is not counted as redundant, hence at least the one is always present in a subsystem.

execution from one component to another (together with the probability of the transfer). Equivalently, the system with replication (Figure 1 on the right) can be formalized as an absorbing DTMC where nodes represent the whole subsystems S_i, and the transitions represent the transfer of execution in between with all the replicated communication links joined into a single transition (see Figure 2, ignoring the annotation for now). Note that since the replicated links are joined in the DTMC, the transfer probabilities remain unchanged with respect to redundancy allocation. In both cases, the DTMC represents a single execution of the system (its reaction to an external event), with possibly many execution scenarios (initiated in different nodes of the DTMC, based on the trigerring event). In summary, the underlying DTMC is determined by the following parameters:

- Execution initiation probability, $q_0 : C \to [0, 1]$, is the probability of initializing the execution in the component (or subsystem); $\sum_{c \in C} q_0(c) = 1$.
- Transfer probability, $p : C \times C \to [0, 1]$, is the probability that the execution continues to component (or subsystem) c_j after component c_i.

Energy and reliability annotation. The energy and reliability-relevant information is added to the DTMC model via model annotation. In case of energy consumption, the annotation is encoded in terms of rewards, and the DTMC extended to a discrete time *Markov Reward Model (MRM)* [28], as discussed below. In case of reliability, the annotation is directly connected to the parameters derived from the DTMC, and used for reliability evaluation, as discussed in Section 5.3. In both cases, the annotation is based on the following parameters of system architecture and execution flow:

- Failure rate $\lambda_c : C \to \mathbb{R}_{\geq 0}$, is the failure intensity of the exponential distribution of failure behavior of a component [29]. Component failures in the model are assumed independent and given per time unit.
- Failure rate $\lambda_l : C \times C \to \mathbb{R}_{\geq 0}$, is the failure intensity of the exponential distribution of failure behavior of a communication link between two components, assumed independent for different links and given per time unit.
- Processing time inside a component per visit, $t_c : C \to \mathbb{R}_{\geq 0}$, measured in a model with no redundancy, given in time units (ms).
- Transfer time for a link per visit, $t_l : C \times C \to \mathbb{R}_{\geq 0}$, measured in a model with no redundancy, given in time units (ms).
- Energy consumption of component processing per visit, $e_c : C \to \mathbb{R}_{\geq 0}$, is the estimated energy dissipation by the component during the execution per single visit of the component, given in Joules (J).
- Energy consumption of an idle component, $e_i : C \to \mathbb{R}_{\geq 0}$, is the estimated energy dissipation by the component when being in the idle state, given in Joules (J) per time unit.
- Energy consumption of a link transfer per visit, $e_l : C \times C \to \mathbb{R}_{\geq 0}$, is the estimated energy dissipation in communication between two components per single interaction. given in Joules (J).
- Trigger rate, $r \in \mathbb{R}$, is the expected number of system executions (occurrence of events trigerring system services) per time unit.

Energy annotated MRM. An example of a MRM (for the system in Figure 1) is given in Figure 2. In the example, the nodes are annotated with state rewards $\rho(c_i)$, and transitions annotated with $p(c_i, c_j)/\tau(c_i, c_j)$ where p denotes the transition probabilities and τ the impulse rewards.

Based on the above, the energy annotated MRM derives state rewards from the energy consumed in component processing e_c, and impulse rewards from the energy consumed in communication e_l. In both cases, the rewards are affected by the redundancy level of the relevant subsystem.

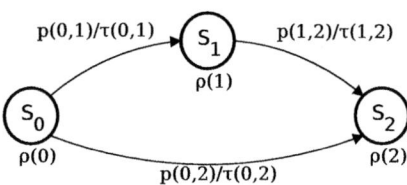

Fig. 2. Markov Reward Model

As the total number of identical components in subsystem S_i is given by $(a(c_i) + 1)$, the *energy consumed in component processing* for the subsystem S_i (node of the MRM) per visit is given by $e_c(c_i) \cdot (a(c_i) + 1)$. The *energy consumed in communication* from a sender subsystem S_i to a recipient S_j (transition in the MRM) is proportional to the number of senders (replicas in S_i), and hence given as $e_l(c_i, c_j) \cdot (a(c_i) + 1)$. In summary, if $c_i, c_j \in C$ are system components (subsystems), and $a \in A$ is a redundancy allocation, then:

– State reward of c_i is defined as $e_c(c_i) \cdot (a(c_i) + 1)$
– Impulse reward of (c_i, c_j) is defined as $e_l(c_i, c_j) \cdot (a(c_i) + 1)$

5   Evaluation of an Architectural Alternative

Each architectural alternative is determined by a single redundancy allocation $a \in A$ (defined in Section 4.1). To quantify the quality of a, we define a quality function $Q : A \rightarrow \mathbb{R}^2$, where $Q(a) = (E^a, R^a)$ s.t. E^a is the quantification of the energy consumption of a (defined in Section 5.2), and R^a denotes the reliability (probability of failure-free operation) of a (defined in Section 5.3). Both E^a and R^a are quantified per a single time unit, which is possible thanks to the trigger rate r, and allows us to reflect also the energy consumed in the idle state. The computation of both E^a and R^a employs the information about the expected number of visits of system components and communication links during the execution (see Section 3 for explanation), which we compute first, in Section 5.1.

5.1   Expected Number of Visits

Expected number of visits of a component, $v_c : C \rightarrow \mathbb{R}_{\geq 0}$, quantifies the expected number of visits of a component (or subsystem) during system execution. Note that $v_c(c)$ corresponds to the expected number of visits of state c_i in the underlying DTMC (as defined in Section 3), i.e. $E[X(c_i)]$. This can be computed by solving the following set of simultaneous equations [26]:

$$v_c(c_i) = q_0(c_i) + \sum_{j \in \mathcal{I}} (v_c(c_j) \cdot p(c_j, c_i)) \tag{3}$$

The formula (3) can be expanded to:

$$v_c(c_0) = q_0(c_0) + v_c(c_0) \cdot p(c_0, c_0) + v_c(c_1) \cdot p(c_1, c_0) + v_c(c_2) \cdot p(c_2, c_0) + ... + v_c(c_n) \cdot p(c_n, c_0)$$
$$v_c(c_1) = q_0(c_1) + v_c(c_0) \cdot p(c_0, c_1) + v_c(c_1) \cdot p(c_1, c_1) + v_c(c_2) \cdot p(c_2, c_1) + ... + v_c(c_n) \cdot p(c_n, c_1)$$
$$v_c(c_2) = q_0(c_2) + v_c(c_0) \cdot p(c_0, c_2) + v_c(c_1) \cdot p(c_1, c_2) + v_c(c_2) \cdot p(c_2, c_2) + ... + v_c(c_n) \cdot p(c_n, c_2)$$

$$\vdots$$

$$v_c(c_n) = q_0(c_n) + v_c(c_0) \cdot p(c_0, c_1) + v_c(c_1) \cdot p(c_1, c_n) + v_c(c_2) \cdot p(c_2, c_n) + ... + v_c(c_n) \cdot p(c_n, c_n)$$

In a matrix form, the transfer probabilities $p(c_i, c_j)$ can be written as $P_{n \times n}$, and execution initiation probabilities $q_0(c_i)$ as $Q_{n \times 1}$. The matrix of expected number of visits $V_{n \times 1}$ can be expressed as:

$$V = Q + P^T \cdot V$$

With the usual matrix operations, the above can be transformed into the solution format:

$$I \times V - P^T \times V = Q$$
$$(I - P^T) \times V = Q$$
$$V = (I - P^T)^{-1} \times Q$$

For absorbing DTMCs which is also the case for the model used in this paper, it has been proved that the inverse matrix $(I - P^T)^{-1}$ exists [18].

Expected number of visits of a communication link, $v_l : C \times C \to \mathbb{R}_{\geq 0}$, quantifies for each link $l_{ij} = (c_i, c_j)$ the expected number of occurrences of the transition (c_i, c_j) in the underlying DTMC (as defined in Section 3), i.e $E[XT(c_i, c_j)]$. To compute this value, we extend the work of Kubat et al. [26] for computing the expected number of visits of system components to communication links. In the extension, we understand communication links as first-class elements of the model, and view each probabilistic transition $c_i \xrightarrow{p(c_i, c_j)} c_j$ in the model as a tuple of transitions $c_i \xrightarrow{p(c_i, c_j)} l_{ij} \xrightarrow{1} c_j$, the first adopting the original probability and the second having probability $= 1$. Then we can apply the above, and compute the expected number of visits of a communication link as:

$$v_l(l_{ij}) = 0 + \sum_{x \in \{i\}} (v_c(c_x) \cdot p(c_x, l_{ij})) \tag{4}$$

$$= v_c(c_i) \cdot p(c_i, c_j) \tag{5}$$

since the execution is never initiated in l_{ij} and the only predecessor of link l_{ij} is component c_i.

5.2   Energy Consumption

The energy consumption of architectural alternative a is computed with respect to two contributing elements: (i) the energy consumed in system execution, and (ii) energy consumed in the idle state.

The *energy consumed in system execution* is represented by the *accumulated reward* defined in Section 3, whose computation employs the state and impulse rewards of the *energy annotated MRM* (defined in Section 4.1) and expected number of visits of both components/subsystems and communication links (defined in Section 5.1). In summary, the energy consumed in system execution is given as:

$$E^a_{exec} = \sum_{c_i \in C} e_c(c_i) \cdot (a(c_i)+1) \cdot v_c(c_i) + \sum_{c_i \in C} \sum_{c_j \in C} e_l(c_i, c_j) \cdot (a(c_i) + 1) \cdot v_l(l_{ij}) \quad (6)$$

Since the MPs together with their redundancies consume certain amount of energy during their idle state as well, the total energy consumption takes into account also the *energy consumed in the idle state*, expressed for a single subsystem S_j and one time unit as $e_i(c_j) \cdot (a(c_j) + 1)$.

Consequently, the total energy consumption of the system for a given redundancy allocation a and a single time unit can be expressed as:

$$E^a = E^a_{exec} \cdot r + \sum_{c_j \in C} e_i(c_j) \cdot (a(c_j) + 1) \quad (7)$$

5.3   Reliability

Having the failure rate λ_c and processing time t_c defined in Section 4.1, the *reliability of a single component c_i* per visit can be computed as [29]:

$$R_c(c_i) = e^{-\lambda_c \cdot t_c(c_i)} \quad (8)$$

When the redundancy levels are employed, the *reliability of a subsystem S_i* (with identical replicas connected in parallel) for the architectural alternative a can be computed as:

$$R^a_c(c_i) = 1 - (1 - R_c(c_i))^{a(i)+1} \quad (9)$$

Similarly, the *reliability of a communication link* per visit is characterized by λ_l and t_l as:

$$R_l(c_i, c_j) = e^{-\lambda_l \cdot t_l(c_i, c_j)} \quad (10)$$

In consideration of a redundancy allocation a, the presence of multiple senders increases the reliability (thanks to the tolerance against commission and value failures) as follows:

$$R^a_l(c_i, c_j) = 1 - (1 - R_l(c_i, c_j))^{a(i)+1} \quad (11)$$

Having the reliabilities of individual system elements (subsystems and links) per a single visit, the reliability of the system execution can be computed analogically to the *accumulated reward* above, based on the expected number of visits, with the difference that we employ multiplication instead of summation [1,26]:

$$R^a_{exec} \approx \prod_{i \in \mathcal{I}} (R^a_c(c_i))^{v_c(c_i)} \cdot \prod_{i,j \in \mathcal{I}} (R^a_l(c_i, c_j))^{v_l(l_{ij})} \quad (12)$$

Finally, the system reliability for a given redundancy allocation a and a single time unit (with respect to trigger rate r) can be expressed as:

$$R^a = (R^a_{exec})^r \quad (13)$$

6   Architecture Optimization with Non-dominated Sorting Genetic Algorithm (NSGA)

The goal of our multi-objective optimization problem is to find the approximate set of solutions $A^* \subseteq A$ that represent a trade-off between the conflicting objectives in $Q : A \rightarrow \mathbb{R}^2$, i.e. the reliability of the system and the energy consumption, and satisfy the set of constraints Ω. In our case, Ω consists of only the constraints on the maximal redundancy levels of system MPs. Different algorithms can be used for solving the optimization problem. In our approach, we employ the *Non-dominated Sorting Genetic Algorithm (NSGA)* [30], which has shown to be robust and have a good performance in the settings related to ours.

For the optimization process, *NSGA* uses an initial *population* of randomly generated *chromosomes* (solutions). Each chromosome encodes a single redundancy allocation alternative $a \in A$. Each *allele* in a *chromosome* represents a redundancy level for a component $c_i \in C$.

The three genetic operators of the evolution process are *selection, cross-over* and *mutation*. NSGA varies from simple genetic algorithm only in the way the selection operator works. The three operators are adapted to the redundancy allocation problem as follows.

6.1   Selection

Before the *selection* operator is applied, the population is ranked on the basis of an individual's non-domination. In a maximization problem a solution a^* is non-dominated if there exists no other a such that $Q_i(a) \geq Q_i(a^*)$ for all objectives, and $Q_i(a) > Q_i(a^*)$ for at least one objective. In other words, if there exists no other feasible variable a which would be superior in at least one objective while being no worse in all other objectives of a^*, then a^* is said to be non-dominated. The set of all non-dominated solutions is known as the non-dominated set.

First, the non-dominated solutions present in the population are identified and assigned a rank value of 0. These solutions will constitute the first non-dominated front in the population, which will be ignored temporarily to process the rest of the population in the same way, finding the solutions which belong to the second non-dominated front. These solution are assigned a higher rank, i.e. the next integer. This process is continued until the entire population is classified into separate fronts.

A mating pool is then created with solutions selected from the population according to the rank that has been assigned to them during the ranking process. The solutions with a lower rank value have a higher chance of being selected to be part of the mating pool than the ones with a higher rank value. This helps the quick convergence of the algorithm towards the optimal solutions. The mating pool will then serve for the random selection of the individuals to reproduce using crossover and mutation.

6.2   Crossover

Crossover is the creation of new solutions $a'_i, a'_j \in A$ from two parents $a_i = [u_{i_1}, u_{i_2}, ..., u_{i_n}]$ and $a_j = [u_{j_1}, u_{j_2}, ..., u_{j_n}]$ coming from existing population by recombining the redundancy levels of components, i.e. for a random k: $a'_i = [u_{i_1}, ..., u_{i_{k-1}}, u_{j_k}, ..., u_{j_n}]$ and $a'_j = [u_{j_1}, ..., u_{j_{k-1}}, u_{i_k}, ..., u_{i_n}]$. After every crossover operation, the solutions are checked for constraints satisfaction in Ω.

6.3   Mutation

Mutation produces a new solution a'_i from existing a_i by switching the allocation of two components, i.e. for randomly selected k, l: $a'_i = [u_{i_1}, ..., u_{i_l}, ..., u_{i_k}, ..., u_{i_n}]$ while the original is $a_i = [u_{i_1}, ..., u_{i_k}, ..., u_{i_l}, ..., u_{i_n}]$. Each newly created chromosome is first checked for constraint satisfaction (for constraints in Ω) before it is allowed to become part of the population. This prevents us from the construction of infeasible solutions.

7   Tool Support

The presented approach, including the NSGA optimization algorithm, has been implemented within the *ArcheOpterix* framework [10], which has been developed with Java/Eclipse and provides a generic platform for specification, evaluation and optimization of embedded system architectures.

ArcheOpterix has a modular structure, with an entry module responsible for interpreting and extracting a system description from a specification, recognizing standard elements like components, services, processors, buses, etc., specified in AADL or XML. It also provides extensions to other elements and domain-specific parameters. The remaining modules allow for plug-in of different quality function evaluators, constraint validators, and optimization algorithms, which makes it a well fitting tool for multi-criteria quality optimization of embedded systems.

8   Illustration of the Approach with a Case Study

8.1   Automotive Control System

An embedded system from the automotive domain is used as a case study for the demonstration of the approach. In the automotive domain reliability is an important quality characteristic, because specific functions (e.g. brake assistance) are safety critical. On the other hand energy consumption is relevant for customer satisfaction, because high energy usage of the electronic systems directly translate to an increased fuel usage for traditional cars or reduced mission times for battery-powered electrical cars. The case study we use in this section has been designed based on already published models [31,32] and models a subsystem which implements an *Anti-lock Brake System (ABS)* and *Adaptive Cruise Control (ACC)* functionality. System parameters required for the model are chosen to closely resemble the reality, including the component failure rates [33], and estimated execution time per visit [34].

Anti-lock Brake System (ABS): ABS is currently used in most of modern cars to minimize hazards associated with skidding and loss of control due to locked wheels during braking. Proper rotation during brake operations allows better maneuverability and enhances the performance of braking.

Adaptive Cruise Control (ACC): Apart from usual automatic cruise control functionality, the main aim of the ACC is to avoid crashes by reducing speed once a slower vehicle in front is detected.

The main components used by the composite system and their interaction diagram are presented in Figure 3. The *ABS Main Unit* is the major decision-making unit regarding the braking levels for individual wheels, while the *Load Compensator* unit assists with computing adjustment factors from the wheel load sensor inputs. Components 4 and 5 represent the components that communicate with wheel sensors while components 7 and 8 represent the electronic control units that control the brake actuators. *Brake Paddle* is the component that reads from the paddle sensor and sends the data to the *Emergency Stop Detection* unit. Execution initialization is possible at the components that communicate with the sensors and user inputs. In this case study the *Wheel Sensors, Speed Limitter, Object Recognition, Mode Switch* and *Brake Paddle* components contribute to the triggering of the service. The captured data from the sensors, are processed by different components in the system and triggers are generated for the actuators like *Brake Actuators* and *Human Machine Interface*.

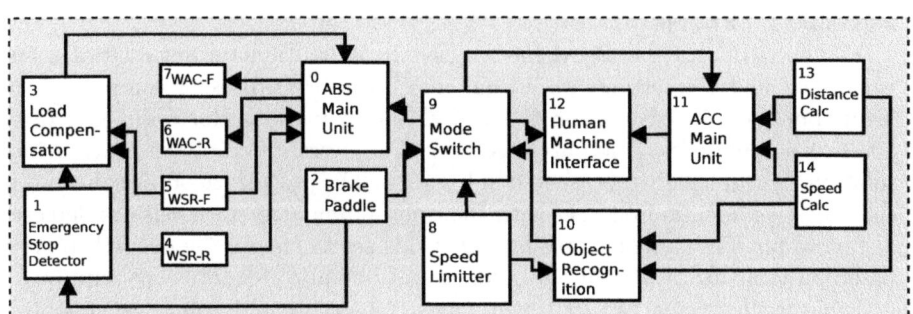

WAC : Wheel Actuator Controllers (Front and Rear)
WSR : Wheel Sensor Readers (Front and Rear)

Fig. 3. Automotive composite system

Parameters of the elements of the considered system, and probabilities of transferring execution from one component to another are illustrated in Table 1. The trigger rate r of the composite system is assumed to be 1 trigger per second.

8.2   Results

Even though the presented case study is a comparatively small segment of an actual automotive system, the possible number of architectural alternatives is $4^{15} \approx 1.07 \cdot 10^9$ (assuming maximum redundancy level of 3), which is too large

Table 1. Parameters of components and communication links

Comp ID	q_0	λ_c	e_c (mJ)	t_c (ms)	e_i (mW)
0	0	$4 \cdot 10^{-6}$	20	33	2
1	0	$6 \cdot 10^{-6}$	10	30	1
2	0.01	$5 \cdot 10^{-6}$	20	10	2
3	0	$8 \cdot 10^{-6}$	25	33	2.5
4	0.17	$8 \cdot 10^{-6}$	30	10	3
5	0.17	$8 \cdot 10^{-6}$	30	10	3
6	0.17	$8 \cdot 10^{-6}$	40	10	4
7	0.17	$8 \cdot 10^{-6}$	40	10	4
8	0.01	$5 \cdot 10^{-6}$	10	20	1
9	0	$5 \cdot 10^{-6}$	10	20	1
10	0	$5 \cdot 10^{-6}$	20	33	2
11	0	$4 \cdot 10^{-6}$	30	28	3
12	0	$7 \cdot 10^{-6}$	40	28	4
13	0.15	$3 \cdot 10^{-6}$	50	33	5
14	0.15	$3 \cdot 10^{-6}$	40	33	4

Trans $c_i \rightarrow c_j$	Prob. $p(c_i, c_j)$	λ_l	e_l (mJ)	t_l (ms)
$0 \rightarrow 7$	0.5	$4 \cdot 10^{-5}$	40	40
$0 \rightarrow 6$	0.5	$5 \cdot 10^{-5}$	40	40
$1 \rightarrow 3$	1	$6 \cdot 10^{-5}$	60	10
$2 \rightarrow 1$	0.75	$5 \cdot 10^{-5}$	60	30
$3 \rightarrow 0$	1	$4 \cdot 10^{-5}$	35	30
$4 \rightarrow 0$	0.7	$4 \cdot 10^{-5}$	60	30
$4 \rightarrow 3$	0.3	$5 \cdot 10^{-5}$	60	30
$5 \rightarrow 0$	0.7	$3 \cdot 10^{-5}$	40	30
$5 \rightarrow 3$	0.3	$5 \cdot 10^{-5}$	50	40
$2 \rightarrow 9$	0.25	$6 \cdot 10^{-5}$	30	40
$8 \rightarrow 9$	0.6	$8 \cdot 10^{-5}$	50	30
$8 \rightarrow 10$	0.4	$12 \cdot 10^{-5}$	40	30
$9 \rightarrow 0$	0.2	$4 \cdot 10^{-5}$	20	10
$9 \rightarrow 11$	0.4	$5 \cdot 10^{-5}$	20	10
$9 \rightarrow 12$	0.6	$5 \cdot 10^{-5}$	30	10
$10 \rightarrow 9$	1	$6 \cdot 10^{-5}$	50	20
$11 \rightarrow 12$	1	$8 \cdot 10^{-5}$	50	20
$13 \rightarrow 10$	0.5	$10 \cdot 10^{-5}$	20	40
$13 \rightarrow 11$	0.5	$12 \cdot 10^{-5}$	20	40
$14 \rightarrow 10$	0.5	$4 \cdot 10^{-5}$	30	40
$14 \rightarrow 11$	0.5	$5 \cdot 10^{-5}$	45	40

to be traversed with an exact algorithm. Therefore we employed the *NSGA* (see Section 6) as a meta-heuristic to obtain a near-optimal solutions in practically affordable time frame.

The execution of the algorithm was set to 25 000 function evaluations, and performed under a settings on a dual-core 2.26 GHz processor computer. The algorithm took 7 seconds for the 25 000 function evaluations and generated 193 non-dominated solution architectures. The distribution of the near-optimal solutions is graphically represented in Figure 4. The prevalence of the solutions in the objective domain, together with their non-dominated trade-offs are depicted in the graph. The designers are provided this set to choose the desired solution based on their utility (trade-off preference of reliability/energy consumption).

Table 2 illustrates two closely related non-dominated solutions generated by the optimization process. The arrays in the second column represent the

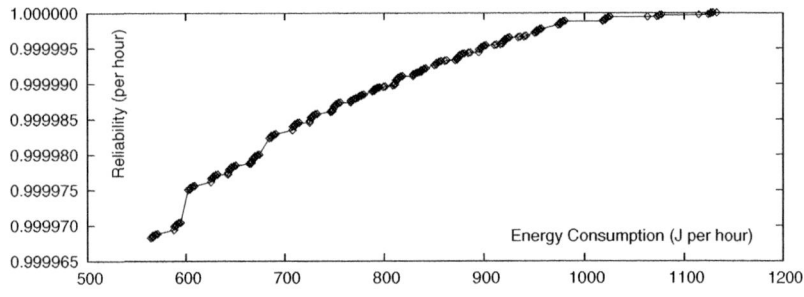

Fig. 4. Distribution of non-dominated solutions

Table 2. Example of two non-dominated solutions

Solution	Redundancy Allocation	Reliability (h^{-1})	Energy Consumption(J/h)
A	[1,0,0,1,1,1,0,0,0,1,1,1,0,1,1]	0.99999828	973.79
B	[1,0,0,1,1,1,0,1,1,1,1,1,1,1,1]	0.99999948	1072.66

redundancy levels for the components (subsystems) ordered by their ID. Note that the reliabilities of the two solutions are very similar while the energy consumption of B is approximately 100 J/h lower than of A. It should be highlighted that the non-obvious change from solution A to solution B has significantly reduced the energy consumption for a very small trade-off of reliability, which would definitely be an interesting information for the system designer.

9   Conclusions and Future Work

In this paper, we have formulated the models for estimating reliability and energy consumption at an architectural level, and combined the two quality attributes in optimizing the redundancy levels of system components. The energy consumption model, formulated in terms of a Markov Reward Model, builds on the expected number of visits in obtaining a point estimate for the accumulated state and impulse reward. The accumulated reward together with the energy consumed in components' idle states then characterizes system energy consumption. The reliability evaluation model extends the Kubat's model [26], applying the concept of subsystems and expected number of visits of system elements. The model is extended to consider also the impact of communication elements of the system. As a result, both estimation techniques enable quantification of the impact of critical design decision on reliability and energy consumption. We have employed this for automatically identifying architecture specification with optimal redundancy level to satisfy both quality attributes. For this identification, the redundancy allocation problem is solved with a multi-objective optimization strategy. We have implemented the architecture evaluation models and used NSGA to find near-optimal architecture solutions. An automotive case study of a composite system of *Anti-lock Brake System (ABS)* and *Adaptive Cruise Control (ACC)* has been used for the validation of our approach.

In future work, we would like to extend the set of investigated design decisions. In addition to the allocation of redundancy levels, also deployment decisions for software components and selection of appropriate architectural elements is interesting. Furthermore, we aim to investigate different optimization strategies such as Ant Colony Strategies, Tabu Search, etc., to compare which of them works better for which problem formulation.

Acknowledgment

This original research was proudly supported by the Commonwealth of Australia, through the Cooperative Research Center for Advanced Automotive Technology (projects C4-501: Safe and Reliable Integration and Deployment Architectures for Automotive Software Systems and C4-509: Dependability optimization on architectural level of system design).

References

1. Goševa-Popstojanova, K., Trivedi, K.S.: Architecture-based approach to reliability assessment of software systems. Performance Evaluation 45(2-3), 179–204 (2001)
2. Benini, L., Bogliolo, A., Micheli, G.D.: A survey of design techniques for system-level dynamic power management. IEEE Trans. VLSI Syst. 8(3), 299–316 (2000)
3. Aydin, H., Melhem, R., Mossé, D., Mejía-Alvarez, P.: Dynamic and aggressive scheduling techniques for power-aware real-time systems. In: Real-Time Systems Symposium, pp. 95–105. IEEE Computer Society, Los Alamitos (2001)
4. Coit, D.W., Smith, A.E.: Reliability optimization of series-parallel systems using a genetic algorithm. IEEE Transactions on Reliability 45(2), 225–266 (1996)
5. Kulturel-Konak, S., Smith, A.E., Coit, D.W.: Efficiently solving the redundancy allocation problem using tabu search. IIE Transactions 35(6), 515–526 (2003)
6. Grunske, L., Lindsay, P.A., Bondarev, E., Papadopoulos, Y., Parker, D.: An outline of an architecture-based method for optimizing dependability attributes of software-intensive systems. In: de Lemos, R., Gacek, C., Romanovsky, A. (eds.) Architecting Dependable Systems IV. LNCS, vol. 4615, pp. 188–209. Springer, Heidelberg (2007)
7. Zhu, D., Melhem, R.G., Mossé, D.: The effects of energy management on reliability in real-time embedded systems. In: International Conference on Computer-Aided Design, pp. 35–40. IEEE Computer Society/ACM (2004)
8. Pop, P., Poulsen, K.H., Izosimov, V., Eles, P.: Scheduling and voltage scaling for energy/reliability trade-offs in fault-tolerant time-triggered embedded systems. In: International Conference on Hardware/Software Codesign and System Synthesis, pp. 233–238. ACM, New York (2007)
9. Bertozzi, D., Benini, L., Micheli, G.D.: Energy-reliability trade-off for NoCs. In: Networks on Chip, pp. 107–129. Springer, US (2003)
10. Aleti, A., Björnander, S., Grunske, L., Meedeniya, I.: ArcheOpterix: An extendable tool for architecture optimization of AADL models. In: Model-based Methodologies for Pervasive and Embedded Software, pp. 61–71. IEEE Computer Society Press, Los Alamitos (2009)
11. Benini, L., Micheli, G.D.: Powering networks on chips. In: International Symposium on Systems Synthesis, pp. 33–38 (2001)
12. Simunic, T., Benini, L., Micheli, G.D.: Energy-efficient design of battery-powered embedded systems. IEEE Trans. VLSI Syst. 9(1), 15–28 (2001)
13. Hong, I., Kirovski, D., Qu, G., Potkonjak, M., Srivastava, M.B.: Power optimization of variable-voltage core-based systems. IEEE Trans. on CAD of Integrated Circuits and Systems 18(12), 1702–1714 (1999)
14. Lu, Y.H., Simunic, T., Micheli, G.D.: Software controlled power management. In: International Workshop on Hardware/Software Codesign, pp. 157–161 (1999)
15. Seo, C., Edwards, G., Malek, S., Medvidovic, N.: A framework for estimating the impact of a distributed software system's architectural style on its energy consumption. In: Working IEEE/IFIP Conference on Software Architecture, pp. 277–280. IEEE Computer Society, Los Alamitos (2008)

16. Qiu, Q., Pedram, M.: Dynamic power management based on continuous-time markov decision processes. In: Design Automation Conference, pp. 555–561. ACM, New York (1999)
17. Vijaykrishnan, N., Kandemir, M.T., Irwin, M.J., Kim, H.S., Ye, W.: Energy-driven integrated hardware-software optimizations using simplepower. In: International Symposium on Computer Architecture, pp. 95–106 (2000)
18. Trivedi, K.S.: Probability and Statistics with Reliability, Queuing, and Computer Science Applications. Prentice-Hall, Englewood Cliffs (1982)
19. Cloth, L., Katoen, J.P., Khattri, M., Pulungan, R.: Model checking markov reward models with impulse rewards. In: Dependable Systems and Networks, pp. 722–731. IEEE Comp. Society, Los Alamitos (2005)
20. Cloth, L., Jongerden, M.R., Haverkort, B.R.: Computing battery lifetime distributions. In: Dependable Systems and Networks, pp. 780–789. IEEE Comp. Society, Los Alamitos (2007)
21. Coit, D.W., Smith, A.E.: Reliability optimization of series-parallel systems using a genetic algorithm. IEEE Transactions on Reliability 45(2), 254–260 (1996)
22. Liang, Y.C., Smith, A.E.: An ant system approach to redundancy allocation. In: Congress on Evolutionary Computation, pp. 1478–1484. IEEE, Los Alamitos (1999)
23. Grunske, L.: Identifying "good" architectural design alternatives with multi-objective optimization strategies. In: International Conference on Software Engineering, ICSE, pp. 849–852. ACM, New York (2006)
24. Zhang, W., Kandemir, M., Sivasubramaniam, A., Irwin, M.J.: Performance, energy, and reliability tradeoffs in replicating hot cache lines. In: Proceedings of the International Conference on Compilers, Architectures and Synthesis for Embedded Systems (CASES 2003), pp. 309–317. ACM Press, New York (2003)
25. Perillo, M.A., Heinzelman, W.B.: Optimal sensor management under energy and reliability constraints. IEEE Wireless Communications, 1621–1626 (2003)
26. Kubat, P.: Assessing reliability of modular software. Operations Research Letters 8(1), 35–41 (1989)
27. Nelson, V.P., Carroll, B.: Fault-Tolerant Computing. IEEE Computer Society Press, Los Alamitos (1987)
28. Katoen, J.P., Khattri, M., Zapreev, S.I.: A markov reward model checker. In: International Conference on the Quantitative Evaluation of Systems(QEST), pp. 243–244. IEEE Computer Society Press, Los Alamitos (2005)
29. Shatz, S.M., Wang, J.P., Goto, M.: Task allocation for maximizing reliability of distributed computer systems. IEEE Trans. on Comp. 41(9), 1156–1168 (1992)
30. Srinivas, N., Deb, K.: Multiobjective optimization using nondominated sorting in genetic algorithms. Evolutionary Computation 2(3), 221–248 (1995)
31. Fredriksson, J., Nolte, T., Nolin, M., Schmidt, H.: Contract-based reusable worst-case execution time estimate. In: The International Conference on Embedded and Real-Time Computing Systems and Applications, pp. 39–46 (2007)
32. Grunske, L.: Towards an Integration of Standard Component-Based Safety Evaluation Techniques with SaveCCM. In: Hofmeister, C., Crnković, I., Reussner, R. (eds.) QoSA 2006. LNCS, vol. 4214, pp. 199–213. Springer, Heidelberg (2006)
33. Assayad, I., Girault, A., Kalla, H.: A bi-criteria scheduling heuristic for distributed embedded systems under reliability and real-time constraints. In: Dependable Systems and Networks, pp. 347–356. IEEE Computer Society, Los Alamitos (2004)
34. Florentz, B., Huhn, M.: Embedded systems architecture: Evaluation and analysis. In: Hofmeister, C., Crnković, I., Reussner, R. (eds.) QoSA 2006. LNCS, vol. 4214, pp. 145–162. Springer, Heidelberg (2006)

QoS Driven Dynamic Binding in-the-many

Carlo Ghezzi, Alfredo Motta, Valerio Panzica La Manna,
and Giordano Tamburrelli

Politecnico di Milano
Dipartimento di Elettronica e Informazione, Deep-SE Group
Via Golgi 42 – 20133 Milano, Italy
{ghezzi,motta,panzica,tamburrelli}@elet.polimi.it

Abstract. Modern software systems are increasingly built out of services that are developed, deployed, and operated by independent organizations, which expose them for the use by potential clients. Services may be directly invoked by clients. They may also be composed by service integrators, who in turn expose the composite artifact as a new service. We envision a world in which multiple providers publish software artifacts which compete with each other by implementing the same "abstract" service (i.e. they export the same API and provide the same functionality), but offering different quality of service. Clients may therefore select the most appropriate services targeting their requirements, among all the competing alternatives, and they may do so dynamically. This situation may be called *dynamic binding in-the-many*. Service selection may be performed by clients by following different strategies, which may in turn affect the overall quality of service invocations.

In this paper we address the problem of analyzing and comparing different service selection strategies and we define a framework to model the different scenarios. Furthermore, we report on quantitative analyses through simulations of the modeled scenarios, highlighting advantages and limitations of each solution.

1 Introduction

Software is rapidly changing in the way it is developed, deployed, operated, and maintained. Applications are often built by integrating components that are produced by independent organizations, or by personalizing and adapting generalized frameworks, rather than developing new solutions in-house and from scratch. Increasingly, applications are built by integrating and composing services that are developed, deployed, operated, and maintained by separate organizations, which offer them as *services* on the market. Services may be invoked directly by clients through some standardized protocols. They may also be composed and integrated by brokers to provide added-value services that are–in turn–exposed for use by potential clients. The long-term vision of *service-oriented computing (SOC)* is that Software as a Service is publicized in an open marketplace through *registries*, which contain the service descriptions that may be of interest for potential clients, and then invoked directly as needed [9].

G.T. Heinemann, J. Kofron, and F. Plasil (Eds.): QoSA 2010, LNCS 6093, pp. 68–83, 2010.

Another key aspect of modern software is its continuous change. Traditionally, change is primarily due to changing requirements, which–in turn–occur because of changes in the business world. Increasingly, however, software is becoming pervasive, and ubiquitous application settings are becoming more and more common. In this context, dynamic environmental change is a dominant factor. It is therefore necessary to develop solutions that may adapt to continuous changes that may arise dynamically, as an application is running and providing service. In conclusion, software increasingly lives in a dynamic and open world, and this poses new challenges to the way it is developed, operated, and evolved [1].

This paper deals with the SOC setting. Although in the current stage most existing approaches are still rather static, continuous evolution is intrinsic in SOC and will play a stronger role in the future. In our work, we envision a world that is fully populated by services that are offered in an open *service marketplace*. Multiple providers publish software artifacts which compete with each other, possibly implementing the same "abstract" service (i.e. they export the same API, which is advertised in registries) but offering different quality of service. Quality may refer to several factors, such as performance, reliability, or cost-per-use. Clients may therefore select the most appropriate services targeting their requirements, among all the competing alternatives, and they may do so dynamically. To support this dynamism, we assume that application components that use external services do not bind to them statically, but rather refer to the required external services through a *required interface*. External services are therefore viewed as *abstract* resources, and the binding to a specific, concrete service may occur dynamically. Since many possible concrete services may be selected for each abstract service, this may be called *binding in-the-many*. The main advantage of a late binding regime is its flexibility. A client may at any time refer to the best possible server, where *best* is defined by some appropriate strategy that may take into account the current state of the world and may maximize the ability of the resulting solution to satisfy the evolving requirements.

This paper focuses on how to support clients in performing dynamic binding to services. In particular, it deals with the service selection problem where clients try to bind to the external services that can ensure the best results in terms of *performance*. In principle, performance attributes might be publicly available as part of the published description of *quality of service* (QoS) that is stored in registries [11]. Clients might use this information to drive their binding policy. In practice, publication of QoS data is unlikely to happen, and even if it does, the published figures might not correspond to the real values. Clients may thus base their binding strategies on the real performance data observed in practice. In this work we describe a first step towards the development of a framework that supports a quantitative analysis of the different strategies that may be followed by clients to perform dynamic binding.

The paper is organized as follows: Section 2 illustrates the service selection problem and the assumptions under which we analyze possible solutions. Section 3 describes different service selection strategies. Section 4 illustrates the simulations we performed to evaluate the different strategies. Section 5 discusses related work. Section 6 concludes the paper summarizing the current limitations of our approach and how they can be tackled by future work.

2   Problem Statement: Assumptions and Formalization

In this section we formalize the service selection problem using an appropriate stochastic framework. For simplicity, we assume that services can be grouped in equivalence classes (called *concrete target sets CTSs*), where all services in a CTS provide the same interface and implement the same functionality. In reality, equivalent services may actually differ in details of their interface, but we can assume that suitable adaptation mechanisms allow clients to abstract away from these technical differences. Adaptation techniques are beyond the scope of this paper but many existing techniques, such as [3,8], tackle this research problem. By relying on these assumptions, any two elements in a CTS are substitutable to one another, since they implement the same abstract service. Any of them can be bound to an abstract service invocation performed by a client, thus reifying a specific dynamic binding. They may differ, however, in the *quality of service* they provide.

Given a CTS, which groups all substitutable implementations of a certain abstract service, we analyze the behavior of competing clients, which need to bind to a concrete service offered by a specific provider to submit their requests. We assume services to be stateless and interactions between clients and services to be of type *request-response*. For simplicity, we measure the execution time of a service invocation as the overall time observed by the client, without further decomposing it into transmission time and service processing time. This simplifying assumption will be removed in future research.

The problem may be formalized as a *multi-client multi-provider stochastic framework*, which is a 6-tuple:

$$< C, P, F1, F2, F3, SS >$$

where:

- $C =< c_1, ..., c_n >$ is a set of *clients*, all of which use the same abstract service,
- $P =< p_1, ..., p_m >$ is a *concrete target set* of substitutable services,
- $F1 : C \times \mathbb{N} \to [0,1]$ is a probabilistic *request submission* function,
- $F2 : C \times \mathbb{N} \to \mathbb{R}$ is a probabilistic *request payload* function,
- $F3 : P \times \mathbb{N} \to \mathbb{R}$ is a *service processing rate* function,
- SS is a service provider selection strategy.

We assume *time* to be modeled discretely by Natural numbers in functions $F1$, $F2$, and $F3$. The intuitive interpretation of the above functions is provided below. Providers are characterized by their time-varying processing rate $F3$, a real number, which defines the speed at which providers process requests coming from clients. Each client, at each time instant, is either *idle* or *busy*. Clients that are busy wait for the completion of their last request. Clients that are idle may submit a new request with probability given by $F1$. Whenever a new request is generated, the client selects one of the available service providers according to the strategy SS. Function $F2$ describes the *payload* of a service request, issued by a certain client at a certain time. The payload is a real number that expresses the complexity of the submitted request. It is used to normalize the service's response time to the complexity of the requests issued by the client. If a client c submits a request with payload $F2(c, t_{start})$ at time t_{start} and the response is received at time t_{stop}, we can compute the service's *timeliness* as:

$$T = (t_{stop} - t_{start})/F2(c, t_{start})$$

Any conceivable strategies used by clients, including the ones we will describe and analyze in this paper, use historical information collected by the client during its past interactions with external services. Such historical information reifies the client's experience and its view of the external world. Each client c traces its history into a vector, the *efficiency estimator* ee_c. The length of this vector corresponds to the cardinality of CTS, and the ith entry in the vector $ee_c(i)$ is a positive real value that represents the client's estimate of the current efficiency of service provider i. In addition to ee_c , client c has a vector jd_c, which stores the number of completed requests it submitted to each of the service providers, since the beginning of time. When the request is completed in normalized time T, vector ee_c associated with client c is updated as follows:

$$ee_c(p) := W \cdot T + (1 - W)ee_c(p)$$

where W is a real value in the interval $[0, 1]$, whose actual value depends on $jd_c(p)$ using the following formula:

$$W = w + (1 - w)/jd_c(p)$$

In the above formula w is a real-valued constant in the interval $[0, 1]$. The term $(1 - w)/jd_c(p)$ is a correcting factor, whose effect becomes negligible when $jd_c(p)$ is sufficiently high. Other functions may be used to update ee_c and could be explored in a future work.

As we assumed, any request generated by clients may be bound to any service provider of a CTS. We may further assume that service providers handle the clients' requests sequentially, for example following a FIFO policy (this assumption can be easily relaxed if necessary). The response time of a certain provider p at a given time t, as observed by clients, obviously deteriorates as the queue of clients' requests waiting to be served grows.

3   Binding Strategies

In this section we illustrate six possible selection strategies through the concepts introduced in the previous section. Each of these strategies defines the binding between the services and clients which issue requests. In particular, two of them (the *Minimum* and the *Probabilistic* strategy) are based on autonomous decisions made by each client, which selects the target service only on the basis of its own locally available information. Conversely, the *Collaborative* strategy allows a simple form of coordination among clients. In the *Proxy-based* approaches the service binding is delegated to a proxy, which assigns providers to clients based on its global knowledge of the current situation. Two strategies are analyzed in this case: *Proxy Minimum* and *Proxy Probabilistic*. Finally, we also analyze an *Ideal* strategy, which assumes an ideal case where all the clients have a perfect instantaneous knowledge on the real services' performance. This strategy, even if not applicable in a real implementation, has been studied in our experiments to show how far can we go if each client tries to maximize its own performance goals in isolation. As introduced in Section 1 we focus on performance expressed in terms of response time. In the following, we describe the selection strategies and we anticipate some remarks on their practical effectiveness. An empirical assessment is reported later in section 4.

3.1   Minimum Strategy

The Minimum Strategy (MS) is the simplest selection strategy in which each client selects the service provider with the minimum locally estimated expected response time. This information is derived by the efficiency estimator ee_c:

$$selected\_provider = p \in P | (min_{p \in P}\{ee_c(p)\})$$

This strategy suffers from a number of drawbacks, since ee_c (1) is different for each client (it depends on its own history) and (2) contains information that may be outdated, because each value $ee_c(p)$ is re-computed only when provider p is used.

This strategy has limitations also from the provider's perspective. In fact, the provider offering best performance figure is likely to be selected by the majority of clients, and hence its performance may deteriorate because of the increased number of issued requests.

3.2   Ideal Strategy

The Ideal Strategy (IS) is a benchmarking strategy used only for the comparison with other strategies. It is based on the following assumptions:

Each time a client needs to select a service, it knows:

- The number of pending requests for each provider p, $pr(p)$.
- The processing rate of each service provider p, $R(p)$.

IS selects the concrete service p which exhibits the maximum value of the current processing capacity cr, defined as:

$$cr(p) = \frac{R(p)}{pr(p)}$$

This strategy is ideal because it assumes complete and accurate knowledge of the available concrete services. It can be seen as an extreme optimal case of MS.

3.3   Probabilistic Strategy

The Probabilistic Strategy (PS) performs service selection with a certain probability. PS uses a probabilistic function based on the efficiency estimator ee_c.
We first define the following function:

$$pd'_c(p) := \begin{cases} ee_c(p)^{-n} & \text{if } jd_c(p) > 0, \\ E[ee_c]^{-n} & \text{if } jd_c(p) = 0 \end{cases}$$

where n is a positive real-valued parameter and $E[ee_c]$ represents the average of the values of $ee_c(p)$ over all the providers that were used in the past. To turn this value into a probability function we define the pd_c as the normalized version of pd'_c:

$$pd_c(p) := \frac{pd'_c(p)}{\sigma}$$

where $\sigma = \sum_{p \in P} pd'_c(p)$

The function pd_c depends on n: the larger n is, the higher the probability to select providers with smaller estimated response time. In extreme cases, where the value of n is very high (e.g., 20), the client behaves like in the Minimum Strategy, always choosing the provider with the best record in ee_c. Using the terminology of reinforcement learning, parameter n defines how much a client is *explorative* in its search. The intuitive advantages of using PS over MS, confirmed by the experiments described later in section 4 are:

1. It guarantees a better load balancing of clients among available providers. In fact, by construction, the probability defines a distribution of client requests with respect to providers. This reduces the size of their associated queues and improves the average response time.
2. It improves the efficiency of the choice with respect to the MS. According to MS, a client performs the same binding to the provider p until the estimated response time of the selected provider (stored in $ee_c(p)$) exceeds the value of the estimate of another provider q. PS is less conservative, and may select a new provider q earlier, avoiding to experience performance deterioration of provider p.

3.4   Collaborative Strategy

According to both MS and PS, the pth entry in the efficiency estimator is updated only if p is used. Thus both strategies are based on information (kept in ee_c), which may not reflect the current situation of available concrete services. Because the ideal strategy cannot be implemented, we try to achieve a better view of the current performance offered by concrete services through the introduction of a simple form of communication among clients in PS. This yields a new algorithm, called Collaborative Strategy (CS). In CS, the set of clients C is partitioned in classes (NCs) according to a *near-to* relation. We assume that each client can communicate only with the clients belonging to the same NC. The communication consists of sharing all the efficiency estimators of clients in a NC in order to derive a new vector called *near-to estimator ne*, computed as the average of all the *ee*s. On the basis of *ne*, the client performs its choice in the same way as in MS or in PS. Each client c keeps its own ee_c and communicates with other clients whenever a new binding occurs, by recomputing *ne*. By grouping together a set of clients which perform their decision on the basis of a common vector we can mitigate the problem arising in PS due to outdated records in ee_c. Two possible collaborative strategies are thus possible: minimum value based and probabilistic. We later show an assessment of the latter, which outperforms the former. In fact, the Collaborative Strategy, as an extended version of PS, inherits all the advantages of PS over MS in terms of efficiency and fair load balancing.

3.5   Proxy-Based Approach

We can try to achieve a global view of the world by introducing a decoupling layer between the clients and the concrete services, i.e. a *proxy*. In proxy-based strategies a proxy is responsible for: (1) selecting the best concrete service within CTS and (2) linking the selected service with the client that issued the request. The proxy can be considered as a binding establishing service. In a configuration without a proxy, the client invokes the selected concrete service directly. To do so, the client has to take into consideration all the different interfaces offered by the various providers to invoke the service, and must implement a particular mapping from the abstract interface into the concrete interfaces offered by concrete services, if needed. The proxy-based solution simplifies the way clients interact with concrete services by letting the proxy handle the nitty-gritty details of the interaction and select the concrete service on their behalf. Furthermore, the proxy can be seen as a load balancer, which tries to distribute load to get the best response time on behalf of clients.

Beside keeping trace of t_{start} and t_{stop} for each requests submitted by clients, the proxy is also in charge of computing two vectors:

- The efficiency estimator *ee* which records the history of interaction with all concrete services. Unlike the previous strategies, *ee* records information about response time for *all* clients.
- The pending requests vector *pr*, which collects all the pending requests sent to each provider.

The main advantage of proxy based solutions is that a single efficiency estimator, which is shared by all clients, is updated more frequently than in the other approaches. For this reason a more accurate performance estimate is obtained for the concrete services. We investigate two possible service selection strategies, Proxy Minimum Strategy (PMS) and Proxy Probabilistic Strategy (PPS) which represent a modified version of the strategies described previously.

The reader might suspect that proxy-based strategies require a centralized component acting as a proxy, thus generating a bottleneck and a single point of failure. This, however, is only a logical view of the architecture. The proxy layer may in fact be physically distributed over a number of nodes for example connected in a token ring structure. Each node of the ring contains:

- the centralized efficiency estimator ee computed as the average of all the ee_i locally stored in each proxy.
- the pr as the sum of all the pr_i maintained by each proxy.

However this is just one possible architecture that has not yet been validated by concrete experiments. The appropriate token speed and the impact of communication delays are beyond the scope of this paper and must be investigated. Future work will focus on these issues.

4   Validation

In this section we illustrate the results obtained by simulating in Matlab the selection strategies introduced in Section 3, to draw some conclusions about their effectiveness.

Given the probabilistic nature of our framework every simulation has been performed 100 times and then the average of results has been considered. We used the following parameters for our simulations:

- $\#C = 100$, number of clients.
- $\#P = 5$, number of service providers.
- time interval= 3 hours.

Each provider has a certain processing rate $F3$ that may assume one of the values in the set $[40, 20, 10]$. The value of the payloads of service invocation $F2$ has a uniform distribution between 50 and 150. Finally for CS we also define the number (5) and the size (20 clients) of the NC classes for all the simulations. In order to compare the different service selection strategies, we focus on service timeliness T. That is, we evaluate the different selection strategies by comparing the resulting values of T, averaged over all requests.

For space reasons, we cannot provide an extensive report on the experimental results we obtained through simulation. In particular, we will only summarize some basic findings regarding parameter tuning in Section 4.1 while section 4.2 will give some detail insights through charts on the different selection strategies.

4.1   Parameters Tuning

The selection strategies presented in Section 3 are characterized by two internal parameters which may affect the selection behavior and the resulting efficiency: (1) w, which defines how to update ee, and affects all the strategies; (2) n, which defines the probability distribution of selection, which affects probabilistic strategies. On the basis of preliminary experiments, concrete values of these parameters are derived and commented in this subsection.

A related study on the importance of such parameters in the context of multi-agent load balancing is described in [10].

Parameter w determines the importance of the last normalized response time with respect to the previous one. The greater w is, the more weight is given to the current record. Given these premises it is interesting to understand how the efficiency of the strategies is influenced by this parameter in different settings of the load of the system.

If the load of the system is fixed and equally distributed among all clients, the setting is completely static and at any invocation the current response time record is the same as the previous. In this case, both pure client-based (MS, PS, IS) and proxy-based strategies (PMS, PPS) are independent of w. Instead, if the load generated by clients changes dynamically, client-based strategies perform better with higher values of w ($w = 0.9$), because in such cases the recently experienced timeliness values weigh more than the previous in the update of ee. Proxy-based strategies are instead less dependent on w, since ee intrinsically keeps a more current view of services' performance.

It is also interesting to understand how n influences the choices of PS and PPS. This may be used to find a good balance between an *explorative* and a *conservative* behavior. In a situation of fixed load, PS achieves a better result with large values of n. This is due to the fact that, whenever there are no changes in the dynamics of the system, it is obviously better to always choose the best provider, hence to reduce PS to MS. On the other hand, if the load is variable when n is too high the results are worse. The same results were obtained for PPS. Good values of n are in the middle of the interval [1 10]. If n is too high, PPS tends not to change the already selected provider p, so if the processing capacity of p decreases, performance may deteriorate. On the other hand, if n is too small PPS does not correctly exploit the knowledge given by ee and pr performing a random selection.

In conclusion, $w = 0.9$ and $n = 6$ are the values used in the simulations described in 4.2.

4.2   Empirical Results

We performed experiments to evaluate the six binding strategies discussed in Section 3. Experiments focus on the following cases:

1. Fixed provider processing rates
2. Variable provider processing rates
3. Heterogeneous client populations

Fixed provider processing rates. In our first experiment (Figure 1) we compare the performance of the six strategies focusing on the case where all the clients have the same request submission function $F1$ and the providers have a constant processing rate $F3$. We fixed $F1$ for the set of clients to one of the values in the set [0.001, 0.003, 0.010], and this value is kept constant over time. Function $F3$ for each of the available concrete services, $[p_1, p_2, p_3, p_4, p_5]$ assumes the values [40, 20, 20, 10, 10], respectively.

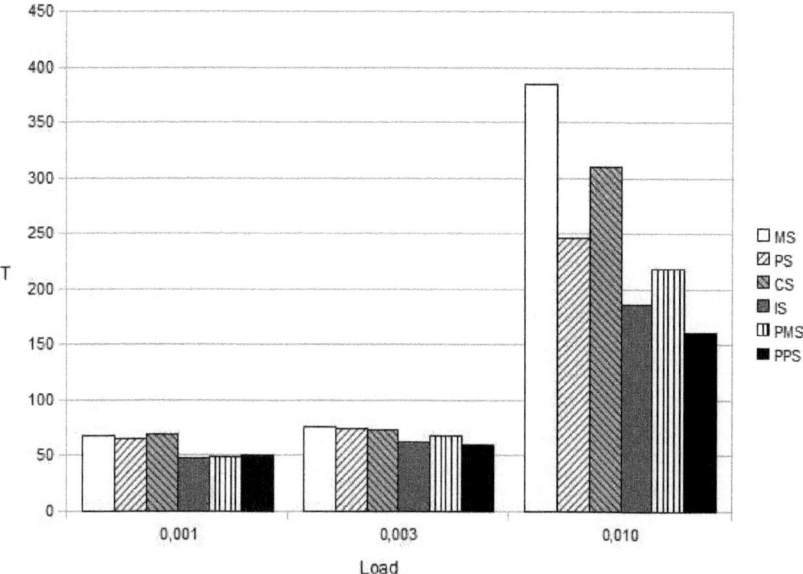

Fig. 1. Performance of selection strategies: fixed provider processing rate and fixed client load

We show the timeliness results provided by the simulation over all the requests made by the clients to the service providers using a certain strategy. Thus, the lowest the bar, the better is the performance of the strategy. From Figure 1 we can draw some conclusions:

- PS performs better than MS, especially as the load of client submissions increases. This is fairly intuitive because all the clients tend to select the same provider that is performing well in that specific instant of time, with the side effect that some clients will wait in a long queue. PS, thanks to its exploration characteristics does not have the same problems and performs reasonably well.
- PS outperforms also CS. NC classes tend to reproduce the same conservative behavior that characterize MS.
- With high load, PPS outperforms IS. Thus, despite its name, IS does not yield the ideal result. Indeed, although IS has a global view of the current providers' performance, it misses a crucial piece of global information, namely the current requests issued by the other clients. Proxy-based strategies, on the other hand, are aware of the current load exerted by clients.

Similar conclusions can be derived by examining Figure 2, which illustrates a situation where clients change their behavior. Specifically, the load is variable among the values [0.001, 0.003, 0.01]: during a 3 hour simulation, the request submission function $F1(c, t)$ of each client randomly changes every 20 minutes

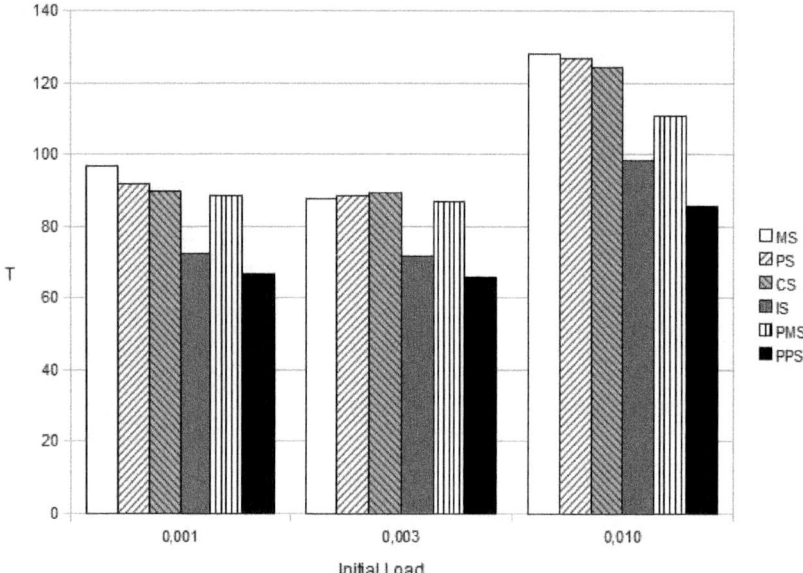

Fig. 2. Performance of selection strategies: fixed provider processing rate and variable client load

and assumes one of the previously specified values. The 3-hour simulation shows slightly different results (but a similar pattern) depending on the initial load chosen for the simulation. A larger simulation period would smooth the differences due to the initial load.

Variable provider processing rates. In Figures 1 and 2 we have seen how the different selection strategies behave depending on changes in the load generated by clients. We now show what happens when concrete services change their behaviors; e.g., a provider decreases or increases its performances. This is exactly the case of Figure 3 where every 20 minutes we change the processing rate of the service providers, which randomly takes a value in the set $[40; 20; 10]$, and this value is kept constant until the next random selection. The results show that the on-client selection strategies (MS, PS and CS) suffer most the changing environment because they do not have enough information for timely reaction. IS turns out to deliver the best results thanks to its complete knowledge of the instantaneous changes in the world. However, PPS still remains very close to IS and it gives evidence of its adaptive capability.

Figure 4 shows the results of a scenario with variable client load in addition to the changing processing rate of the providers. This change increases the unpredictability of the system, but the different strategies behave like in the previous case, although here PPS performs better than IS.

Heterogeneous client populations. In the next examples we are going to relax the hypothesis that all the clients use the same request submission function $F1$.

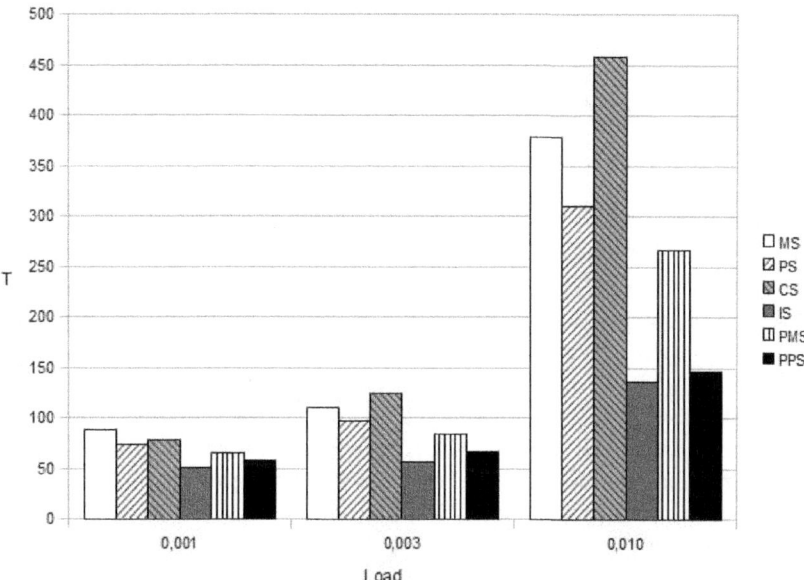

Fig. 3. Performance of selection strategies: variable provider processing rate and fixed client load

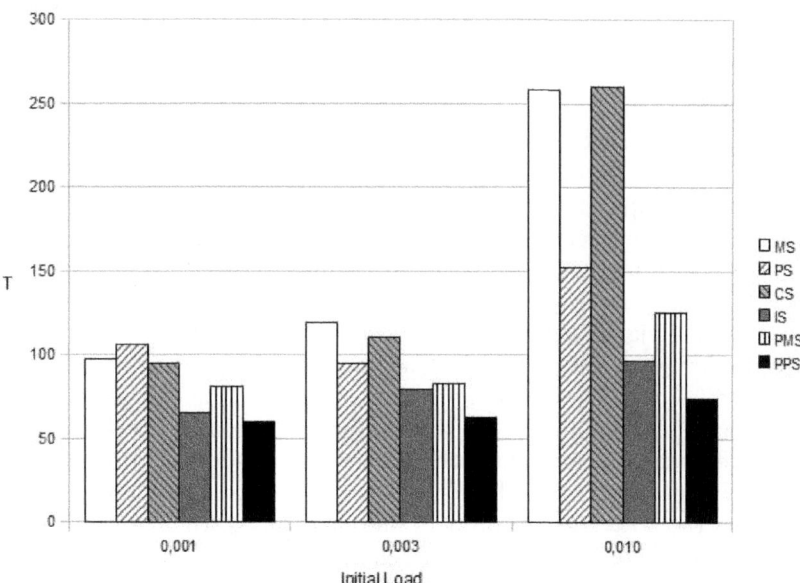

Fig. 4. Performance of selection strategies: variable provider processing rate and variable client load

Specifically, we consider the set of clients C to be partitioned in two populations: the first, called C1, which submits a low number of requests ($F1(c,t) = 0,001 \; \forall c \in C1, \; t \in \mathbb{N}$) and the second, called C2, which submits a higher number of requests ($F1(c,t) = 0,01 \; \forall c \in C2, \; t \in \mathbb{N}$).

Figure 5 shows the performance of $C1$ and $C2$ using the different strategies in a setting where the processing rate of the providers is fixed.

As shown in Figure 5, the two different classes perform equally in any of the service selection strategies. This is fairly intuitive because the processing capacities of the providers and the load of the system are fixed. As a consequence, the performance estimation, represented by the efficiency estimator ee, is always updated.

The last results we report (Fig. 6) illustrate the case where we modify the environment at run-time by changing the processing rate $F3$ of the service providers in order to see if the class $C1$ of clients that submit requests with less frequency still performs like the class of clients $C2$. Figure 6 shows that the clients of class $C2$ (high load) that are using MS, CS and PS perform better than the clients belonging to class $C1$ (low load). This shows that the more one issues requests to the service providers, the more local efficiency estimators are updated, hence the closer one gets to selecting the best service provider. However this is an undesirable behavior, because in principle a fair strategy should not distinguish clients with different submission rates. Proxy-based approaches (both PMS and PPS) solve this problem. In fact the ee vector is the same for all the clients and it is stored in the proxy, and obviously the two classes of clients will have the same performance. Notice also that IS, thanks to its complete knowledge, is always up-to-date, thus even if clients of class $C1$ submit less requests than clients of class $C2$, it always chooses the best service provider.

5   Related Work

The problem of supporting automatic service composition has become a hot research theme in the recent years. Many recent papers deal with service selection, focusing on particular aspects that differ from this study.

Most of them concentrate on the *Web Service* scenario where delivering QoS is a critical and significant challenge because of its dynamic and unpredictable nature. Service composition here is done using the performances declared by the external service provider assuming that those values do not change at run-time. This is also the main difference with our research work, which does not rely on declared performance data, but rather on values measured at run-time. In other words we cannot assume that the declared level of performance is guaranteed. For this reason, the strategies we propose automatically select the services at run-time based on response time measurements which reflect the current situation.

In this context both Liu et al. [5] and Yu et al. [12] reason on how to satisfy end-to-end QoS constraints by modeling service composition as a graph. The former solves the problem using a genetic algorithm which produces a set of paths defining the optimal composition among services that satisfy the global QoS

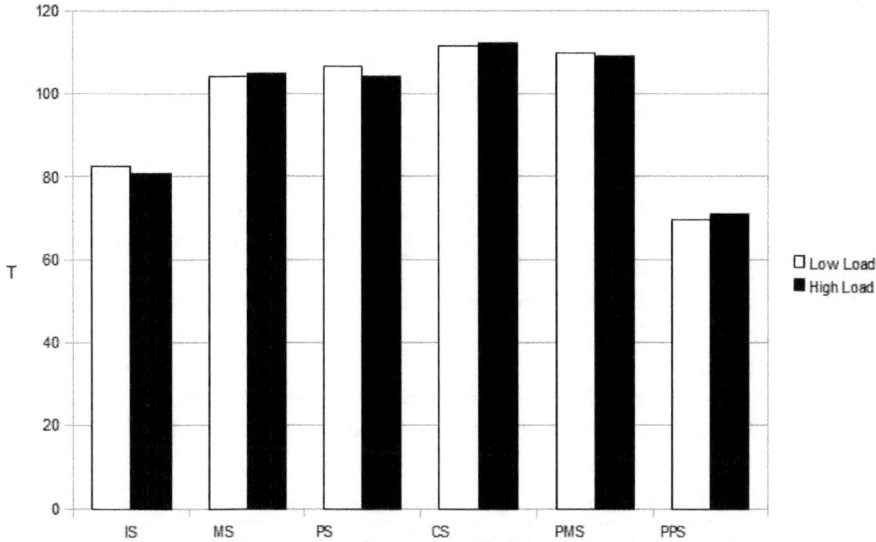

Fig. 5. Service Selection strategies performances of two populations of clients: C1 (low value of F1) and C2 (high value of F1). Providers have fixed processing rate.

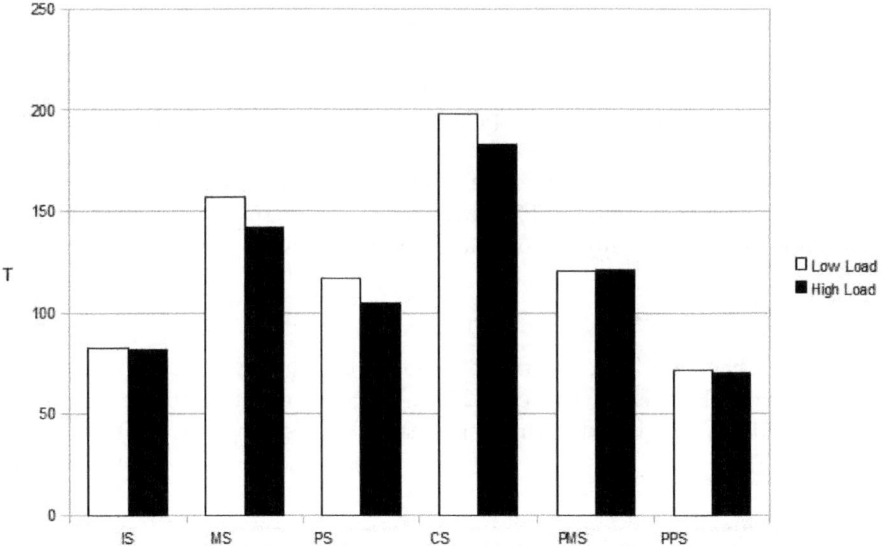

Fig. 6. Service Selection strategies performances with two heterogeneous population of clients: C1 (low value of F1) and C2 (high value of F1). Providers have variable processing capacities.

constraints on the basis of declared parameters. The latter proposes a broker-based architecture that can solve a multi-dimension multi-choice knapsack problem (MMKP) or a multi-constrained optimal path (MCOP) problem. We do not analyse end-to-end QoS because we concentrate on the substitution of a single service trying to optimize the expected performance of the new one.

Single service substitution is studied in [7], [4] and [6]. In [7] link analysis is applied to rank the QoS of the available services. In [4] a centralized service selector is proposed that collects user's feedback in order to rank the services. Finally, [6] relies on a centralized entity that ranks the available services using a recommendation system which exploits the item based collaborative filtering approach (see also [2]). None of these papers uses performance data to select external services, as instead we discussed here.

Finally, an important aspect of service substitution is to identify possible interaction mismatching [8] and to produce the correct mapping of the interfaces [3]. These, however, are out of the scope of the work we described here.

6   Conclusions

In this paper we addressed the issue of dynamically reconfiguring a composite service-based application in order to optimize its performance through dynamic binding. We focused on a number of binding strategies and we evaluated them via simulation. This is an initial but encouraging step towards understanding dynamically adaptable software applications.

We plan to extend this work in a number of interesting directions. First, we wish to refine our model and enrich its experimental assessment. For example, we would like to improve its accuracy by decomposing the response time observed by clients into network latency and service response time. Next, we wish to explore a distributed architecture for the proxy-based strategies, to eliminate a possible single point of failure that would arise in a centralized solution. Last, we wish to explore other reconfiguration strategies through which one can react to performance violations, other than dynamic binding, which may restructure the internals of the application or dynamically discover and add new service providers.

Acknowledgments

This research has been partially funded by the European Commission, Programme IDEAS-ERC, Project 227977-SMScom and by Project Q-ImPrESS (FP7-215013) funded under the European Union's Seventh Framework Programme (FP7).

References

1. Baresi, L., Di Nitto, E., Ghezzi, C.: Toward open-world software: Issue and challenges. Computer 39(10), 36–43 (2006)
2. Bianculli, D., Binder, W., Drago, L., Ghezzi, C.: Transparent reputation management for composite web services. In: ICWS 2008, pp. 621–628. IEEE Computer Society, Washington (2008)

3. Cavallaro, L., Di Nitto, E., Pradella, M.: An automatic approach to enable replacement of conversational services. In: ICSOC/ServiceWave, pp. 159–174 (2009)
4. Huebscher, M.C., McCann, J.A.: Using real-time dependability in adaptive service selection. In: Proceedings of the Joint International Conference ICAS-ICNS 2005. 76 p. IEEE Computer Society Press, Washington (2005)
5. Liu, S., Liu, Y., Jing, N., Tang, G., Tang, Y.: A dynamic web service selection strategy with QoS global optimization based on multi-objective genetic algorithm. In: Zhuge, H., Fox, G.C. (eds.) GCC 2005. LNCS, vol. 3795, pp. 84–89. Springer, Heidelberg (2005)
6. Manikrao, U.S., Prabhakar, T.V.: Dynamic selection of web services with recommendation system. In: NWESP 2005: Proceedings of the International Conference on Next Generation Web Services Practices, 117 p. IEEE Computer Society, Washington (2005)
7. Mei, L., Chan, W.K., Tse, T.H.: An adaptive service selection approach to service composition. In: ICWS 2008: Proceedings of the 2008 IEEE International Conference on Web Services, pp. 70–77. IEEE Computer Society, Washington (2008)
8. Motahari Nezhad, H.R., Benatallah, B., Martens, A., Curbera, F., Casati, F.: Semi-automated adaptation of service interactions. In: WWW, pp. 993–1002 (2007)
9. Di Nitto, E., Ghezzi, C., Metzger, A., Papazoglou, M., Pohl, K.: A journey to highly dynamic, self-adaptive service-based applications. Automated Software Eng. 15(3-4), 313–341 (2008)
10. Schaerf, A., Shoham, Y., Tennenholtz, M.: Adaptive load balancing: a study in multi-agent learning. J. Artif. Int. Res. 2(1), 475–500 (1994)
11. Skene, J., Davide Lamanna, D., Emmerich, W.: Precise service level agreements. In: ICSE 2004, pp. 179–188 (2004)
12. Yu, T., Zhang, Y., Lin, K.-J.: Efficient algorithms for web services selection with end-to-end qos constraints. ACM Trans. Web 1(1), 6 (2007)

A Hybrid Approach for Multi-attribute QoS Optimisation in Component Based Software Systems

Anne Martens[1], Danilo Ardagna[2], Heiko Koziolek[3],
Raffaela Mirandola[2], and Ralf Reussner[1]

[1] Karlsruhe Institute of Technology, Karlsruhe, Germany
{martens,reussner}@kit.edu
[2] Politecnico di Milano, Dipartimento di Elettronica e Informazione, Milano, Italy
{ardagna,mirandola}@elet.polimi.it
[3] ABB Corporate Research, Ladenburg, Germany
heiko.koziolek@de.abb.com

Abstract. Design decisions for complex, component-based systems impact multiple quality of service (QoS) properties. Often, means to improve one quality property deteriorate another one. In this scenario, selecting a good solution with respect to a single quality attribute can lead to unacceptable results with respect to the other quality attributes. A promising way to deal with this problem is to exploit multi-objective optimization where the objectives represent different quality attributes. The aim of these techniques is to devise a set of solutions, each of which assures a trade-off between the conflicting qualities. To automate this task, this paper proposes a combined use of analytical optimization techniques and evolutionary algorithms to efficiently identify a significant set of design alternatives, from which an architecture that best fits the different quality objectives can be selected. The proposed approach can lead both to a reduction of development costs and to an improvement of the quality of the final system. We demonstrate the use of this approach on a simple case study.

1 Introduction

One of the today issues in software engineering is to find new effective ways to deal intelligently with the increasing complexity of software-intensive computing system. In this context a crucial role is played by the achievement of quality requirements, such as performance and availability.

In recent decades, software architecture (SA) has emerged as an appropriate level for dealing with software qualities [10,31] and several efforts have been devoted to the definition of methods and tools able to evaluate quality at SA level (see, for example, [3,25,15,31]). However, each method usually addresses a single quality attribute (e.g., performance or availability), while a major challenge in system development is finding the best balance between different, possibly conflicting quality requirements that a system has to meet and cost constraints (e.g., maximize performance and availability, while minimizing cost).

For these multi-attribute problems, there is usually no single global solution, and a promising way to deal with them is to exploit multi-objective optimisation [16,6]

G.T. Heinemann, J. Kofron, and F. Plasil (Eds.): QoSA 2010, LNCS 6093, pp. 84–101, 2010.

where the objectives represent different quality attributes. The aim of these techniques is to devise a set of solutions, called Pareto optimal solutions or Pareto front [16], each of which assures a trade-off between the conflicting qualities. In other words, while moving from one Pareto solution to another, there is a certain amount of sacrifice in one objective(s) to achieve a certain amount of gain in the other(s). This activity is time consuming, thus the software architect needs an automated method that efficiently explores the architectural design space with respect to the multiple quality attributes. Previous approaches in this direction use evolutionary algorithms [27], however, the derived optimisation process is time-consuming.

To overcome these drawbacks, this paper proposes a method where different design alternatives are automatically generated and evaluated for different quality attributes, providing the software architect with a powerful decision making tool enabling the selection of the SA that best fits multiple quality objectives. The proposed approach is centered around a hybrid approach, where an initial SA of the system (fulfilling its functional requirements) is taken as input. Based on this initial solution, a search problem is formulated by defining "degrees of freedom". The identification of a significant set of design alternatives is then based on a combined use of analytical optimisation techniques and evolutionary algorithms [6]. This hybrid approach extends the work presented in [27], introducing a step based on analytical optimisation whose goal is to derive very efficiently an approximated Pareto front with respect to a simplified search space. The obtained results are used as input candidates for an evolutionary optimisation of the original search problem. In this way, more accurate estimates for availability and performance metrics and a larger Pareto optimal solution set can be obtained. The advantages of this hybrid approach are shown in a case study.

The proposed method can lead both to a reduction of development costs and to an improvement of the quality of the final system, because an automated and efficient search is able to identify more and better design alternatives.

The remainder of the paper is organized as follows. Section 2 introduces the adopted architectural model and quality prediction techniques. Section 3 describes the optimisation process. Experimental results are presented in Section 4. Section 5 reviews other literature proposals. Conclusions are finally drawn in Section 6.

2 Background: Architecture Modelling and Analyses

In this section, we present the architectural model and the existing quality analyses methods our approach is based on. To quickly convey our contributed concepts to the reader, we introduce an example system.

Our approach requires a component-based architecture model with performance, availability, and costs annotations as input. Balsamo et al. [3] and Koziolek [25] have surveyed many different methods for specifying performance models, and Smith and Williams [31] have provided a set of guidelines on how to obtain performance models during early development stages and on how to refine such models as the implementation progresses. For reliability, Gokhale [17] provides a survey.

In our approach, we adopt the Palladio Component Model (PCM) [5], but our approach could be extended to consider other architectural performance and availability models and analysis methods. The PCM is beneficial for our purposes as it is specifically designed for component-based systems. Thus, the PCM naturally supports many architectural degrees of freedom (e.g., substituting components, changing component allocation, etc.). Additionally, the model-driven capabilities of the PCM allow an easy automated generation of alternative architecture candidates.

The example system in this paper is the so-called business reporting system (BRS), which lets users retrieve reports and statistical data about running business processes from a data base. It is loosely based on a real system [33]. Fig. 1 shows some parts of the PCM model of the BRS visualised using annotated UML diagrams. It is a 4-tier system consisting of several software components. In an open workload usage scenario, requests arrive according to a Poisson process with a rate equal to 0.2 req/sec. Users issue three types of requests, that lead to varying execution paths in the system.

Components are annotated with software cost (*Cost*) in K€. The initial system is deployed to four servers annotated by costs (*HCost*) in K€, availability (*HA*) and processing rate (*PR*) in GHz. Fig. 1 also shows an excerpt of the behaviour in the lower half of the figure. The behaviour contains the CPU resource demands (*demand* in sec on a 2.6GHz CPU, log normally distributed with coefficient of variation equal to 2) and failure probabilities (*FP*) for actions. `ExternalCallActions` model calls to other components. The components are allocated on four different servers. The complete model can be found at [36].

In order to provide SAs with a priori performance and availability guarantees, if the application include any loops, they are annotated with a discrete probability distribution and an upper bound for their number of execution exists. In the following, we briefly explain the analysis methods for the considered quality criteria performance, availability, and costs:

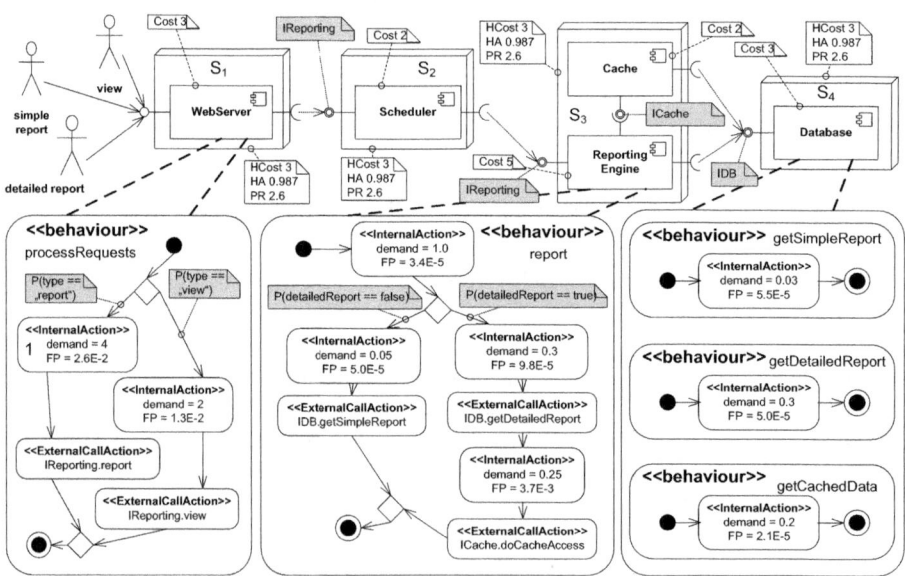

Fig. 1. Business Reporting System: PCM instance of the case study system

- **Performance:** For the analytic optimisation, we model the software system by introducing an M/G/1 queue for each physical server. For the evolutionary optimisation, we use an automated transformation of PCM models into a discrete-event simulation (SimuCom [5]) to derive response times. The performance model is in the class of extended queueing networks, so that we can analyse models containing resource demands specified as arbitrary distribution functions. However, the simulation can be time-consuming to derive stable results.
- **Availability:** For the analytic optimisation, we consider the well known serial/parallel formula [2] applied to the PCM model. In particular, the availability is evaluated by considering the set of components involved, the physical servers supporting the execution, and the probability of invocations. For the evolutionary optimisation, we use an automated transformation of PCM models into absorbing discrete time Markov chains (DTMC) and solve them with the PCM Markov solver [8].
- **Costs:** We annotate constant costs to each component and each server configuration. The software architect can choose whether costs values represent procurement costs, total costs of ownership, or other. If a server specified in the model is not used, i.e., no components are allocated to it, its costs do not add to the overall costs. The goal of this simplistic model is to allow costs to be considered, not to provide a sophisticated costs estimation technique. For the latter, existing costs estimation techniques such as COCOMO II [7] could be integrated here to obtain more accurate values.

Although the example in Fig. 1 is not particularly complicated, it is not obvious how to change the architectural model efficiently to improve the quality properties. For example, the software architect could increase the processing rate of server S_1, which would result in better performance but higher costs. The software architect could also change the component allocation ($4^5 = 1024$ possibilities) or incorporate other component specifications with different QoS attributes.

The design space for this example is huge. Manually checking the possible design alternatives in a trial-and-error approach is laborious and error-prone. The software architect cannot easily create design alternatives that are even locally optimal for all quality criteria. Finding global optima is practically impossible because it requires modelling each alternative. In practice this situation is often mitigated by overprovisioning (i.e., incorporating fast and expensive hardware resources), leading to unnecessarily high costs.

3 Optimisation Process

To present our hybrid optimisation approach, we first give an overview in Section 3.1. In Section 3.2, we describe the search problem. Then, we describe in detail the analytical optimisation (Section 3.3) and the evolutionary optimisation (Section 3.4).

3.1 Overview

Our approach starts considering as input an initial architectural model of the system, named *initial candidate* in Fig. 2. In our case, this is a complete PCM model instance as shown in Fig. 1. The optimisation process starts with the *search problem formulation*. In this work, we consider three degree of freedom types: (1) allocation of components, (2) server configuration, and (3) component selection. The result of this step is a set of system-specific degrees of freedom that describe the search problem.

In the second step, a simplified version of the search problem is optimised using analytic techniques. The impact of a degree of freedom (or a combination of them) is evaluated by analytic models, and the Pareto optimal candidates are derived very efficiently by solving a mixed integer linear programming problem. The result of this step is a set of candidates that are globally Pareto-optimal with respect to the simplified search space. In the third step, the results of the analytic optimisation are used as input candidates for an evolutionary optimisation of the original search problem. Evolutionary optimisation is more time consuming, but it can consider the whole search space and obtain more accurate estimates for availability and performance metrics.

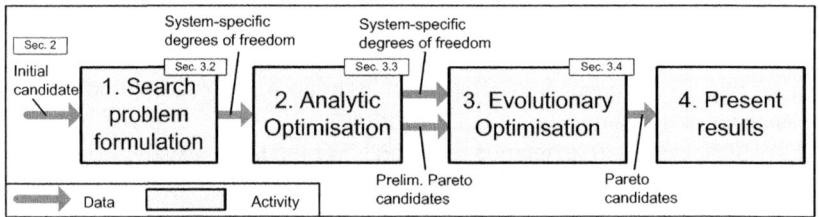

Fig. 2. Hybrid Optimisation Process Overview

The results of the evolutionary optimisation phase is a set of Pareto-optimal candidates. The Pareto-optimal candidates are presented to the software architect, who can study the remaining optimal trade-offs between possibly conflicting objectives.

3.2   Search Problem Formulation

Candidate solutions can be evaluated for optimal trade-offs, i.e. for Pareto-optimality [16]. A candidate architecture is Pareto-optimal, if it is superior to all other candidate in at least one quality criterion. More formally: Let a be a candidate solution, let DS be the set of all possible candidates, and let q be a quality criterion with a value set D_q, an evaluation function $f_q : DS \rightarrow D_q$ so that $f_q(c)$ denotes the quality property of a $c \in DS$ for the quality criterion q, and an order $\leq_q$ on D_q so that $c_1 \leq_q c_2$ means that c_1 is better than or equal to c_2 with respect to quality criterion q. Then, a candidate solution a is Pareto-optimal iff $\forall b \in DS \; \exists q : f_q(a) \leq_q f_q(b)$. If a candidate solution is not Pareto-optimal, then it is Pareto-dominated by at least one other candidate solution in DS that is better or equal in all quality criteria. The optimisation problem can be formulated as follows for a set of quality criteria $Q = \{q_1, ..., q_m\}$: $\min_{c \in DS} [f_{q_1}(c), ..., f_{q_m}(c)]$. In this work, we consider three quality criteria: $q_1 = T$ = mean response time, $q_2 = A$ = availability measured as the probability of success of each request, and $q_3 = C$ = cost.

In our approach, the following degrees of freedom can be considered:

Allocation of components to available servers: The mapping of components to servers can be changed. This is an integral part of most performance-prediction models and has large effects on the performance of a system. When reallocating components, the number of servers can change as well. In our example, the `Scheduler` component could be allocated to S_1, so that S_2 could be removed and its cost can be saved. The software architect can specify the maximum number of servers to be considered.

Server configuration: The available hardware resources (CPU, HDD, ...) can be changed in a certain range. In this work, we model a discrete set of servers with different CPU processing rates and costs. Thus, components can be allocated to servers with different processing rates.

Component selection: If functionally-equivalent components with different non-functional properties are available, they can be exchanged. Currently, we deem that a component B can replace a component A if B provides (i.e., implements) all interfaces provided by A and if B requires at most the interfaces required by A.

More degrees of freedom that could be considered in an automated approach are described in [27]. In the search problem formulation step, the initial candidate model is automatically analysed for instantiations of these degrees of freedom, called system-specific degrees of freedom. The found set of system-specific degrees of freedom defines the search space. If desired, the software architect can also manually remove some of them.

3.3 Analytical Optimisation

The analytical optimization step starts by evaluating the quality metrics of each component i included in the initial candidate by means of M/G/1 and availability formula. Then, a binary decision variable x_j is introduced for each "atomic" design alternative which can be obtained from the degrees of freedom. x_j is equal to 1 if the corresponding design alternative is implemented in the system, and 0 otherwise. The optimization problem which can be introduced in this way is combinatoric in nature, since a Pareto optimal solution can be obtained by selecting a combination of atomic design alternatives.

For example, S_1 alternative configurations for the reference system in Fig. 1 can be modelled introducing the binary variables x_1 (CPU downgrade to 2.4 GHz), x_2 (CPU upgrade to 2.8 GHz), x_3 (CPU upgrade to 3 GHz). Down/upgrades of servers S_2, S_3, and S_4 can be modelled analogously with variables x_4 to x_{12}. Likewise, the alternative components selection can be modelled by introducing two binary variables x_{13} and x_{14} equal to 1 iff the `WebServer` is replaced by alternative `WebServer2` or `WebServer3` implementation.

The limit of the analytical optimisation with respect to the evolutionary search is in the evaluation of the *allocation* of components to servers degree of freedom. The analytical problem formulation cannot remove a server from the system if no components are allocated to it. The aim of the analytical optimisation is to derive quickly an approximated Pareto front which will be further refined by the evolutionary search. As it will be discussed in Section 4, providing approximated Pareto solutions to the evolutionary search allows to improve the whole analysis process. For the sake of simplicity in the following we assume that the application under study includes a single initial component and a single end component. Furthermore, loops are peeled and transformed into a number of branches with varying number of repetitions according to the annotated probability distribution [1]. In this way the application PCM model is transformed into a Directed Acyclic Graph (DAG).

Let us denote with $\mathcal{I}$ the set of indexes of the system components and with $\mathcal{J}$ the set of indexes for the atomic design alternatives arising from the degrees of freedom definition. Let us denote by $\tilde{C}$ the cost of the initial candidate and let δ_j^c be the cost variation of the initial candidate for implementing the design alternative j.

In the following optimization problem formulation we will consider only the average response time performance metric, availability optimization can be formalized similarly. Let us denote with $\tilde{t}_i$, the average response time for component i invocation in the initial candidate and let $\delta_{j,i}^t$ be the variation of the response time (evaluated by means of M/G/1 formula) for component i if the design alternative j is implemented. For example, if S_1 CPU frequency is raised to 2.8 GHz (x_2 design alternative), then the WebServer service demands for the two invocations and S_1 utilization are initially equal to 4 sec, 2 sec and 0.52 respectively, are reduced by a factor $2.8/2.6 = 1.08$. Thus, the initial response times equal to 8.33 sec, and 4.16 sec become 7.18 sec and 3.59 sec and hence the deltas are equal to -1.15 sec, and -0.57 sec.

Some of the atomic design alternatives could be in conflict. For example, since only one server CPU can be changed at one instance, the following constraint has to be introduced for S_1:

$$x_1 + x_2 + x_3 \leq 1$$

Formally, we introduce an exclusive set es_k for each combination of atomic design alternatives which are in conflict among each other, because they concern the same software component and/or the same physical server where components are deployed. A parameter $es_{k,j} = 1$ is introduced indicating that the atomic design alternative j is in the exclusive set k, while $es_{k,j} = 0$ otherwise.

Note that the size of exclusive sets could grow exponentially, since taking into account all of the atomic choices is also combinatorial in nature. However, since the number of possibly conflicting atomic design alternatives is usually significantly lower than the number of degrees of freedom, the analytic problem can be formulated and solved efficiently, as it will be shown in Section 4.2.

If we denote by t_i the execution time of component i according to the selection of atomic design choices, we have:

$$t_i = \tilde{t}_i + \sum_{j \in \mathcal{J}} \delta_{j,i}^t x_j, \forall i; \qquad \sum_{j \in \mathcal{J}} es_{k,j} x_j \leq 1, \forall k$$

Let us denote with π_i the probability of execution of component i which can be derived from the sum of the transition probabilities of the paths in the DAG from the initial component to i. The execution time T of the whole application can then be computed as $T = \sum_{i \in \mathcal{I}} \pi_i \cdot t_i$, while the cost C corresponding to a given combination of atomic choices is given by $C = \tilde{C} + \sum_{i \in \mathcal{I}} \sum_{j \in \mathcal{J}} \delta_j^c \cdot x_j$.

If $\overline{T}$ and $\overline{C}$ denote a bound for the application execution and system cost respectively, than the Pareto-optimal solutions can be obtained by solving iteratively the problems shown in Fig. 3 according to Algorithm 1.

(P1) $\min C$	(P2) $\min T$
subject to: $C = \tilde{C} + \sum_{i \in \mathcal{I}} \sum_{j \in \mathcal{J}} \delta_j^c \cdot x_j$ $t_i = \tilde{t}_i + \sum_{j \in \mathcal{J}} \delta_{j,i}^t x_j, \ \forall i$ $\sum_{j \in \mathcal{J}} es_{k,j} x_j \le 1, \ \forall k$ $\sum_{i \in \mathcal{I}} \pi_i \cdot t_i \le \overline{T}$	subject to: $t_i = \tilde{t}_i + \sum_{j \in \mathcal{J}} \delta_{j,i}^t x_j, \ \forall i$ $T = \sum_{i \in \mathcal{I}} \pi_i \cdot t_i$ $\sum_{j \in \mathcal{J}} es_{k,j} x_j \le 1, \ \forall k$ $\tilde{C} + \sum_{i \in \mathcal{I}} \sum_{j \in \mathcal{J}} \delta_j^c \cdot x_j \le \overline{C}$

Fig. 3. The Analytic Optimisation Problems for Performance and Cost

Algorithm 1 requires as input the upper $\overline{T}^{upper}$ and lower bound $\overline{T}^{lower}$ response time for the application under study, which can be computed easily by considering the maximum and minimum $\delta_{j,i}^t$ for each component i. Then, the Algorithm starts minimizing the system cost with the goal to provide a response time lower than $\overline{T}^{upper}$ (i.e., solving problem (P1), see step 4). Let x^* be the corresponding optimum solution (i.e., the set of atomic design alternatives to be implemented) and C^* be the corresponding cost. Then, the first Pareto solution is obtained by solving (P2) setting $\overline{C} = C^*$ (see step 6). Let T^* be optimum response time obtained. Indeed, no other atomic design alternative combination can lead to a better response time with a lower cost, hence x^* computed at step 6 is a Pareto global optimum solution. The process is then iterated by solving (P1) again and setting as constraint $\overline{T} = T^* - \epsilon$, where $\epsilon > 0$ is any sufficiently small constant. $IC + x^*$ at step 7 denotes the solution obtained by applying to the initial candidate IC the set of atomic design alternatives x^*.

---

input : $\overline{T}^{upper}, \overline{T}^{lower}$
output: $Paretos$
1 $\overline{T} \leftarrow \overline{T}^{upper}$;
2 $Paretos \leftarrow \emptyset$;
3 **while** $\overline{T}^{lower} \le \overline{T}$ **do**
4   Solve (P1). Let be x^* the optimum solution found and C^* its cost ;
5      $\overline{C} \leftarrow C^*$;
6   Solve (P2). Let be x^* the optimum solution found and T^* the application execution time ;
7      $Paretos \leftarrow Paretos \bigcup \{IC + x^*\}$;
8      $\overline{T} \leftarrow T^* - \epsilon$
9 **end**
10 **return** $Paretos$;

Algorithm 1. Analytical Pareto-optimality Algorithm

For the availability analysis the analytical problem formulation can be derived similarly. The main difference is that the delta values have to be derived for independent application execution paths (i.e., each path from the source to the sink) and the optimization has to be iterated for each execution path. The set of initial candidates provided to the evolutionary optimization is obtained as union of the analytical solutions of individual execution paths. It can be shown that (P1) and (P2) are NP-hard, since they are equivalent to a knapsack problem. The solution complexity grows exponentially with the number of binary variables. However, current solvers are very efficient and (P1) and (P2) solutions can be computed very quickly for realistic design problems of reasonable size.

3.4   Evolutionary Optimisation

If all degrees of freedoms presented in Section 3.2 have to be considered, then the analytical optimization model becomes a mixed integer non-linear problem and we cannot rely on efficient solvers as for the linear case to determine software architectures quality trade-offs. For this type of problems, metaheuristic optimisation techniques have been successfully applied in software engineering [19]. In this work, we use evolutionary optimisation (see, e.g. [6, p. 284]), as it has been considered useful for multi-objective problems [12]. Other metaheuristics could be used as well. More details on this choice can be found in [27].

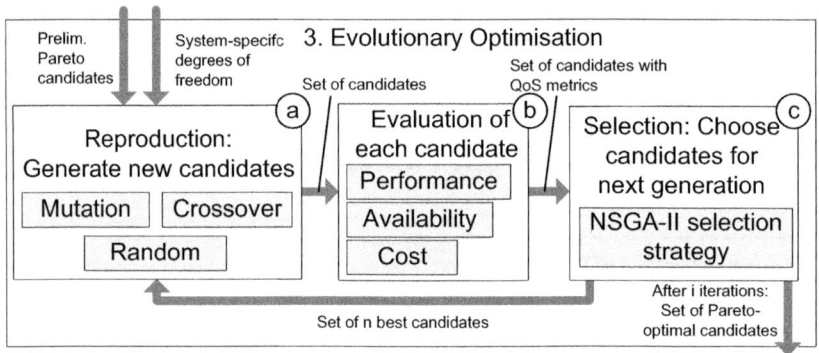

Fig. 4. Evolutionary optimisation process

Fig. 4 shows the main steps of our evolutionary search. The method is described here exemplary for our current realisation in the PEROPTeryx tool [36] with the NSGA-II evolutionary algorithm [14] as implemented in the Opt4J framework [26] with an extended reproduction step.

The process starts with an input population derived from the analytical optimisation step. Individuals are then modified along system-specific degrees of freedom (see Section 3.1). As the software model contains all required annotations, all steps of the search can be completely automated. The population size n and the number of iterations i can be configured. If the input population size $|Paretos|$ is less than n, additional

$n - |Paretos|$ random candidates are generated. The evolutionary search then iterates the following steps:

(a) **Reproduction:** Based on the currently available candidates in the population, new candidate solutions are derived by "mutation" or "cross-over" or they are randomly created. With mutation, one or several design options are varied. With cross-over, two good candidate solutions are merged into one, by taking some of each candidates design option values for the cross-over. In addition to the original NSGA-II, in order to diversify the search, duplicate candidates are removed from the population and are replaced by candidates randomly generated based on the available design options.

(b) **Evaluation:** Each yet unevaluated candidate is evaluated for each quality attribute of interest. In our case, performance, availability and/or costs metrics are predicted as described in Section 2. As a result, each candidate is annotated with the determined quality properties (i.e. mean response time, availability, and/or cost).

(c) **Selection:** After the reproduction phase, the population has grown. In the selection phase, the population is again reduced by just keeping the n most promising candidates based on the NSGA-II selection strategy. After i iterations, the search ends here and returns the Pareto-optimal candidates found so far.

More details on the evolutionary optimisation (such as the genetic encoding) can be found in [27]. Over several iterations, the combination of reproduction and selection lets the population converge towards the real front of globally Pareto-optimal solutions. The result of the optimisation is a set of Pareto-optimal candidates with respect to all candidates evaluated before. If the search also keeps a good diversity of candidates, the result set can be near to the global optima. However, in general, evolutionary optimisation cannot guarantee globally Pareto-optimal solutions [27].

4   Experimental Results

This section reports the results of the quality optimisations performed for the BRS system to demonstrate the applicability and usefulness of our approach and is organised as follows. Section 4.1 describes the degrees of freedom adopted. Sections 4.2 and 4.3 summarize the analytical optimisation and evolutionary optimisation. Finally, Section 4.4 presents and discusses the results of the hybrid approach.

Notice that we do not compare our prediction results from the models with actual measurements from the system implementation. For our validation, we assume that the underlying modelling and prediction methods are sound and deliver accurate prediction results as discussed in other papers [5,8].

4.1   Search Problem Formulation

We defined two separate search problems: (1) optimise performance and cost, (2) optimise availability and cost. The following degrees of freedom are considered:

Component allocation: For the evolutionary optimisation of (1), all components can be freely allocated to up to five servers. For the analytic optimisation of (1) the problem can be defined considering only one allocation degree of freedom: The Cache component can be allocated to server S_3 or S_4. For (2), we do not consider component allocation as a degree of freedom. With free component allocation, the optimal solution would be to deploy all components on one server, so that only this server's availability affects the system. However, the inevitable performance degradation would not be taken into account.

Component selection: The `Webserver` can be realised using third party components. The software architect can choose among three functional equivalent implementations: `Webserver2` with cost 4 and `Webserver3` with cost 6. Both have less resource demand than the initial `Webserver`. `Webserver2` has better availability for the requests of type "view", while `Webserver3` has better availability for the requests of type "report".

Server configuration: Four different server configurations C_1 to C_4 with varying processor speed (PR in GHz), hardware availability (probability HA), and cost $HCost$ available.

The exact values considered in the case study can be found at [36]. A performance and availability optimisation has been omitted for space reasons, but works analogously. In principle, it is also possible to optimise all three quality criteria at once to determine a three-dimensional Pareto candidate set.

4.2 Analytic Optimisation

The degrees of freedom are mapped into an optimization problem including 24 binary variables: x_1-x_3, x_4-x_6, x_7-x_9, and x_{10}-x_{12} specify physical servers up/downgrades. x_{13} and x_{14} are introduced to model the two `WebServer` component alternative implementations. x_{15} is associated with the allocation of the `Cache` component to S_4. x_{16}-x_{18} model S_1 down/upgrades joint with the `WebServer2` implementation. Similarly x_{19}-x_{21} model S_1 down/upgrades joint with the `WebServer3` implementation. Finally x_{22}-x_{24} model the `Cache` component allocation on S_4 with the joint down/upgrades of servers S_3 and S_4. Four exclusive sets have to be introduced which are defined as follows:

- es_1: prevents conflicting design alternatives for server S_1 down/upgrades and the different implementation of the `WebServer` component (i.e., includes variables x_1-x_3, x_{13}-x_{14}, and x_{16}-x_{21}).
- es_2: avoids conflicting design alternatives associated with server S_2 down/upgrades (i.e., includes variables x_4-x_6).
- es_3: enumerates conflicting design alternatives for server S_3 down/upgrades and the different allocations of the `Cache` component (i.e., includes x_7-x_9, x_{15}, and x_{22}-x_{24}).
- es_4: prevents conflicting design alternatives associated with server S_4 down/upgrades and the different allocations of the `Cache` component (i.e., includes variables x_{10}-x_{12}, x_{15}, and x_{22}-x_{24}).

The analytical optimization step is performed by running *CPLEX* [20], a state of the art integer linear programming solver based on the branch and cut technique [32]. At each iteration of Algorithm 1, the solver identifies the global optimum solution of problems

(P1) and (P2). The initial Pareto front can be determined very efficiently in 0.14 sec for the performance vs. cost analysis and 0.54 sec for the availability vs. cost analysis on a single core of an Intel Nehalem @2.6 GHz.

4.3 Evolutionary Optimisation

For performance prediction, we use the SimuCom simulation [5]. A stop criterion based on the confidence of the mean response time T was used in all but one evaluation. The simulation of candidate stopped when the 90% confidence interval $Conf$, determined with the batching algorithm of [9], was within +/-10% of the mean value: $Conf \subset [0.9T, 1.1T]$. Before calculating the confidence interval, the samples had to pass an independence test ("run test algorithm" [24]). For availability and cost prediction, we use the PCM Markov solver [8] and the PCM costs solver, respectively.

For the evolutionary optimisation, our prototype PEROPTeryx tool follows the process described in Section 3.4. The number or candidates per iteration was set 25% higher than of optimal candidates found by the previous, analytical step to leave room for more optimal solutions. Table 1 shows the statistics of the optimisation runs (cand. = candidate(s), it. = iteration) which have been performed single threaded on on a single core of an Intel Core 2 T7200 CPU @ 2GHz. The stop criterion of the search was a manually chosen maximum number of iterations. The results had to be inspected to determine whether the search had converged up to then.

Table 1. Statistics of the Evolutionary Optimisation with Analytic Input

Search problem	input cand.	cand. per it.	cand. total	optimal cand.	iter- ations	dura- ation d	mean d per cand.
Performance and Cost	19	25	151	16	10	46 min	18.3 sec
Availability and Cost	12	15	130	10	15	5 min	2.3 sec

4.4 Results

The results of the performance and cost optimisation for the BRS system are presented to the software architect as shown in Fig. 5. Based on this set of Pareto-optimal candidates, software architects can make well-informed trade-off decisions and choose one candidate based on their quality requirements. One resulting solution with a good trade-off is shown in Fig. 6. It is superior to the initial candidate both in average response time ($T = 4.9sec$) and cost ($C = 22$). Thus, the hybrid optimisation could successfully improve the BRS system's architecture.

More detailed results for the optimisation of performance and cost are shown in Fig. 7. The series □ marks the 19 candidates of the analytic optimisation as evaluated with the analytic approach. The series ◇ marks the same 19 candidates as evaluated with SimuCom (thus, every candidate has the same cost, but updated mean response time). We observe that all analytic result values deviate from the simulation results by 40% on average (25% to 97% percent) but are always conservative. The deviation is larger for lower costs. Still, the form of the Pareto-curve is preserved and can serve as a valuable input for the evolutionary search. The series △ marks the 9 new optimal candidates

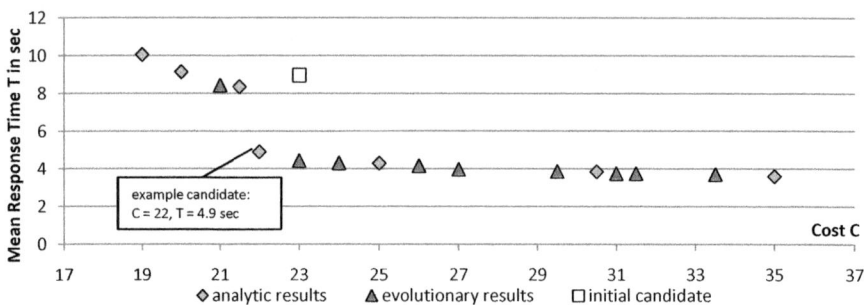

Fig. 5. Performance and cost optimisation: Results and comparison to initial candidate

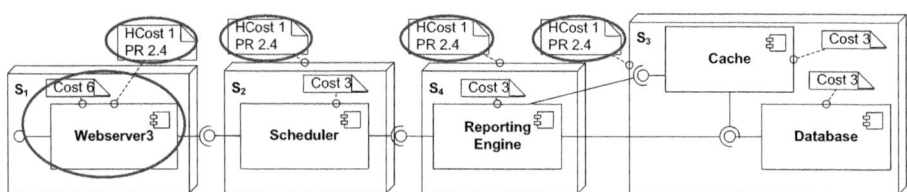

Fig. 6. Performance and cost optimisation: Example PCM Model for one Pareto-optimal candidate. Circles mark the changes compared to the initial candidate.

found by the evolutionary optimisation. They dominate 12 of the analytic candidates. The 143 further candidates evaluated by the evolutionary optimisation are not shown.

Hence, the hybrid approach is superior to the analytic optimisation alone, because the Pareto-front can be refined and additional Pareto solutions can be found. To assess the benefit of the hybrid approach to an evolutionary optimisation, we compared the results to a evolutionary optimisation with the same number of iterations from random candidates. The hybrid approach finds a superior Pareto-front (see Fig. 8), because 1) more optimal candidates are found and 2) all Pareto-optimal candidates found by the evolutionary optimisation from random candidates are dominated by the results of our hybrid approach. Thus, the evolutionary optimisation from random candidates would require more iterations to find a Pareto-front of similar quality, which is more time-consuming.

The results for the optimisation of availability and cost are shown in Fig. 9. The series ◇ marks the 12 optimal solutions found by the analytical optimisation (some overlap each other), as evaluated with the PCM Markov solver. The series × marks the additional 118 candidates evaluated by the evolutionary optimisation. Three new optimal candidates have been found. All analytical optimal solutions stay undominated. Again, the hybrid results is superior to the analytic results alone. The results of a comparison with an evolutionary optimisation from random candidates can be found at [36]. The evolutionary optimisation from random candidates only finds an inferior Pareto-front in the same number of iterations.

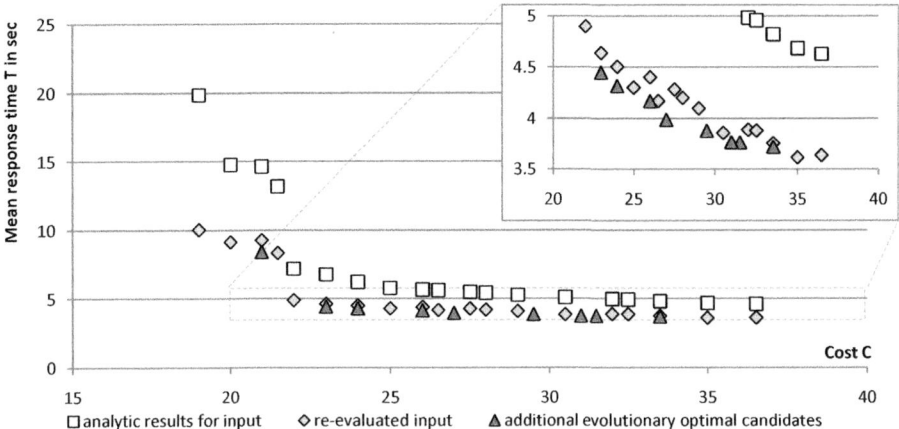

Fig. 7. Performance and cost optimisation: Analytic and simulation performance results

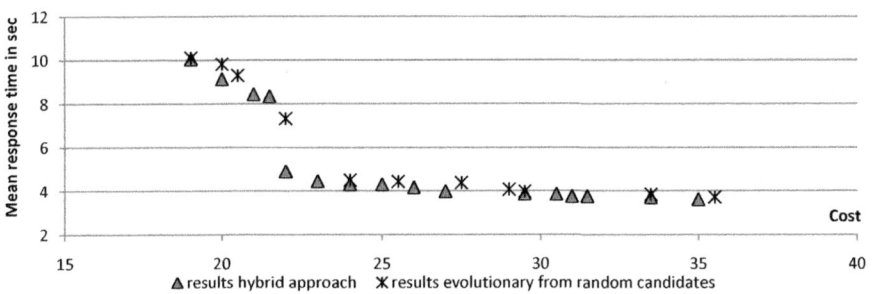

Fig. 8. Performance and cost optimisation: Hybrid vs. evolutionary search comparison

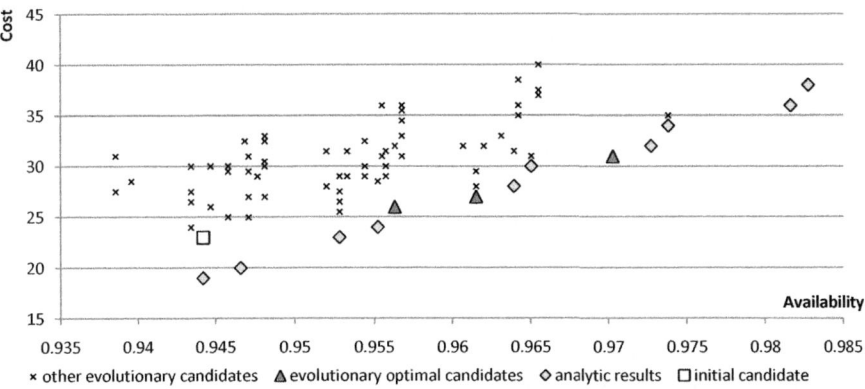

Fig. 9. Availability and cost optimisation: Results and comparison to initial candidate

5   Related Work

Our approach is based on software performance prediction [31,3,25], architecture-based software availability analysis [17], and search-based software engineering [19]. We categorize closely related approaches into: (i) Scenario based SA analysis, (ii) rule-based approaches, and (iii) metaheuristic-based approaches.

Scenario based SA analysis approaches: The definition of a SA model can embody not only the software qualities of the resulting system, but also the trade-offs decisions taken by designers [4,11,35]. The efforts to explore such trade-offs have produced the so-called scenario-based architecture analysis methods, such as SAAM and ATAM [22,23] and others reviewed in [15]. These methods analyze the SA with respect to multiple quality attributes exploring also trade-offs concerning software qualities in the design. The outputs of such analysis include potential risks of the architecture and the verification result of the satisfaction of quality requirements. These methods provide qualitative results and are mainly based on the experience and the skill of designers and on the collaboration with different stakeholders. With respect to these works, our goal is to provide the software architect with a tool able to analyze the multiple objective problem in a quantitative way by allowing the automatic generation of several design architectures.

Rule-based approaches: Xu et al. [34] present a semi-automated approach to find configuration and design improvement on the model level. Based on a LQN model, performance problems (e.g., bottlenecks, long paths) are identified in a first step. Then, rules containing performance knowledge are applied to the detected problems.

McGregor et al. [28] have developed the ArchE framework. ArchE assists the software architect during the design to create architectures that meet quality requirements. It helps to create architectural models, collects requirements (in form of scenarios), collects the information needed to analyse the quality criteria for the requirements, provides the evaluation tools for modifiability or performance analysis, and suggests improvements.

Cortellessa et al. [13] propose an approach for automated feedback generation for software performance analysis, which aims at systematically evaluating performance prediction results using step-wise refinement and the detection of performance problem patterns. However, at this point, the approach is not automated.

Parsons et al. [30] present a framework for detecting performance anti-patterns in Java EE architectures. The method requires an implementation of a component-based system, which can be monitored for performance properties. Then, it searches for EJB-specific performance antipatterns in this model.

Kavimandan et al.[21] present an approach to optimise component allocation in the context of distributed real-time embedded component-based systems. They use heuristic rules to deploy components together that have a compatible configuration. In total, only allocation is considered as a degree of freedom, but the authors also mention that their approach could be combined with other approaches.

All rule-based approaches share a common limitation. The model can only be changed as defined by the improvement rules. However, especially performance is a complex and cross-cutting quality criterion. Thus, optimal solutions could lie on search paths not accessible by rules.

Metaheuristic-based approaches: Grunske [18] studies the improvement of two quality criteria, namely availability and costs, to allow well-informed trade-off decisions. Evolutionary computing is applied to search for good design solutions. However, only redundancy of components is studied as a degree of freedom to improve availability.

Menascé et al. [29] have developed the SASSY framework for generating service-oriented architectures based on quality requirements. Based on an initial model of the required service types and their communication, SASSY generates an optimal architecture by selecting the best services and potentially adding patterns such as replication or load balancing. As the allocation of components is irrelevant in SASSY's service architecture, the quality evaluations are simpler and allocation degrees of freedom cannot be considered. Thus, the approach is not suitable for component-based architectures in general.

6   Conclusions

In this paper, a hybrid approach for multi-attribute QoS optimisation of component based software systems has been proposed. The approach is promising. Both for performance vs. cost and availability vs. cost analyses, the hybrid approach is able to exploit the approximated analytical Pareto front providing a larger number of solutions with a more accurate estimate of performance and availability metrics. At the same time, the hybrid approach is less time-consuming than a evolutionary optimisation starting from random candidates. Hence, the integration of the analytical and evolutionary approaches is effective.

The proposed approach can lead both to a reduction of development costs and to an improvement of the quality of the final system, because an automated and efficient search is able to identify more and better design alternatives, and allows the software architect to make optimal trade-off decisions.

Future work will extend the analytical problem formulation in order to consider applications with parallel components execution and/or which can be modelled by means of closed queueing networks. Furthermore, the evolutionary search will be implemented as a parallel algorithm and an automated stop criterion will be developed. Ongoing work focuses on the integration of the analytic technique in the PCM software suite and on the QoS analyses of real industrial case studies.

Acknowledgments. This work reported in this paper has been partially supported by the EU FP7 Q-ImPrESS project.

References

1. Ardagna, D., Pernici, B.: Adaptive service composition in flexible processes. IEEE Trans. on Soft. Eng. 33(6), 369–384 (2007)
2. Avizienis, A., Laprie, J.C., Randell, B., Landwehr, C.: Basic concepts and taxonomy of dependable and secure computing. IEEE Trans. on Dependable and Secure Computing 1(1), 11–33 (2004)

3. Balsamo, S., Di Marco, A., Inverardi, P., Simeoni, M.: Model-Based Performance Prediction in Software Development: A Survey. IEEE Trans. on Software Engineering 30(5), 295–310 (2004)
4. Bass, L., Clements, P., Kazman, R.: Software Architecture in Practice, 2nd edn. Addison-Wesley, Reading (2003)
5. Becker, S., Koziolek, H., Reussner, R.: The Palladio component model for model-driven performance prediction. Journal of Systems and Software 82, 3–22 (2009)
6. Blum, C., Roli, A.: Metaheuristics in combinatorial optimization: Overview and conceptual comparison. ACM Computing Surveys 35(3), 268–308 (2003)
7. Boehm, B.W., Abts, C., Brown, A.W., Chulani, S., Clark, B.K., Horowitz, E., Madachy, R., Reifer, D.J., Steece, B.: Software Cost Estimation with Cocomo II. Prentice-Hall PTR, Upper Saddle River (2000)
8. Brosch, F., Zimmerova, B.: Design-Time Reliability Prediction for Software Systems. In: International Workshop on Software Quality and Maintainability, pp. 70–74 (2009)
9. Chen, E.J., Kelton, W.D.: Batching methods for simulation output analysis: a stopping procedure based on phi-mixing conditions. In: Winter Simulation Conference, pp. 617–626 (2000)
10. Clements, P.C., Kazman, R., Klein, M.: Evaluating Software Architectures. SEI Series in Software Engineering. Addison-Wesley, Reading (2001)
11. Clements, P.C., Northrop, L.: Software Product Lines: Practices and Patterns. SEI Series in Software Engineering. Addison-Wesley, Reading (August 2001)
12. Coello Coello, C.A.: A comprehensive survey of evolutionary-based multiobjective optimization techniques. Knowledge and Information Systems 1, 269–308 (1999)
13. Cortellessa, V., Di Marco, A., Eramo, R., Pierantonio, A., Trubiani, C.: Approaching the model-driven generation of feedback to remove software performance flaws. In: EUROMICRO Conf. on Softw. Engineering and Advanced Applications, pp. 162–169. IEEE Computer Society, Los Alamitos (2009)
14. Deb, K., Agrawal, S., Pratap, A., Meyarivan, T.: A fast elitist non-dominated sorting genetic algorithm for multi-objective optimization: NSGA-II. In: Deb, K., Rudolph, G., Lutton, E., Merelo, J.J., Schoenauer, M., Schwefel, H.-P., Yao, X. (eds.) PPSN 2000. LNCS, vol. 1917, pp. 849–858. Springer, Heidelberg (2000)
15. Dobrica, L., Niemela, E.: A survey on software architecture analysis methods. IEEE Trans. on Software Engineering 28(7), 638–653 (2002)
16. Ehrgott, M.: Multicriteria Optimization. Springer, Heidelberg (2005)
17. Gokhale, S.S.: Architecture-based software reliability analysis: Overview and limitations. IEEE Trans. on Dependable and Secure Computing 4(1), 32–40 (2007)
18. Grunske, L.: Identifying "good" architectural design alternatives with multi-objective optimization strategies. In: Intl. Conf. on Softw. Engineering, pp. 849–852. ACM, New York (2006)
19. Harman, M.: The current state and future of search based software engineering. In: Briand, L.C., Wolf, A.L. (eds.) Workshop on the Future of Softw. Engin., pp. 342–357. IEEE, Los Alamitos (2007)
20. IBM ILOG. IBM ILOG CPLEX (2010),
    http://www-01.ibm.com/software/integration/optimization/cplex/about/
21. Kavimandan, A., Gokhale, A.S.: Applying model transformations to optimizing real-time QoS configurations in DRE systems. In: Quality of Softw. Architectures, pp. 18–35. Springer, Heidelberg (2009)
22. Kazman, R., Bass, L., Abowd, G., Webb, M.: SAAM: A method for analyzing the properties of software architectures. In: Intl. Conf. on Softw. Engineering, pp. 81–90. IEEE, Los Alamitos (May 1994)

23. Kazman, R., Klein, M., Barbacci, M., Longstaff, T., Lipson, H., Carrière, S.: The architecture tradeoff analysis method. In: Intl. Conf. on Engineering of Complex Computer Systems, pp. 68–78. IEEE, Los Alamitos (1998)
24. Knuth, D.E.: The Art of Computer Programming. Seminumerical Algorithms, vol. 2. Addison-Wesley, Reading (1969)
25. Koziolek, H.: Performance evaluation of component-based software systems: A survey. Performance Evaluation (in Press) (Corrected Proof) (2009)
26. Lukasiewycz, M.: Opt4j - the optimization framework for java (2009),
    `http://www.opt4j.org`
27. Martens, A., Koziolek, H., Becker, S., Reussner, R.H.: Automatically improve software models for performance, reliability and cost using genetic algorithms. In: WOSP/SIPEW International Conference on Performance Engineering. ACM, New York (2010)
28. McGregor, J.D., Bachmann, F., Bass, L., Bianco, P., Klein, M.: Using arche in the classroom: One experience. Technical Report CMU/SEI-2007-TN-001, Software Engineering Institute, Carnegie Mellon University (2007)
29. Menascé, D.A., Ewing, J.M., Gomaa, H., Malex, S., Sousa, J.P.: A framework for utility-based service oriented design in SASSY. In: WOSP/SIPEW International Conference on Performance Engineering, pp. 27–36. ACM, New York (2010)
30. Parsons, T., Murphy, J.: Detecting performance antipatterns in component based enterprise systems. Journal of Object Technology 7(3), 55–90 (2008)
31. Smith, C.U., Williams, L.G.: Performance Solutions: A Practical Guide to Creating Responsive, Scalable Software. Addison-Wesley, Reading (2002)
32. Wolsey, L.: Integer Programming. John Wiley and Sons, Chichester (1998)
33. Wu, X., Woodside, M.: Performance Modeling from Software Components. SIGSOFT Softw. Eng. Notes 29(1), 290–301 (2004)
34. Xu, J.: Rule-based automatic software performance diagnosis and improvement. In: International Workshop on Software and Performance, pp. 1–12. ACM, New York (2008)
35. Yang, J., Huang, G., Zhu, W., Cui, X., Mei, H.: Quality attribute tradeoff through adaptive architectures at runtime. Journal of Systems and Software 82(2), 319–332 (2009)
36. Details on case study for the hybrid optimisation approach (2010),
    `https://sdqweb.ipd.kit.edu/wiki/PerOpteryx/Hybrid_Optimisation_Case_Study`

Using QoS-Contracts to Drive
Architecture-Centric Self-adaptation*

Franck Chauvel, Hui Song, Xiang Ping Chen, Gang Huang, and Hong Mei

Key Laboratory of High Confidence Software Technologies, Ministry of Education
School of Electronics Engineering and Computer Science
Peking University, Beijing, 100871, PRC
{franck.chauvel,songhui06,chenxp04,huanggang,meih}@sei.pku.edu.cn

Abstract. Self-adaptation is now a promising approach to maximize
the satisfaction of requirements under changing environmental conditions. One of the key challenges for such self-adaptive systems is to automatically find a relevant architectural configuration. Existing approaches
requires a set of adaptation strategies and the rough estimation of their
side-effects. However, due to the lack of validation methods for such
strategies and side-effects, existing approaches may lead to erroneous
adaptations. Instead of side-effects, our solution leverages quality contracts whose accuracy can be separately established and which can be
dynamically composed to get a quality prediction of any possible architectural configurations. To support self-adaptation, we propose a reactive
planning algorithm which exploits quality contracts to dynamically discover unforeseen architectural configurations. We illustrate our approach
using a running HTTP server adapting its architecture with respect to
the number and the similarity of incoming requests.

1   Introduction

The growing complexity of software systems and the need of continuously-
running systems have resulted in the emergence of self-adaptive systems (SAS).
Such systems adjust their internal architecture with respect to their execution
environment in order to meet their functional or non-functional requirements.
SAS are mainly built as a control-loop [6] which includes monitoring the running
system, analyzing the collected data, planning the needed reconfigurations, and
executing those reconfigurations.

Correctly planning the needed changes of the running system according to the
environmental conditions is critical to get an effective self-adaptation. Existing
approaches search among a finite set of predefined architectural changes named

* This work is partially sponsored by the National Key Basic Research and Development Program of China under Grant No. 2009CB320703; the National Natural
Science Foundation of China under Grant No. 60821003, 60873060; the High-Tech
Research and Development Program of China under Grant No. 2009AA01Z16; and
the EU FP7 under Grant No. 231167.

G.T. Heinemann, J. Kofron, and F. Plasil (Eds.): QoSA 2010, LNCS 6093, pp. 102–118, 2010.

adaptation rules in Plastic [1] and [14], *strategies/tactics* in Rainbow [11,7], *architectural aspects* by Morin et al. [15] or *actions* in [20,13]. In the presence of multiple and conflicting requirements, the selection takes into account the expected quality side-effects of each change in order to ensure a good trade-off between the desired quality properties (side-effects are modeled as help/hurt values and utility functions in Rainbow [11,7], MADAM [10], DiVA [9] and [20,13]).

The two key challenges in planning design are thus the definition of a set of possible architectural changes and the estimation of their side-effects on the desired quality properties with respect to the environmental conditions. However, although both of these activities are critical for SAS, they remain hand-crafted and highly error-prone: Ensuring that no architectural changes have been overlooked and that their side-effects are realistic remains extremely difficult [6].

Our contribution is to avoid the enumeration of architectural modifications and consequently the estimation of their side-effects. Instead, our solution leverages quality contracts whose accuracy can be independently established and which can be dynamically composed to get quality predictions for any meaningful architectural configuration.

Our solution combines a reactive planning algorithm with the parametric contracts proposed by Firus et al. [8]. The planning algorithm dynamically searches for an architectural change that better fits the environment and the quality objectives, whereas the parametric contracts predict the quality of each resulting architectural configuration. For the sake of interoperability, our prototype leverages standard model-driven techniques and can thus be connected to various execution platforms. We illustrate our approach on an HTTP server deployed on the Fractal platform [4], which adapts its architecture to the number and the density of incoming requests.

The remainder of the paper is organized as follows. Section 2 illustrates the limitations of existing techniques using the HTTP server. Section 3 gives an overview of our approach. Section 4 presents how we model contracts and component-based architectures whereas our self-adaptation algorithm is formalized in Section 5. Section 6 presents our prototype implementation and the related experimental results. Finally Section 7 discusses additional related works before Section 8 concludes and outlines some future works.

2   Motivating Example

This section illustrates on an running scenario the limitations of existing approaches while designing SAS.

Let us consider an HTTP server made of two main components: a listener component (L) reads HTTP requests on a socket and transmits them to a data server component (DS) that returns the corresponding HTTP responses. In addition, three optional components may be inserted: A cache component (C) reduces the response time by caching solved requests ; a filter component (F) detects harmful requests (e.g. containing SQL code) and a dispatcher component (D) enables the combination of several data servers. Figure 1a illustrates several possible architectural configurations of the HTTP server.

The number of possible architectural configurations is potentially infinite since multiple instances of each component definition can be combined. From the functional point of view, a first constraint enforces that filter components (if deployed) protect cache components to avoid caching harmful requests. Another constraint establishes that both filtering and caching must happen only once for each data server. From the non-functional point of view, three main requirements must be met, namely the "minimization of the overall response time" (R.T.), the "maximization of the security level" (S.L.), and the "minimization of the memory consumption" (M.).

A first solution to the design of such a SAS is described in C2 [17], Plastic [1] or Genie [2]. It requires to statically identify a small set of frozen architectural configurations (also known as architectural modes) ; each one resulting from a trade-off between quality objectives and environmental conditions. In Figure 1a, four modes are selected: *Idle*, *Normal*, *Effort* and *Best Effort*. The *Idle* mode only includes one listener and one data server to handle the smallest workload ($w < low$). When the workload increases ($low \leq w < medium$), the system switches to the *Normal* mode to add a cache and a filter. If the workload keeps increasing, the system uses the *Effort* mode ($medium \leq w < high$) where two additional data servers are both cached and filtered. For heavier workloads ($w \geq high$), the system uses the *Best Effort* where a group of 5 servers is cached and filtered. The resulting behavior of the HTTP server is a meshed automaton where each state is a frozen architectural mode and each transition is triggered by a given state of the environment.

A better solution initially proposed in Rainbow [11,7] but also used in DiVA [9] and by Sykes et al. [20,13], is to identify adaptations strategies, their triggering conditions, and their respective costs or benefits with respect to the quality objectives. Table 1b outlines the adaptation strategies needed to deploy (rep. undeploy) each optional component (cache, filter, dispatcher and extra data servers) and their possible side effects on the quality objectives (memory in kB, reponse-time in ms, and security level).

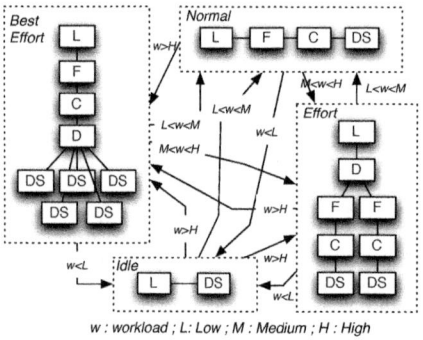

w : workload ; L: Low ; M : Medium ; H : High

Strategy	Side-Effects		
	R.T.	M.	S.L.
AddCache	-50	+200	0
RemoveCache	+100	-200	0
AddFilter	+50	+200	+1
RemoveFilter	-50	-200	-1
AddDispatcher	+10	+25	0
RemoveDispatcher	-10	-25	0
AddServer	-200	+500	0
RemoveServer	+200	-500	0

(a) Using Predefined Configurations   (b) Using Adaptation Strategies

Fig. 1. Existing approaches for self-adaptation applied on the HTTP server

Predefined configurations (Figure 1a) enable a straightforward planning that consists in triggering the relevant transition in the automaton with respect to the current environment. In addition, it ensures that the functional constraints (e.g. the filter components protect the cache components) are respected. However, establishing that the predefined set of configurations is complete remains very difficult and configurations may easily be overlooked [6].

Adaptation strategies (Figure 1b) require the designer to roughly evaluate their quality side-effects (using absolute deviation or utility functions). However, estimating such side-effects at design time is difficult and error prone. Quality side-effects do not only depend on the selected strategy but also on the architectural configuration on which this strategy is applied, and on the environmental conditions. In the HTTP server for instance, the benefits of deploying a cache (row 1 of Tab. 1b) depends on the similarity of incoming requests and on its position with respect to the dispatcher (if deployed). In addition, using strategies that are only applicable on one environmental condition would roll back to the first solution.

Our solution is an alternative to these two solutions and avoids both the enumeration of predefined configurations and the rough estimations of quality side-effects.

3   Approach Overview

By contrast with existing approaches, which either predefine configurations or estimate quality side-effects, our approach leverages "composable" quality contracts whose accuracy can be separately established. Our solution gradually explores the possible architectural configurations by composing additional components, and concurrently builds the related quality model by composing their quality models (quality contracts).

As shown in Figure 2, we modify (on a model of the running system) the current configuration ($L - DS$ in Figure 2) by adding (resp. removing) one component instance and by rebuilding all the possible connection schemes between the remaining components. The use of quality contracts consequently enables the evaluation of the quality of each resulting configuration. Further details about the exploration of the configuration space are given in Section 5.

The key point of our approach is that the quality evaluation is based on complete architectural configurations and not on the expected side effects of the modification which led to new configurations. Such evaluation is made using quality contracts [8], that specify the quality of each individual component definition (L, F, C, D, and DS) as do classical performance models (c.f. Section 4.1 for further details on contracts). Contracts bring us the four following benefits:

1. They allow designers to specify compositional quality model for each component definition which accuracy can be established during unit testing [8].
2. They ensure (theoretically [3]) that all possible connections between components makes sense form the syntactic, behavioral, quality and semantic perspective. They thus ensure that the algorithm only explores meaningful configurations.

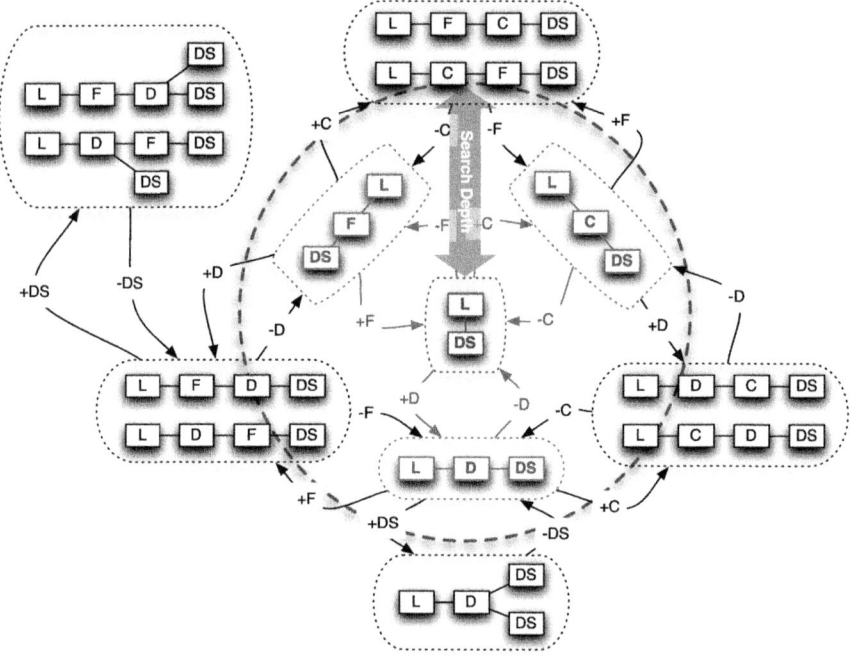

Fig. 2. Approach Overview: Gradual Exploration of the Configurations Space

3. They allow designers to express complex architectural constraints (such as Cache/Filter order) by propagating data on components interfaces.
4. They reduce the number of possible connection schemes, by providing a restrictive interface matching mechanism.

4   Modeling Self-adaptive Systems

This section presents the two main inputs required by our algorithm, namely: (i) the software architecture model specifying the available component definitions (such as Listener, Cache, etc.) and including the contracts specifying the possible connections and, (ii) the adaptation policy specifying the quality objectives that the system must try to satisfy and their relationship with the contracts.

4.1   Modeling Software Architecture

UML 2.x [16] is now the *de facto* standard commonly used by both academics and industrials to described software architectures. However, since UML goes beyond the scope of component-based software architecture, we extracted a minimal subset of concepts needed to perform architecture centric self-adaptation.

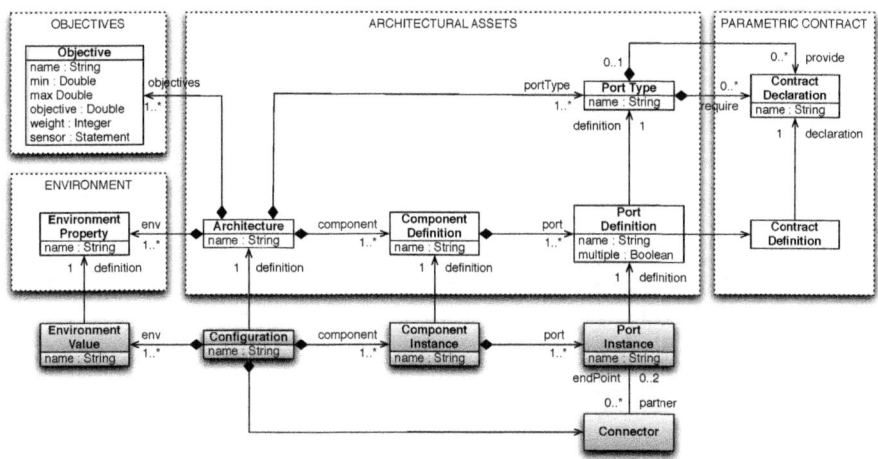

Fig. 3. Modeling Architectural Assets, Contracts, Objectives, and Environmental Properties

Figure 3 formalizes this subset of concepts. In the central frame, an *Architecture* contains a set of *Component Definitions* defining the potential connection points (so called "port") of component. For the sake of conciseness, Figure 3 does not include the definition of functional interfaces but they are needed and encapsulated into the contract definitions.

As explained by Beugnard et al. [3] the notion of contract is a suitable abstraction to describe and specify various properties on component interfaces, including syntax, behavior, synchronization, performances/quality and potentially semantics. Contracts formalize the relationship between provided and required interfaces (in an "assume/guarantee" manner).

Modeling Performances and Quality using Contracts. Non-functional properties such as performance or quality of service (QoS) are commonly modeled as crisp values added on components interfaces (CQML, QoSCL or SLA). By contrast, parametric contracts [8] advocate the use of numerical functions, which capture dependencies between provided and required interfaces. Then, once components interfaces are bound (to build a configuration), these functions can be evaluated to get a end-to-end quality prediction. Parametric contracts enable the encapsulation of different mathematical models for different QoS properties (ad-hoc, probabilistic, markovian, etc.) and their combination using function composition. Our contribution is not the definition of a new formalism to model QoS, but rather focuses on the use of parametric contract to enable self-adaptation.

The top part of Figure 4 provides several illustrative examples of parametric contracts applicable on the HTTP server. The response time (RT) of the data server is defined as the average time to process a given workload (as a number of requests per sec). It is worth to note that the parametric contracts presented

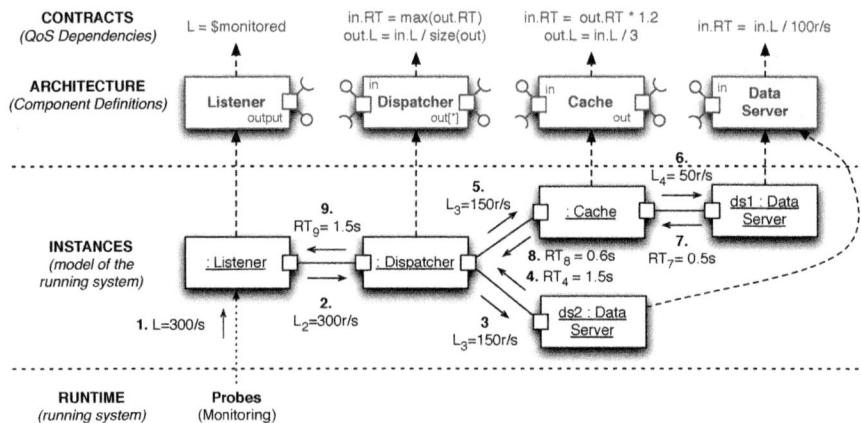

Fig. 4. End-to-End Quality Evaluation using Parametric Contracts

here are over-simplified, realistic and accurate models are proposed in [8]. In Figure 3, each *Contract Definition* encapsulates the imperative description of a function (the related abstract syntax is not detailed here).

Figure 4 illustrates such end-to-end QoS evaluation on a simplified example. At first, the running system is monitored to get initial data (e.g. the load delivered by the listener). Thanks to the parametric contracts, this initial load can be propagated to the other component instances (messages 2, 3, 5 and 6 at the instance level). For example, the dispatcher equally balances the load between its two outputs. Contracts then enable to compute the response time of the data servers and to back propagate it to the listener instance (messages 4, 7, 8 and 9).

Modeling Architectural Constraints using Contracts. Contracts can also be used to enforce architectural constraints. For the record, the HTTP server includes two functional constraints: *"filtering requests must happen before caching to avoid caching harmful requests"* and *"filtering and caching must happen only once for each data server"*. To enforce such constraints, component interfaces in the HTTP must specify if the HTTP requests have already been filtered and/or cached. For instance, the cache component assumes that its incoming HTTP requests have not yet been cached and guarantees that the requests which are transmitted to its backbone have been cached. Listing 1 illustrates the realization of such constraints using contracts.

Listing 1. Excerpt of the contracts needed to order cache and filter instances

```
1  cache.input
       provides processRequest(r1 : Request)
3          assume !cached(r1)

5  cache.output
       requires processRequest(r2 : Request)
7          guarantee cached(r2) and (isFiltered(r1) <=> isFiltered(r2))
```

4.2   Modeling Environment and Objectives

The quality objectives (class *Objective* in Figure 3) are modeled as numeric properties. They include a validity interval (defined by the *min* and *max* attributes) as well as an objective value. Although any value within the range may be used as an objective, only the bounds are used in practice since they reflect the "minimize" and "maximize" requirements respectively.

Listing 2. Minimization of the response time

```
1    issue response_time : Real
     is
3        range is [0, 20]
         objective is 0
5        priority is 5
         sensor
7        do
             value := component.select{ c | c.isKindOf("Listener") }.first()
                 .output.rt
9        end
     end
```

Listing 2 shows an excerpt of the textual syntax used in our prototype to model objectives. It describes the *response time* of the HTTP server as a real value over $[0, 20]$ which optimal value is 0 and which priority is 5 (in $[0, 10]$). The last element defines the contract used to evaluate the response time on a given configuration. The response time of the HTTP Server is measured as the "rt" contract required by the port output of the listener component (See section 4.1).

Additional information such as deployment parameters (CPU speed, bandwidth, etc.) can be stored in our model as environmental properties and then used to further parameterize the quality contracts.

5   Self-adaptation Algorithm

The section formalizes the algorithm which exploits the quality contracts at runtime to enable self-adaptation.

5.1   Problem Formalization

In order to formalize the SAS problem and our self-adaptation algorithm, let us formalize the concepts introduced by Figure 3:

- $\mathcal{E}$ is the execution environment.
- $\mathcal{D}$ is the set of possible component definitions.
- $\mathcal{C}$ is the set of possible component instances.
- $new : \mathcal{D} \rightarrow \mathcal{C}$ is a function which creates a new instance of a given component definition.
- $\mathcal{P}$ is the set of port instances.
  - $match(p_1, p_2) : \mathcal{P} \times \mathcal{P} \rightarrow \mathbb{B}$ is a predicate which checks if two connection points are compatible i.e. if they can be bound together. This represent the enforcement of constraints using contracts.

- $pending(p) : \mathcal{P} \to \mathbb{B}$ is a predicate which checks if a connection point is pending, i.e. if it is not connected to any other connection points.
- $connectable(p) : \mathcal{P} \to \mathbb{B}$ is a predicate which checks if a (multiple) connection point is still connectable i.e. if it can still accept new bindings.

Then, let $\mathcal{K}$ be the set of architectural configurations where each element is a structure $k = \langle C_k, P_k, \beta_k \rangle$ such as:

- $C_k \subset \mathcal{C}$ is the set of component instances involved in the configuration k.
- $P_k \subset \mathcal{P}$ is the set of ports available in the configuration k.
- $\beta_k \subset P_k \times P_k$ is a reflexive relation which maps each connection point to his partners.

Finally, let $\mathcal{O}$ be the set of quality objectives where each objective is a structure $o = \langle w_o, v_o \rangle$ such as w_o is the priority (weight) associated to the objective, and v_o is the optimal value. $\mathcal{O}$ forms an n-dimensions space where the overall distance to the objectives (Δ) of a configuration k under a given environment $\mathcal{E}$ is defined as:

$$\Delta(\mathcal{E}, \mathcal{O}, k) = \sqrt{\sum_{o \in \mathcal{O}} \left(w_o \times |v_o - eval(o, k)| \right)^2}$$

where $eval(o, k)$ stands for the evaluation of a dimension o on a given configuration k using the parametric contracts.

As shown by Equation 1 below, the decision problem of SAS is to find the configuration k which minimizes the distance to the objectives.

$$\Delta(\mathcal{E}, \mathcal{O}, k) = \min_{k' \in \mathcal{K}} \left(\Delta(\mathcal{E}, \mathcal{O}, k') \right) \tag{1}$$

5.2 Planning Algorithm

We use a *a reactive planning algorithm* to explore gradually the space of configurations. By contrast with traditional planning which searches for a sequence of actions satisfying predefined objectives, reactive planning searches for a single action which contributes to better satisfy the objectives.

We only consider two kinds of possible actions: adding and removing a component instance from a given configuration. To ensure the exploration of all possible connection schemes, our algorithm recomputes all of them after each addition or removal. More formally, we define two sets of actions:

- $\mathcal{A}^{\oplus}$ is the set of possible additions of a new instance. Each addition action is a structure $s = \langle \oplus, k, d \rangle$ where k is the target configuration and d the component definition to instantiate. The action execution is provided by the function $\chi : \mathcal{A}^{\oplus} \to \mathcal{K}$ such as $\chi(\langle \oplus, k, d \rangle) = \langle C_k + \{new(d)\}, P_k, \beta_k \rangle$.
- $\mathcal{A}^{\ominus}$ is the set of possible removals of a component instance. Each removal action is a structure $s = \langle \ominus, k, c \rangle$ where k is the target configuration and c the component instance to remove. The removal execution is provided by the function $\chi : \mathcal{A}^{\ominus} \to \mathcal{K}$ such as $\chi(\langle \ominus, k, d \rangle) = \langle C_k - \{any(d, C_k)\}, P_k, \beta_k \rangle$.

Here $any(d, C_k)$ is a random choice of a component instance in C_k such as its definition is d. Since we recompute all the possible connection schemes after each removal, it is not necessary to try to remove each instance of the same definition.

For a given configuration $k \in \mathcal{K}$ and a set of component definitions $\mathcal{D}$ we define the set possible actions $\mathcal{A}(k, \mathcal{D})$ as:

$$\mathcal{A}(k, \mathcal{D}) = \bigcup_{d \in \mathcal{D}} (\{\langle \oplus, k, d \rangle\} \cup \{\langle \ominus, k, d \rangle\})$$

According to the previous definitions, the planning problem addressed by our algorithm is to find the sequence of n actions $(a_1, \ldots, a_n)$ which execution best fits the quality objectives, as formalized by Equation 2 below:

$$\Delta(\mathcal{E}, \mathcal{O}, k) = \min_{a \in \mathcal{A}(k, D)^n} (\Delta(\mathcal{E}, \mathcal{O}, \chi(a))) \tag{2}$$

Algorithm 1 formalizes our solution for the problem above. Given the current configuration k, the set of actions that can be undergone on it ($\mathcal{A}$), and number n of actions to perform, it explores (recursively w.r.t. the length n) all the possible sequences of actions and their resulting configurations. For each resulting configuration, it evaluates the distance to the objectives (Δ) of each possible connection scheme (see line 6) and keeps the best one.

The enumeration of possible connection schemes is performed by algorithm 2. On line 1, it first filters the set of possible connections to remove the ones which cannot be instantiated on the current configuration (only multiple ports support multiple connection). Then, it recursively selects one of the possible connection and instantiates it until no more connections are possible (See line 9). At each step, we keep only the valid configurations (see line 5) i.e. the configurations which form a connected graph of components.

5.3   Worst Case Complexity

In terms of the number of analyzed configurations, the worst situation occurs when all the ports are multiple (i.e. potentially bounded to several other ports) and when all the ports share the same type (i.e. they provide and require the same interfaces with similar contracts). In such a situation, exploring all the possible bindings between a given set of components is boiled down to exploring all the possible connected graphs between their ports [12]. The overall worse case complexity, with respect to the number of objectives, the number of definitions, and the search depth is given by the following formula:

$$O\left[search\left(\mathcal{A}, n, k\right)\right] = \sum_{i=1}^{n} \left(|\mathcal{O}| \times \mathbf{C}_i^{2 \cdot |\mathcal{D}| + i - 1} \times O\left[allConnectionSchemes\left(k_i, \beta_i\right)\right]\right)$$

$$\in O\left(n \times |\mathcal{O}| \times (2 \cdot |\mathcal{D}|)! \times 2^{(n \cdot |P_k|)^2}\right)$$

Algorithm 1. $search(\mathcal{A}, n, k) \rightarrow k_{\perp}$

Input: $\mathcal{A}$ a set of possible actions
Input: $n \in \mathbb{N}^{+}$ the maximal depth of the search
Input: $k \in \mathcal{K}$ the current configuration
Output: $k_{\perp} \in \mathcal{K}$ the best derived configuration

$k_{\perp} \leftarrow k$
while $\mathcal{A} \neq \varnothing$ **do**
    $a \leftarrow any(\mathcal{A})$
    $k' \leftarrow \chi(a)$
    $\beta \leftarrow \{(p_1, p_2) \in P_{k'} \times P_{k'} \mid p_1 \neq p_2 \wedge match(p_1, p_2)\}$
6   **foreach** $k'' \in allConnectionSchemes(k', \beta)$ **do**
        if $\Delta(\mathcal{E}, \mathcal{O}, k'') < \Delta(\mathcal{E}, \mathcal{O}, k_{\perp})$ **then**
            $k_{\perp} \leftarrow k''$
        end
    end
    if $n > 1$ **then**
        $k'' \leftarrow search(\mathcal{A} - \{\mathsf{C}(a)\}, n - 1, k')$
        if $\Delta(\mathcal{E}, \mathcal{O}, k'') < \Delta(\mathcal{E}, \mathcal{O}, k_{\perp})$ **then**
            $k_{\perp} \leftarrow k''$
        end
    end
    $\mathcal{A} \leftarrow \mathcal{A} - \{a\}$
end
return $k_{\perp}$

Algorithm 2. $allConnectionSchemes(k, \beta) \rightarrow R$

Input: $k \in \mathcal{K}$ a configuration without any connector
Input: $\beta \in (P_k)^2$ the set of possible connectors to create
Output: $R \in \wp(K)$ the resulting set of complete configurations

1 $\beta' \leftarrow \{\{p_1, p_2\} \in \beta \mid connectable(p_1) \wedge connectable(p_2)\}$
while $\beta \neq \varnothing$ **do**
    $b \leftarrow choice(\beta')$
    $\beta_k \leftarrow \beta_k \cup \{b\}$
5   **if** $valid(k)$ **then**
        $R \leftarrow R \cup \{k\}$
    end
    if $\exists \{p_1, p_2\} \in \beta'$, $connectable(p_1) \wedge connectable(p_2)$ **then**
9        $R \leftarrow R \cup allConnectionSchemes(k, \beta')$
    end
    $\beta_k \leftarrow \beta_k - \{b\}$
    $\beta' \leftarrow \beta' - \{b\}$
end

Although the complexity is exponential when the number of possible connectors explodes, our algorithm remains applicable since the depth search is not supposed to be larger than 2 (generally 1), as we illustrate using the HTTP server where all components definition share the same port types.

6   Experimental Evaluation

6.1   Prototype Implementation

We provide a first prototype of our algorithm as a Java library named "Brain" [1]. It is built upon the ECore framework: the architectural definitions, the contracts and the objectives (See Figure 3) are initially defined as a standard ECore model which can thus be reused for other purposes. Brain also provides a textual syntax for contracts and the related interpreter which enables the end-to-end evaluation of quality contracts.

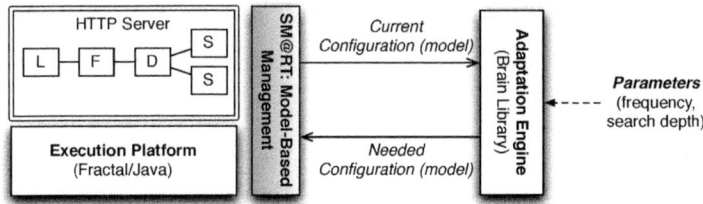

Fig. 5. Deployment and Configuration of the Adaptation Framework on the Fractal Platform

Figure 5 depicts the deployment and the configuration of the Brain library on the Fractal platform. The monitoring and modification of the real running system are done using the SM@RT tool [2] [19] which enables the generation of a synchronization engines between a running system and its model based view. During the runtime, this synchronization engine monitors the running system and instantiates the relevant instance model (the gray part of Figure 3). In addition, the synchronization engine also deploys automatically the new configuration calculated by the Brain library by computing the difference between the current and the new configuration. The HTTP server is implemented on the Fractal platform [4] as a composite component extended with a specific controller. This "Brain" controller combines the Brain library and the synchronization engines generated by SM@RT to monitor and adjust the running system at a given frequency.

---

[1] Available at http://code.google.com/p/pku-brain/
[2] Available at http://code.google.com/p/smatrt

6.2   Experimental Setups

We carried out two experiments aiming at ensuring the feasibility and the effectiveness of our approach respectively.

In the first experiment, we defined two adaptation policies (A and B) which differ only from the weight related to each quality dimension (our approach does not require the definition of architectural modifications). As shown by Figure 6, the first adaptation policy focuses on the response time of the server and thus balances the quality dimensions as follows: $R.T. = 9$, $M. = 1$ and $S.L. = 1$. In contrast, the policy B targets a consensus between those three dimensions and therefore defines equal weights ($R.T. = 5$, $M. = 5$ and $S.L. = 5$). Finally we monitor the architectural configurations which are produced by these two policies with respect to a load increasing and decreasing.

The second experiment compares our approach with a set of predefined architectural configurations. We implement the fixed set of configurations presented in Figure 1a (c.f. Section 2) and a selection engine selecting the best of these configurations. For the sake of the comparison, both our planning algorithm and the static selection engine evaluate the configurations using the same set of contracts. In Figure 7, our adaptive planning algorithm found different but better fitting configurations, by accepting to spend more memory in order to save response time.

6.3   Discussion

Feasibility.   Figure 6 illustrates the feasibility of our approach. On the top part, using Policy A, the adaptation algorithm first increases the number of

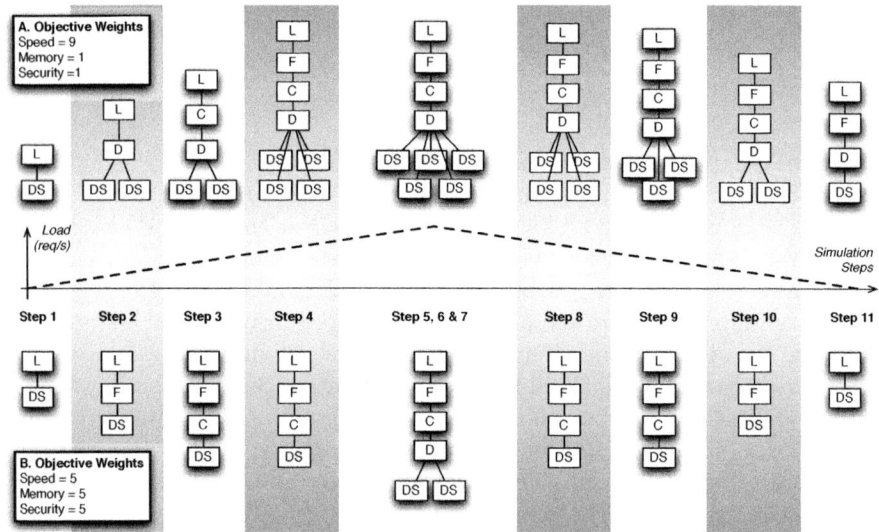

Fig. 6. Driving Self-Adaptation Using Weighted Quality Objectives

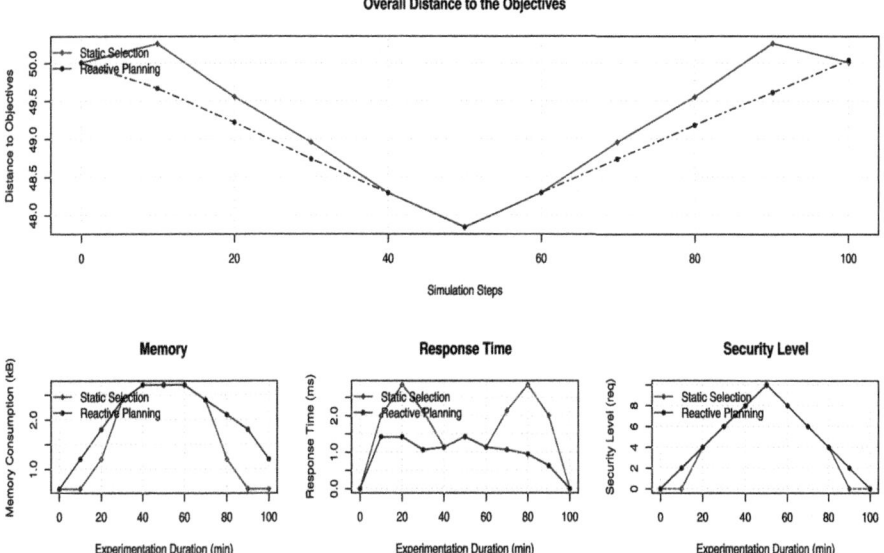

Fig. 7. Adaptation relevance: Predefined Configurations vs. Reactive Planning

data servers connected to the dispatcher component in order to balance the load increase (step 2, 4 and 5). In contrast, using Policy B, the adaptation algorithm first deploys a filter and a cache (step 2 and 3) and finally increases the number of data servers (5). The use of such objective-based policies boils down the management of adaptation to weight modifications.

Effectiveness. By avoiding the static specification of architectural modifications, our approach simplifies the specification of the desired self-adaptive behavior. In addition it also increases the effectiveness of self-adaptation. As shown in Figure 7, our planning algorithm discovers new architectural configurations which result in a better trade-off with respect to the quality objectives. By contrast with side-effects, the specification of parametric contracts must be the responsibility of a QoS expert and since their accuracy can be independently established, they therefore enforce both the separation of concerns and the accuracy of the adaptation.

Performance. The theoretical complexity of the planning algorithm limits its applicability due to the combinatorial explosion of the number of possible configurations in the most complex cases. Possible applications of this algorithm exclude large scale architectures where the number of similar component (similar port/interface type) is maximal. The HTTP server example illustrates such a situation, since each possible configuration is potentially valid. Above all, the benefits of building self-adaptation upon parametric contracts is not related to a specific exploration algorithm such as our reactive planning algorithm.

7   Related Works

As explained in Section 2, existing approaches can be divided in two categories. Solutions from the first category advocate the definition, at design time, of a set of architectural configurations which freezes the adaptation space. For instance, C2 [17], Genie [2] and Plastic [1] address architecture-centric self-adaptation in that way. Our approach avoids such static enumeration of predefined architecture configurations and can explore dynamically unforeseen configurations.

Solutions in the second category (Rainbow [11,7], MADAM [10], Sykes et al. [20,13], DiVA [9]) proposed to combine, at runtime, predefined architectural actions. Although this results in a potentially infinite set of architectural configurations, it requires the designers to roughly evaluate at design time the side-effects of such architectural actions. Our approach to self-adaptation leverage quality contracts as third-party quality-models. By contrast with side-effects evaluation, the accuracy of such quality contracts can be separately assessed as shown in [8].

Caporuscio et al. proposes PMF [5] a framework to manage the performance of software systems at run time using model-based performance evaluation. PMF goes further than C2 and Rainbow and MADAM since it generates new configuration using performances models. However, the objectives are fixed at design time while our approach supports their dynamic evolution as shown in Figure 6.

Finally, Ramirez et al. propose Plato [18] a framework which generates new configurations fitting the environmental conditions using genetic algorithms. Plato shares some similarities with our approach but requires the designer to provide a global fitness function to evaluate architectural configurations. By contrast, our approach relies on local quality contracts which can be obtained from components provider.

8   Conclusion

One of the key challenges of the development of SAS is to correctly plan how to adjust the current architectural configuration to better fit the environmental conditions and maximize the satisfaction of the requirements. Current approaches either require the enumeration, at design time, of a fix set of predefined configurations or of a set architectural modifications and their expected side-effects. Both remains difficult and error-prone activities and may lead to erroneous adaptation.

This paper addresses these two limitations by exploring at runtime the possible changes which can be undergone on the current architectural configuration of the system. Our algorithm dynamically searches for modifications of the current configuration and concurrently modifies the related quality model needed to evaluate the resulting configurations. This is achieved by combining a reactive planning algorithm with quality contracts.

Although the complexity of our algorithm prohibits its use for large scale systems (such as Multi Agent systems), we illustrated its use to dynamically adapts an HTTP server. Compared to the traditional design-time selection of configurations, it provides a better adaptation effectiveness with regard to the quality objectives and avoids the rough estimation of architectural modifications at design time.

As future works we plan to address the automated discovery of quality models to easy the integration of third-party components and improve adaptation capabilities of legacy systems.

References

1. Batista, T., Joolia, A., Coulson, G.: Managing Dynamic Reconfiguration in Component-Based Systems. In: Morrison, R., Oquendo, F. (eds.) EWSA 2005. LNCS, vol. 3527, pp. 1–17. Springer, Heidelberg (2005)
2. Bencomo, N., Grace, P., Flores, C., Hughes, D., Blair, G.: Genie: Supporting the Model Driven Development of Reflective, Component-based Adaptive Systems. In: ICSE: Proceedings of the 30th international conference on Software engineering, pp. 811–814. ACM Press, New York (2008)
3. Beugnard, A., Jezequel, J., Plouzeau, N., Watkins, D.: Making components contract aware. Computer 32(7), 38–45 (1999)
4. Bruneton, E., Coupaye, T., Leclercq, M., Quema, V., Stefani, J.: The Fractal Component Model and its Support in Java. Software Practice and Experience, special issue on Experiences with Auto-adaptive and Reconfigurable Systems 36(11-12), 1257–1284 (2006)
5. Caporuscio, M., Di Marco, A., Inverardi, P.: Model-based System Reconfiguration for Dynamic Performance Management. Journal of Systems and Software 80(4), 455–473 (2007); Software Performance, 5th International Workshop on Software and Performance
6. Cheng, B.H.C., de Lemos, R., Giese, H., Inverardi, P., Magee, J.: Software Engineering for Self-Adaptive Systems: A Research Roadmap. In: Cheng, B.H., de Lemos, R. (eds.) Software Engineering for Self-Adaptive Systems. LNCS, vol. 5525, pp. 1–26. Springer, Heidelberg (2009)
7. Cheng, S., Garlan, D., Schmerl, B.: Architecture-based Self-Adaptation in the Presence of Multiple Objectives. In: Proceedings of the Intl. Workshop on Self-Adaptation and Self-Managing Systems, pp. 2–8. ACM Press, New York (2006)
8. Firus, V., Becker, S., Happe, J.: Parametric Performance Contracts for QML-specified Software Components. In: Proceedings of the 2nd Int. Workshop on Formal Foundations of Embedded Software and Component-based Software Architectures (FESCA 2005), vol. 141, pp. 73–90 (2005)
9. Fleurey, F., Solberg, A.: A Domain Specific Modeling Language Supporting Specification, Simulation and Execution of Dynamic Adaptive Systems. In: Schürr, A., Selic, B. (eds.) MODELS 2009. LNCS, vol. 5795, pp. 606–621. Springer, Heidelberg (2009)
10. Floch, J., Hallsteinsen, S., Stav, E., Eliassen, F., Lund, K., Gjorven, E.: Using Architecture Models for Runtime Adaptability. IEEE Software 23(2), 62–70 (2006)
11. Garlan, D., Cheng, S., Huang, A., Schmerl, B., Steenkiste, P.: Rainbow: Architecture-based Self-Adaptation with Reusable Infrastructure. Computer 37(10), 46–54 (2004)
12. Harary, F., Palmer, E.: Graphical Enumeration. Academic Press, London (1973)

13. Heaven, W., Sykes, D., Magee, J., Kramer, J.: A Case Study in Goal-Driven Architectural Adaptation. In: Goos, G., Hartmanis, J., Leeuwen, J.V. (eds.) Software Engineering for Self-Adaptive Systems. LNCS, vol. 5525, p. 127. Springer, Heidelberg (2009)
14. Mei, H., Huang, G., Lan, L., Li, J.G.: A Software Architecture Centric Self-Adaptation Approach for Internetware. Science in China, Series F: Information Sciences 51(6), 722–742 (2008)
15. Morin, B., Barais, O., Nain, G., Jézéquel, J.M.: Taming Dynamically Adaptive Systems using Models and Aspects. In: ICSE: 31st Intl. Conference on Software Engineering, pp. 122–132. IEEE, Los Alamitos (May 2009)
16. OMG: OMG Unified Modeling Language (OMG UML), Superstructure, V2.1.2. OMG Available Specification (ptc/03-08-02), Object Management Group (November 2007)
17. Oreizy, P., Gorlick, M., Taylor, R., Heimhigner, D., Johnson, G., Medvidovic, N., Quilici, A., Rosenblum, D., Wolf, A.: An Architecture-Based Approach to Self-Adaptive Software. IEEE Intelligent Systems and Their Applications 14(3), 54–62 (1999)
18. Ramirez, A.J., Knoester, D.B., Cheng, B.H., McKinley, P.K.: Applying Genetic Algorithms to Decision Making in Autonomic Computing Systems. In: Proceedings of the 6th intl. conference on Autonomic Computing (ICAC 2009), pp. 97–106. ACM, New York (2009)
19. Song, H., Xiong, Y., Chauvel, F., Huang, G., Hu, Z., Mei, H.: Generating Synchronization Engines between Running Systems and Their Model-Based Views. In: Bencomo, N., Blair, G., France, R. (eds.) MRT 2009: Proceedings of the Workshop on Models at Runtime 2009. Springer, Heidelberg (2009) (to be published)
20. Sykes, D., Heaven, W., Magee, J., Kramer, J.: From goals to components: a combined approach to self-management. In: SEAMS 2008: Proceedings of the 2008 international workshop on Software engineering for adaptive and self-managing systems, pp. 1–8. ACM, New York (2008)

Is BPMN Really First Choice in Joint Architecture Development? An Empirical Study on the Usability of BPMN and UML Activity Diagrams for Business Users

Dominik Birkmeier and Sven Overhage

Component and Service Engineering Group,
Business Informatics and Systems Engineering Chair,
University of Augsburg,
Universitaetsstrasse 16, 86159 Augsburg, Germany
{dominik.birkmeier,sven.overhage}@wiwi.uni-augsburg.de

Abstract. Joint architecture development plays a key role in service-oriented computing as it facilitates the coordination of business processes with the software architectures of applications. To better support business users in the communication of business process semantics, the Object Management Group advises to adopt the newly standardized Business Process Modeling Notation (BPMN) instead of the UML Activity Diagram. A main reason for this advice is that BPMN is presumed to be more usable for business users than the technically-oriented Activity Diagram. Adopting a new process modeling language, however, is a significant expense factor for businesses and consolidated findings on whether such presumptions hold true in practice are missing. In this paper, we present results from an empirical study, in which we examined the application of BPMN and the UML Activity Diagram by business users during a model creation task. Results indicate that the UML Activity Diagram is at least as usable as BPMN since neither user effectiveness, efficiency, nor satisfaction differ significantly.

1 Motivation

The success of service-oriented computing (SOC) strategies considerably depends on the joint development approach that brings diverse stakeholders together to shape a company's service-oriented architectures [1]. To support the communication of relevant business process semantics and so ensure a tight coordination with the software architecture of applications, stakeholders should use a process modeling language that can straightforwardly be understood and applied both by IT and business parties. The growing demand for such an integral process modeling language, amongst others, led to the development of the Business Process Modeling Notation (BPMN), which is said to bridge the communication gap between IT and business departments [2,3].

Not only is BPMN directly applicable for the design of service-oriented software architectures as it supports an automated conversion of modeled processes into the machine-readable Business Process Execution Language (BPEL). BPMN advocates such as the Object Management Group (OMG) furthermore claim that, at the same time, it is understandable and readily usable for all business users, even for "the business people who will manage [...] those processes" [2]. The well-established UML Activity Diagram (UML AD) in contrast is deemed as too technically oriented and hence

G.T. Heinemann, J. Kofron, and F. Plasil (Eds.): QoSA 2010, LNCS 6093, pp. 119–134, 2010.

useful for designers only [4]. With the adoption of BPMN as core standard to develop a business modeling framework around, the OMG deliberately decided not to use the UML AD as its recommended language to model business processes anymore.

While the BPMN success story is likely to continue in light of this development, transitioning to a new business process modeling language comes with significant efforts and costs for companies. The promised advantages of BPMN therefore have to be thoroughly confirmed. While BPMN's integration into the SOC technology is unquestioned, it has to be proven if it is also more usable for business users and better allows them to communicate process semantics in joint architecture development scenarios than the UML AD. To date, however, a superior usability of BPMN has neither been backed with sound theoretical arguments nor consolidated empirical findings. As authors who conducted analytical comparisons have in fact highlighted considerable similarities between the concepts of both languages [4,5], the presumed superiority merely stands as an unproven claim.

In this paper, we analyze the usability of BPMN 1.1 and UML AD 2.x for business users using results of a comparative empirical study. In order to efficiently participate in a joint architecture development scenario, business users not only need easy-to-understand models, but a basic knowledge of the underlying modeling techniques as well. Building upon a standardized usability definition, we therefore test the conservative hypothesis that UML AD is at least as usable as BPMN in a model creation task. To confirm that BPMN indeed is more usable, we then try to falsify this proposition. During the empirical study, we therefore conducted a controlled experiment, in which each participant had to model the same process. The process was predetermined as part of the experiment design and documented in natural language. We measured to what extent participants were able to express relevant process semantics with the two modeling languages.

Building upon such a confirmatory, quantitative research method [6], the remainder of this paper is organized as follows: next, we describe related work to further motivate the research gap. In section 3, we introduce the theories and definitions relevant for our study in order to derive and refine our proposition. We then describe the experiment setting (section 4) and analyze the obtained data in detail (section 5). We conclude by summarizing central findings and discussing implications for practice and academia.

2   Related Work

How to evaluate and compare conceptual modeling languages (and process modeling languages in particular) has already been addressed in literature. General recommendations thereby advise to combine analytical with empirical approaches to get a complete picture [7]. With respect to its usability for business users, BPMN so far has only been analyzed from an analytical perspective, however. Analyses of BPMN against a semiotic quality framework with several linguistic evaluation categories revealed that it is easily applicable for simple modeling scenarios, but especially its advanced modeling concepts are likely to complicate a successful usage by business users [8,9]. Compared to the UML AD, BPMN was judged to be somewhat superior with respect to its learnability and precision. Overall, however, the UML AD was found to be equally suited to improve the communication between IT and business departments [8].

Analytical evaluations of BPMN, which use the workflow patterns as introduced by van der Aalst et al. [10] as a benchmark, found the expressive power to be comparable to those of established process modeling languages [5,4]. Especially, they attested a notable similarity between the constructs of BPMN and UML AD regarding their expressive power. The authors of one study nevertheless considered BPMN to be more usable for business users since "although the UML 2.0 development included a more focused effort to upgrade the Activity Diagram in terms of its use for business people, it is still more technically oriented" [4]. They did not elaborate on why this might be the case, except for stating that this is due to the design of the language constructs, though.

In contrast to analytical evaluations, empirical studies on the usability of BPMN for business users are rarely found. One study was devoted to comparatively evaluate BPMN against Event-Driven Process Chains (EPC). It measured the comprehension and problem-solving capacities of students as surrogates for business users [11]. While no significant differences were identified, the study admittedly had a differing focus: it aimed at examining teaching effects and therefore compared the performance of trained participants in the EPC group versus untrained participants in the BPMN group. To the best of our knowledge, there currently is no empirical study that focuses on confirming that the usability of BPMN for business users is (a) higher than that of other process modeling notations in general or (b) higher than that of UML AD in particular.

3   Theory and Propositions

Before analyzing if BPMN is indeed more usable for business users than other process modeling languages, we first have to clarify what the term "usability" means and how it is to be measured in a controlled experiment. For our study, we adopted the usability definition from the International Organization for Standardization (ISO), which defines usability as the "extent to which a product can be used by specified users to achieve specified goals with effectiveness, efficiency and satisfaction in a specified context". In our study, we focus on a joint architecture development scenario (as the specified context) and examine the ability of business users (as the specified users) to express the semantics of business processes in a model (as the specified goal).

Effectiveness generally is determined by the accuracy and completeness with which the participants were able to reach the defined goal [12]. Thereby, accuracy is to be measured as the extent to which the quality of the users' output conforms to specified criteria, while completeness is to be measured as the degree of target achievement [12,13]. In the context of a business process modeling task, effectiveness can be interpreted as the quality of the resulting model [14]. To measure the quality of the models obtained during our study, we took several types of modeling faults from literature and aggregated them into a framework which covers accuracy and completeness (see section 5.1). Thereby, we focused on capturing modeling faults which complicate the communication of process semantics to other parties in a joint architecture development scenario.

Efficiency generally is to be determined as the level of effectiveness in relation to the expenditure of resources like physical effort, time, materials, or financial cost [12]. We measured it as effectiveness in relation to the time necessary to produce the process model. *Satisfaction* generally is to be measured by means of the users' attitude towards the usage of the product, e.g. as the extent to which users are free from discomfort [12]. It was measured by questioning users during a post-test survey.

As part of the study design, we also had to account for any intervening variables as they could influence the model quality in addition to the used modeling language and so bias the results. Generally, the quality of conceptual models is influenced by a variety of factors [15,16,17], which are summarized in Figure 1. The human factor has an influence on the quality of the resulting process model, as different perceptions and interpretations of reality, diverging professional experiences, or varying perceptions of model quality may affect the selection of the modeling language and the modeling process. As such effects cause variations in the resulting process models, differences between individual users have to be controlled, e.g. by increasing the sample size.

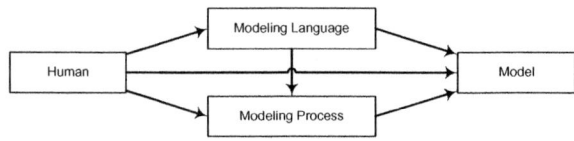

Fig. 1. Factors that affect the quality of a conceptual model [17]

Apart from the human factor, the quality of a business process model is mainly influenced by the chosen modeling language, especially by its expressive power and complexity [18]. The expressive power of a modeling language thereby is determined by its ontological completeness and its ontological clarity. A modeling language is ontological complete, if it is possible to represent all relevant aspects of a domain with its language constructs. A modeling language is ontologically clear if there are no redundant or superfluous constructs and constructs are not overloaded (i.e. cannot be used to model different domain aspects). The complexity of a language is determined by the number of constructs and the number of ways to combine them [18].

Regarding complexity and completeness, many similarities between BPMN and UML AD become obvious [4]. Both, e.g., use the same construct to model process steps and model control flow branches in a similar way (see Figures 4 and 5 for examples). There are, however, also differences, like the modeling of events or the data flow, which in BPMN has to be separated from the control flow [2]. Moreover, BPMN only offers a reduced set of core constructs and uses variations of these to depict similar process patterns. E.g., it comprises similar elements to model different kinds of events or to depict branches of the control flow. Both the reduced set of core constructs as well as the separation of control and data flow, have been used as a rationale to claim a superior usability of BPMN for business users [3,4]. Introducing variants of constructs, however, reduces the ontological clarity of a language as apparently similar constructs exhibit differing semantics. Therefore, it remains to be validated whether the presumed superior usability of BPMN actually holds in practice.

With its properties, the modeling language also influences the modeling process, in which the perceived reality is transcribed and communicated as a written model. This process largely depends on the successful mapping of domain aspects onto modeling constructs, which has to be achieved with limited human cognitive capacity [19]. If the semantics of modeling constructs is imprecise or the mapping is complicated due to the language complexity, however, the quality of the resulting model is likely to be compromised. Here, BPMN might have a negative influence as, e.g., the semantics of the UML AD in version 2.x has been more clearly defined than in BPMN [20] and the separation of control and data flow introduces additional complexity.

While it is not possible to conduct a more detailed analysis of BPMN versus UML AD in light of the above-mentioned theory due to space limitations, we already raised reasonable doubts whether BPMN might indeed be better usable for business users as claimed by BPMN advocates. In order to substantiate their claim, an empirical inter-language comparison [14] would have to result in a falsification of the proposition *P: For business users, UML AD is at least as usable as BPMN during model creation.* Based on the discussed definition of usability, P can be further refined into:

P1. Business users model at least as effectively with UML AD as with BPMN,
P2. Business users model at least as efficiently with UML AD as with BPMN,
P3. Business users will be at least as satisfied with UML AD as with BPMN.

If at least one of these propositions can be falsified, the claim that BPMN is more usable than UML AD can be corroborated.

4   Experiment Setting

The experiment conducted to examine the stated propositions followed the design used by Batra et al. [21]. In a related research topic they evaluated representations with different data modeling techniques in an empirical examination. The main variable examined in the experiment is the notation used for model creation by the participants. Besides the modeling language, we additionally introduced three different training levels to simulate an environment of different experiences as it is usually found in practice [22]. The analysis, however, concentrates on one source of variation, namely the modeling method, within a completely randomized design [23,24].

Experiment Design. Figure 2 depicts the design of the experiment. It started with a pre-test survey on prior domain and modeling knowledge, whose results were used to identify and exclude possible outliers afterwards. Two equally large groups were

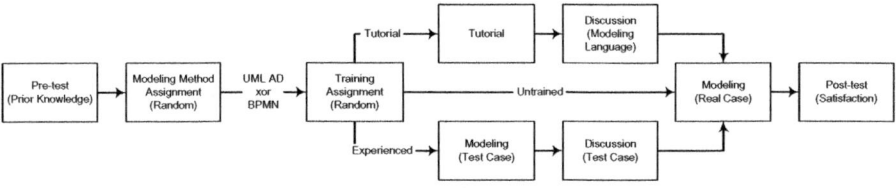

Fig. 2. The experiment design

selected at random and allocated to different modeling techniques. Next, the participants in each group were randomly assigned to undergo different trainings. Depending on the assignments, short tutorials in BPMN or UML AD were provided for one third of the participants. Each of them took 45 minutes and included one small test case. Both were held by the same instructor and were congruent with regard to their content and explanations. To simulate a second level of training, another third of the participants had to create a model of a complex test case without a detailed tutorial and was urged to discuss individual experiences afterwards. Finally, the remaining participants were left completely untrained. The actual case was modeled by all participants at the same time. There was no time restriction; however, time was recorded for the following analysis. A survey on user satisfaction completed the experiment. Parts of the experiment were repeated with the same participants on a control case, which has marginal differences from the main case in its representational complexity [25].

Participants. Participants in the experiment were 30 graduate students in business administration. As surrogates for business users, they were randomly chosen out of over 40 volunteers for the study and split into two groups with 15 subjects each. The pre-test survey revealed that all of them had slightly different backgrounds in process modeling, but none was an approved expert or freshman. Following Gemino and Wand [19], we agree that the use of students is appropriate for such a type of study and in fact beneficial, as "prior knowledge on the problem solving (domain understanding) [...] might have confounded the results". For that reason, such a substitution, moreover, is common standard in related studies [21,26,19].

Materials. Several materials were provided for the participants of the study. A pre-test survey aimed at identifying prior knowledge. During the model creation task students were supplied with several large empty pages to create the models, a page with instructions, and four sheets of information on the application of the modeling language. The information sheets described the available modeling primitives and common patterns, as well as an end-to-end example. They have been independently compared and validated by several faculty members with experience in both modeling languages.

Prior knowledge on the utilized business domain by some participants "might create substantial difficulties in an experimental study" [14]. Thus, we decided to choose an equally well-known example from everyday life, which, nevertheless, was complex and non-straightforward (see Figures 4 and 5). In doing so, we accounted for prior

Table 1. Complexity characteristics of the process to be modeled

		Count
Primitive	Flow element	18
	Data element	12
Basic control flow pattern	Sequence (regular / conditional)	4 (3/1)
	Parallel split	1
	Synchronization	4
	Exclusive choice	3
	Simple merge	3
Structural pattern	Arbitrary Cycle	1

domain knowledge as an intervening variable while testing a process with representative complexity [14]. As shown in Table 1, the case contains all basic control flow patterns from van der Aalst et al. [10], as well as one structural pattern. Its complexity, thus, is comparable to most of the reference business processes found in the German standard reference on business information systems for e-commerce [27].

Figure 3 depicts four questions from the post-test survey, which were created to gather information on the users' satisfaction with their respective modeling language. On the first question, a high value indicates a highly satisfied user, whereas on the last three questions small values are favorable.

Q1 - Do you think you have understood the modeling language thoroughly?	(not at all) 1 ... 2 ... 3 ... 4 ... 5 ... 6 (completely)
Q2 - Do you think the modeling language is challenging for you?	(not at all) 1 ... 2 ... 3 ... 4 ... 5 ... 6 (completely)
Q3 - Do you think the concept of the modeling language is difficult?	(not at all) 1 ... 2 ... 3 ... 4 ... 5 ... 6 (completely)
Q4 - Do you think the application of the modeling language is difficult?	(not at all) 1 ... 2 ... 3 ... 4 ... 5 ... 6 (highly)

Fig. 3. An excerpt of the post-test survey on user satisfaction

Statistical tools and methods. For the analysis of the obtained data, we mainly applied the programming language and software environment R for statistical computing and graphics. In addition, we utilized SPSS for various calculations and GGobi for interactive graphics. Hypothesis testing was primarily performed via Student's t-tests. Where necessary, a Kolmogorow-Smirnow test or Bartlett's test helped to check for normality or equal variance conditions respectively.

5 Results

5.1 Scoring

Three raters graded the quality of the created models by comparing them with an adequate solution [21]. Therefore, sample solutions were independently prepared by four experienced modelers and consolidated (see Figures 4 and 5). As every model is created from a subjective view and generally there is no one solution [17], tolerated variations from the sample solutions were defined for the grading process. Only differentiations exceeding these tolerances were marked as deficient.

For the grading process, we defined types of modeling faults that compromise the quality of a business process model. We thereby concentrated on identifying fault types that complicate the communication of process semantics to other parties as this is a main goal in joint architecture development scenarios. Building upon a survey of the literature on conceptual and business process modeling [28,14], we identified various fault types and aggregated them into a framework (see Figure 6). Broadly, this framework distinguishes between violations of the language grammar (formal mistakes) and faults made during the application of the language in the modeling process (content-related mistakes). The fault categories correspond to the modeling language and the modeling process which were identified as influence factors earlier on (see Figure 1).

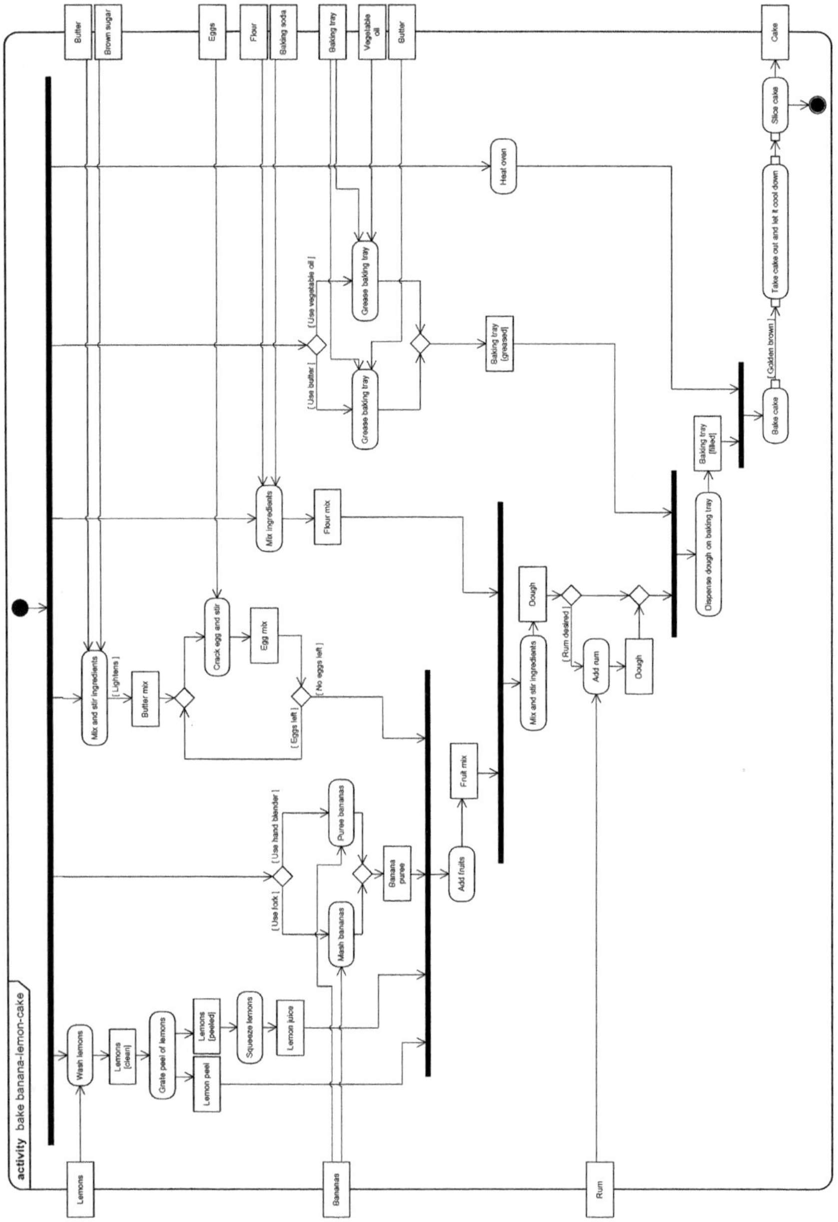

Fig. 4. Sample solution using UML AD

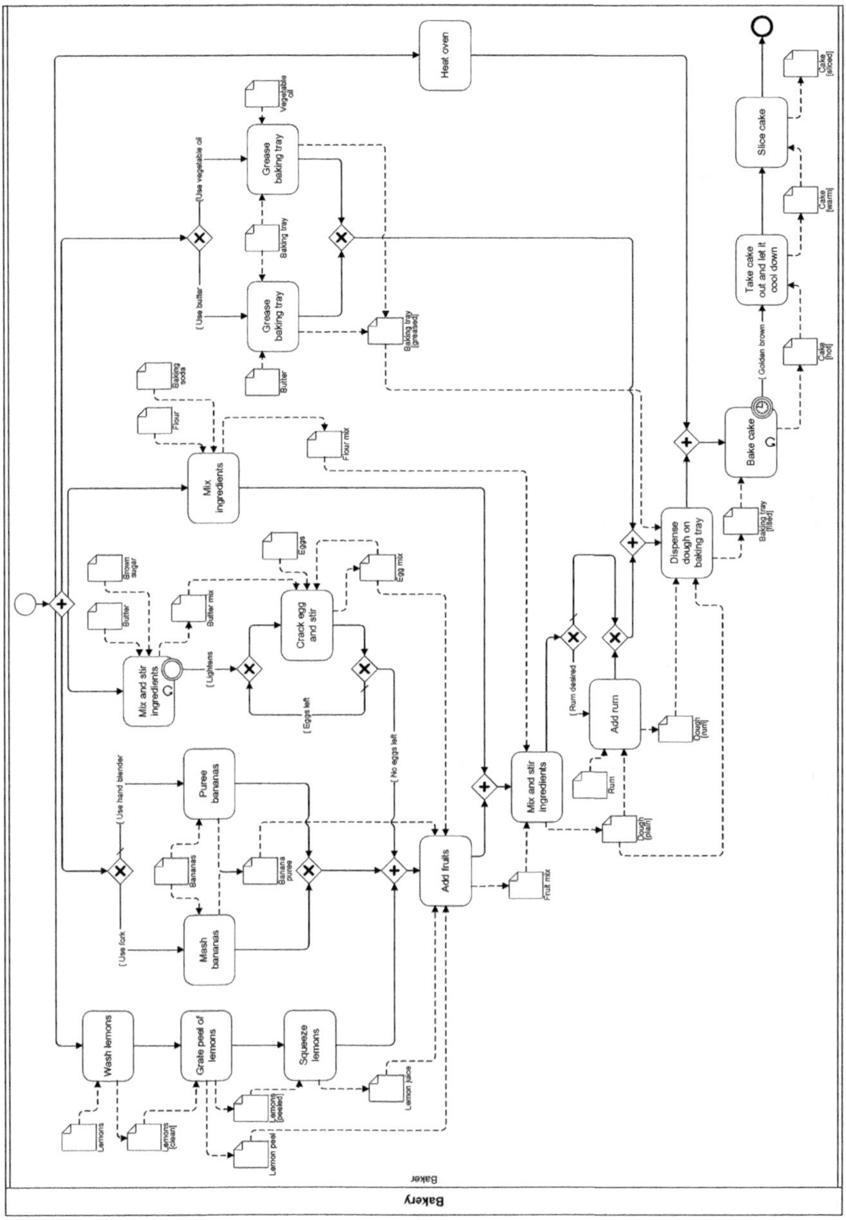

Fig. 5. Sample solution using BPMN

In accordance with linguistic theory, we distinguished violations of the language grammar into syntax, semantic, or pragmatic faults [29]. Consecutive syntax and semantic faults of the same type were recorded as repetitive fault if they occurred more than three times. Pragmatic faults were counted wherever participants incorrectly modeled flow patterns (e.g. loops) due to an allowed but inadequate combination of language elements. Formal mistakes stemming from an incorrect understanding of the modeling language in general make the communication of process semantics difficult. For this reason, they were included into the grading process.

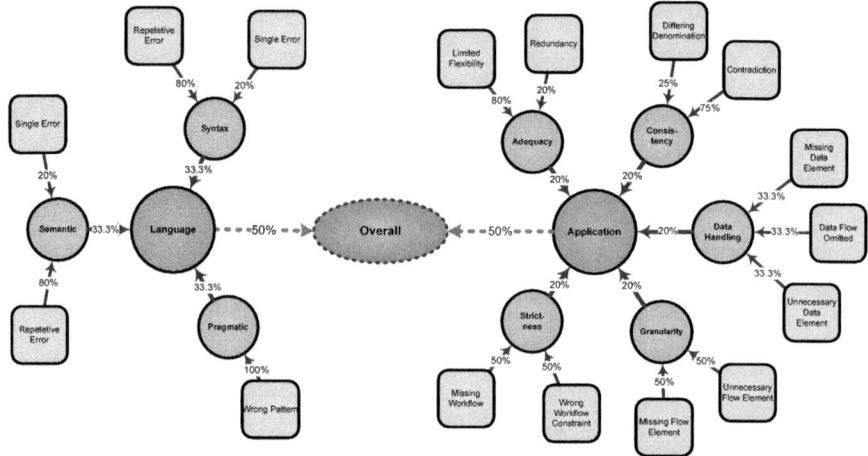

Fig. 6. Fault types for the grading of processes and aggregation scheme

Regarding the application of a process modeling language, we considered the criteria adequacy, consistency, strictness, granularity, and data handling during the grading process. The *adequacy* of a process model is compromised if it contains redundant process elements or the flexibility is unnecessarily limited by modeling independent workflows in sequence. Especially the latter fault has significant consequences for the quality of a software architecture, as flows that could run in parallel are specified to run in sequence. The *consistency* is affected if participants include contradictions or differing denominations into their models. Such faults make the design of an adequate software architecture difficult as they cause a need for further inquiry of stakeholders.

The *strictness* criterion is violated if wrong workflow constraints are introduced into the model or workflows are omitted completely. Leaving out individual process steps or unnecessarily splitting them up violates the *granularity* criterion, which demands a complete and minimalistic mapping of process steps from reality to the model. Having such a tight mapping is important to ensure compliance of the resulting software architecture with the underlying reality. Similarly, the *data handling* criterion ensures informational equivalency [14]. It is compromised if superfluous data objects are included into the model, relevant data objects are left out, or relevant data flows are omitted.

Before applying the framework for grading the quality of created business process models, it was evaluated by faculty members who were experienced in teaching business process modeling. Any necessary adjustments were discussed and implemented.

During the grading process, faults in the elementary categories were identified and counted for each of the process models created during the study.

5.2 Measuring

We determined the effectiveness of BPMN and UML AD by building upon the results of the grading process. To evaluate the model quality not only in regard to elementary but also in regard to compound categories of the framework (see Figure 6), aggregated scores had to be built. This was done in four steps. First, the counted occurrences of faults were scaled to each form a score between 0 (worst) and 100 (best). In doing so, a score of 100 in one of the elementary categories is equal to zero faults. A score of 0 is assigned for the highest amount of faults in one category over all models. For each model, a score was calculated in all of the elementary fault categories. The approach uses a linear transformation and, thus, no information is changed or lost. The standard transformation is performed using the following formula where EFC is an abbreviation for elementary fault category and $\#E$ denotes the number of faults counted in one EFC:

$$Score_{EFCX} = 100 \cdot \left[1 - \left(\frac{\#E_{EFCX} - \min_{\forall EFC}(\#E)}{\max_{\forall EFC}(\#E) - \min_{\forall EFC}(\#E)} \right) \right]$$

In step two, the scores of the elementary categories were aggregated to obtain scores for the compound categories as introduced above. In step three, they were further combined to form language and application scores. The consolidation of the latter ones to an overall score completes the aggregation. In all aggregation steps, the weights depicted in Figure 6 were used. Most of the weights are balanced, except where equal weights would be unreasonable. While the overall score is an interesting nice-to-have, it was not used for the analysis as the level of aggregation turned out to be highly abstract. Instead, we decided to evaluate the effectiveness of each modeling language on varying levels of aggregation to get a complete picture.

Since the time needed to complete the model creation task was recorded (in minutes), the efficiency could be calculated for every criterion by dividing the effectiveness scores through time. The corresponding unit is points per minute. Satisfaction was straightforwardly measured as each question of the post-test survey was recorded on a scale from 1 to 6 and hence was directly usable.

5.3 Analysis

The three propositions concerning effectiveness, efficiency, and satisfaction were tested on the obtained data. As described above, mainly t-tests were used since they are rather robust towards violations of its preconditions [30]. Nevertheless, whenever an assumption is violated, test results have to be interpreted more carefully. In accordance with the state of the art, we interpreted test results with p-values smaller than 5% to be statistically significant.

Effect of intervening variables. The effect of intervening variables was examined using an analysis of covariance (ANCOVA) technique [31]. Two possible covariate factors might have an influence on the analysis: prior domain knowledge and the assigned training. Domain knowledge information was recorded in the surveys. The analysis showed that domain knowledge was comparable between subjects and had no significant influence on the results. Therefore, it is disregarded in the further analysis.

The different experience levels, which were intentionally introduced and monitored through the assigned trainings, constitute the second possible covariate factor. The analysis revealed neither an influence on the scores investigated to examine the effectiveness, nor on the satisfaction measures. On the other hand, the experience has a significant influence on the time needed for the model creation task. This complies with our expectations. Consequently, the training has an impact on the efficiency scores (points per minute) as well. Nevertheless, as the analysis showed, the influence of the language used for model creation stays the same regardless whether the experience level is considered or not. Therefore, it is safe to be removed from the further analysis as well.

Table 2. Tests and summary statistics for effectiveness and efficiency measures

Variable		Effectiveness ND[1]	EV[2]	t test[3] t	p-value	Summary Statistics[6] Min	Max	Mean	Med[4]	SD[5]	Efficiency ND[1]	EV[2]	t test[3] t	p-value	Summary Statistics[7] Min	Max	Mean	Med[3]	SD[4]
Overall	AD	✓	✓	-1,331	0,903	95	99	97,3	97	1,29	✓	✓	-0,825	0,792	0,97	2,14	1,39	1,25	0,373
	BPMN	✓				94	98	96,7	97	1,45	✓				0,84	1,92	1,28	1,27	0,305
Language	AD	✓	✓	-0,541	0,703	94	100	98,1	99	2,09	✓	✓	-0,806	0,786	0,97	2,16	1,40	1,26	0,377
	BPMN	✓				92	100	97,6	99	2,61	✓				0,82	1,94	1,29	1,27	0,309
Application	AD	✓	✓	-1,241	0,888	94	99	96,8	97	1,52	✓	✓	-0,856	0,800	0,98	2,12	1,38	1,25	0,371
	BPMN	✓				93	99	96,1	96	1,71	✓				0,87	1,89	1,27	1,27	0,299
Syntax	AD	✗	n/a	0,318	0,376	94	100	98,5	99	1,60	✓	✓	-0,712	0,759	0,99	2,16	1,40	1,26	0,373
	BPMN	✓				94	100	98,7	99	1,84	✓				0,83	1,96	1,31	1,30	0,318
Semantics	AD	✓	n/a	0,741	0,233	94	100	98,8	100	2,11	✓	✓	-0,704	0,756	0,97	2,16	1,40	1,28	0,373
	BPMN	✗				97	100	99,3	100	1,22	✓				0,86	1,96	1,32	1,30	0,309
Pragmatics	AD	✓	✓	-0,970	0,830	86	100	96,8	100	5,03	✓	✓	-0,985	0,833	0,93	2,17	1,38	1,27	0,386
	BPMN	✓				83	100	94,9	97	5,85	✓				0,76	1,89	1,25	1,21	0,306
Adequacy	AD	✓	✓	-2,131	0,979	91	100	97,4	98	2,44	✓	✓	-0,973	0,830	0,99	2,07	1,38	1,26	0,364
	BPMN	✓				94	100	95,7	95	1,99	✓				0,88	1,85	1,27	1,27	0,285
Consistency	AD	✓	n/a	1,125	0,136	91	100	97,9	100	3,08	✓	✓	-0,654	0,741	0,97	2,17	1,39	1,27	0,378
	BPMN	✗				94	100	99,0	100	2,00	✓				0,88	1,96	1,31	1,27	0,311
Strictness	AD	✗	n/a	-1,987	0,971	97	100	99,1	100	1,39	✓	✓	-0,877	0,806	1,00	2,10	1,41	1,27	0,379
	BPMN	✓				93	100	97,8	98	2,04	✓				0,87	1,96	1,30	1,30	0,318
Granularity	AD	✓	✓	0,603	0,276	81	100	94,0	95	4,47	✓	✓	-0,658	0,742	0,90	2,10	1,34	1,19	0,378
	BPMN	✓				88	98	94,9	95	3,31	✓				0,81	1,96	1,26	1,23	0,300
Data Handling	AD	✓	✓	-2,033	0,974	90	99	96,1	98	3,44	✓	✓	-1,119	0,864	0,98	2,15	1,36	1,27	0,365
	BPMN	✓				82	99	93,1	93	4,56	✓				0,86	1,83	1,23	1,23	0,290

[1] Normally Distributed, [2] Equal Variances, [3] One-tailed, [4] Median, [5] Standard Deviation, [6] Unit: points (0-100), [7] Unit: points per minute

Proposition 1. Table 2 contains an overview of descriptive statistics and testing results. Considering the p-values for the one-tailed t-test, it becomes obvious that the results are rather unambiguous, as for none of the criteria the difference is close to being significant. Thus, the stated proposition cannot be falsified and the claimed superiority of BPMN over UML AD remains unsupported with regard to its effectiveness. A closer look at the results reveals that the UML AD group has higher means in language and application scores, as well as in four of the lower aggregated criteria. Wherever differences in medians are present, UML AD scores are higher as well.

While the language scores are rather equal, Figure 7 reveals that especially the application of UML AD seems to be more successful. An examination of the contrary hypothesis, of BPMN being at least as effective for business users as UML AD, leads to deeper insights. Such a hypothesis will be significantly rejected for the criteria adequacy, strictness, and data handling.

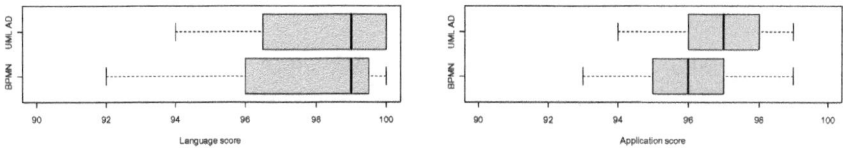

Fig. 7. Boxplots showing the effectiveness of participants

Proposition 2. As discussed, the basis of all efficiency indicators is the time needed to finish the model creation task. The mean modeling time needed by subjects to perform the task is between 74 and 80 minutes. A t-test showed no significant difference in model creation time between BPMN and UML AD (p-value: 0.492).

The statistical results on efficiency shown in Table 2 are even more distinct than those for effectiveness. All reported p-values are larger than 74% and thus, they are far from rejecting the claimed proposition. For every single criterion the means in the UML AD group are higher than those in the BPMN group. However, this is quite opposite for the medians, which are higher for the BPMN group except for pragmatic faults and data handling. Overall, business users modeling with UML AD are at least equally efficient as with BPMN.

Proposition 3. Finally, the examination of the post-test survey gives information about the average satisfaction of business users with the different modeling notations. As discussed, a high value on question 1 and low values on the other three are favorable. For all questions the means and medians of BPMN and UML AD are relatively close to each other and thus no clear tendency can be seen. This observation is validated by the p-values of the respective tests, which range between 0.39 and 0.79 and, hence, are far from indicating significant differences. Consequently there is no reason to discard the stated proposition and, hence, also no evidence to conclude that business users are less satisfied with UML AD as with BPMN.

As we failed to reject any of the refined propositions (*P1*, *P2* and *P3*), the main proposition *P* (*UML AD is at least as usable as BPMN*) cannot be falsified as well. A subsequent examination of the control process supported these results.

5.4 Limitations

The study can be easily replicated and hence an independent confirmation of the results is possible. However, as for any empirical study there are some limitations as to what extent the results can be generalized. On the one hand, the number of samples is still limited. We plan to increase the sample size and validate our results in further experiment settings in order to increase the external validity of our findings. Additionally, our examination is based on a model creation task. Results for an analysis of usability in model interpretation tasks, in the sense of recall, comprehension, and problem solving, might be different. As business users are the primary source of information about a company's business processes and will hence likely play a major role during the creation of models in joint architecture development scenarios, however, we decided to concentrate on model creation as the more demanding task first.

6 Conclusions

In this paper, we evaluated the usability of BPMN and UML AD for business users based on an empirical comparison, in which we examined their ability to express and communicate business process semantics in a joint architecture development scenario. The goal of this examination was to judge if BPMN is indeed more usable for business users than UML AD, as it is commonly claimed by BPMN advocates. Starting from a brief comparative discussion of both languages, we raised doubts whether this claim actually can be substantiated. With the analysis of the data obtained during our model creation task, these doubts became justified as the usage of BPMN did neither led to significantly different results in user effectiveness, efficiency, nor satisfaction. In contrast, examinations revealed that it was the usage of UML AD which in fact led to significantly better results in some of the quality criteria.

Above all, UML AD turned out to be superior in expressing flexible processes, in which independent activities are allowed to run in parallel. The usage of BPMN instead promoted a rather sequential modeling style in which unrelated activities run one after the other. Taken over into the software architecture, however, such a sequential modeling unnecessarily degrades the performance of the resulting application. One of the reasons for the observed differences is that the UML AD has adopted the semantics of Petri Nets and, e.g., supports an independent start of unrelated activities [20]. In BPMN, the use of a single start event is preferred to initiate the process flow [2]. A second reason is that the branching and synchronization of parallel workflows is done with a graphically significant construct in UML AD, while in BPMN an apparently insignificant gateway symbol is used. A second remarkable observation concerns the separation of control and data flow in BPMN, which introduces additional complexity and apparently mislead participants to leave out parts of the data flow. Originally being introduced as a means to separate concerns [3], this concept turned out to be inferior to a combined modeling of data and control flow as present in UML AD. To design service-oriented architectures, however, a close knowledge of the data flow is important.

The presented results have implications for both practice and academia. For practice, they signal that BPMN should not all too easily be judged to be more usable than UML AD. Although this currently is often done in literature [8,3,4] and even standardization organizations such as the OMG seem to have jumped to that conclusion, there are indications that BPMN still has shortcomings, which are likely to hinder its efficient adoption by business users in practice. Where business users are unable to use a modeling language adequately, however, the goal of achieving an efficient communication between business users and developers is compromised. Taking into account that our results especially revealed that the use of BPMN implied a decrease of process flexibility, it may be doubted that it really is first choice in joint architecture development.

While the presented study revealed several insights to better discuss the usability of BPMN and UML AD, it also left a need for further research. Amongst others, we were unable to confirm our theoretically motivated doubt that reducing the number of modeling constructs and instead introducing variants generally leads to a higher rate of faults due to a reduction of grammar clarity. Future research should hence concentrate on further examining the empirical indications identified in this paper. In order to better judge the usability of BPMN and UML AD for business users, a deeper understanding of their individual strengths and weaknesses has to be gained. Therefore, extended empirical studies of model creation products and processes as well as model interpretation products and processes should be conducted [14]. Consolidated findings of such studies could provide a basis for merging BPMN and UML AD, which is eventually being planned in the future to form a truly unified process modeling notation that combines the strengths of both languages [4].

References

1. Krafzig, D., Banke, K., Slama, D.: Enterprise SOA: Service-Oriented Architecture Best Practices. Prentice-Hall, Upper Saddle River (2005)
2. OMG: Business Process Modeling Notation Specification. Final Adopted Specification dtc/06-02-01, Object Management Group (2006)
3. Weske, M.: Business Process Management: Concepts, Languages, Architectures. Springer, Heidelberg (2007)
4. White, S.A.: Process Modeling Notations and Workflow Patterns. In: Fischer, L. (ed.) The Workflow Handbook 2004, pp. 265–294. Future Strategies Inc., Lighthouse Point (2004)
5. Wohed, P., van der Aalst, W.M.P., Dumas, M., ter Hofstede, A.H.M., Russell, N.: On the Suitability of BPMN for Business Process Modelling. In: Dustdar, S., Fiadeiro, J.L., Sheth, A.P. (eds.) BPM 2006. LNCS, vol. 4102, pp. 161–176. Springer, Heidelberg (2006)
6. Creswell, J.W.: Research Design: Qualitative, Quantitative, and Mixed Methods Approaches, 3rd edn. Sage Publications, Thousand Oaks (2008)
7. Gemino, A., Wand, Y.: Evaluating Modeling Techniques based on Models of Learning. Communications of the ACM 46, 79–84 (2003)
8. Nysetvold, A.G., Krogstie, J.: Assessing Business Processing Modeling Languages Using a Generic Quality Framework. In: Castro, J., Teniente, E. (eds.) Proceedings of the CAiSE 2005 Workshops. Faculdade de Engenharia da Universade do Porto, vol. 1, pp. 545–556 (2005)
9. Wahl, T., Sindre, G.: An Analytical Evaluation of BPMN Using a Semiotic Quality Framework. In: Castro, J., Teniente, E. (eds.) Proceedings of the CAiSE 2005 Workshops. Faculdade de Engenharia da Universade do Porto, vol. 1, pp. 533–544 (2005)
10. van der Aalst, W.M.P., ter Hofstede, A.H.M., Kiepuszewski, B., Barros, A.P.: Workflow Patterns. Distributed and Parallel Databases 14, 5–51 (2003)
11. Recker, J., Dreiling, A.: Does It Matter Which Process Modelling Language We Teach or Use? An Experimental Study on Understanding Process Modelling Languages without Formal Education. In: Proceedings of the Australasian Conference on Information Systems, Toowoomba, Australia (2007)
12. ISO: Ergonomic Requirements for Office Work with Visual Display Terminals (VDTs) - Part 11 : Guidance on Usability. ISO Standard ISO 9241-11:1998(E), International Standard Organization (1998)
13. Frøkjær, E., Hertzum, M., Hornbæk, K.: Measuring Usability: Are Effectiveness, Efficiency, and Satisfaction Correlated? In: Proceedings of the CHI 2000 Conference on Human Factors in Computing Systems, pp. 345–352. ACM Press, New York (2000)
14. Gemino, A., Wand, Y.: A Framework for Empirical Evaluation of Conceptual Modeling Techniques. Requirements Engineering 9, 248–260 (2004)
15. Topi, H., Ramesh, V.: Human Factors Research on Data Modeling: A Review of Prior Research, an Extended Framework and Future Research Directions. Advanced Topics in Database Research 3, 188–217 (2002)

16. Soffer, P., Hadar, I.: Reusability of Conceptual Models: The Problem of Model Variations. In: EMMSAD, Proceedings of the Eighth CAiSE/IFIP8, 1. International Workshop on Evaluation of Modeling Methods in Systems Analysis and Design (on CD), Austria (2003)
17. Hadar, I., Soffer, P.: Variations in Conceptual Modeling: Classification and Ontological Analysis. Journal of the Association for Information Systems 7, 569–593 (2006)
18. Wand, Y., Weber, R.: On the Ontological Expressiveness of Information Systems Analysis and Design Grammars. Journal of Information Systems 3, 217–237 (1993)
19. Gemino, A., Wand, Y.: Complexity and Clarity in Conceptual Modeling: Comparison of Mandatory and Optional Properties. Data & Knowledge Engineering 55, 301–326 (2005)
20. OMG: Unified modeling language specification: Version 2. Revised Final Adopted Specification ptc/05-07-04, Object Management Group (2005)
21. Batra, D., Hoffler, J.A., Bostrom, R.P.: Comparing Representations with Relational and EER Models. Communications of the ACM 33, 126–139 (1990)
22. Recker, J.: BPMN Modeling - Who, Where, How and Why. BPTrends 5, 1–8 (2008)
23. Cobb, G.W.: Introduction to Design and Analysis of Experiments. Springer, New York (1998)
24. Dean, A., Voss, D.: Design and Analysis of Experiments. Springer, New York (1999)
25. Bodart, F., Patel, A., Sim, M., Weber, R.: Should Optional Properties Be Used in Conceptual Modelling: A Theory and Three Empirical Tests. Information Systems Research 12, 384–405 (2001)
26. Kim, Y.G., March, S.T.: Comparing Data Modeling Formalisms. Communications of the ACM 38, 103–115 (1995)
27. Becker, J., Schuette, R.: Handelsinformationssysteme, 2nd edn. Verlag Moderne Industrie, Frankfurt (2004)
28. Schuette, R., Rotthowe, T.: The Guidelines of Modeling - An Approach to Enhance the Quality in Information Models. In: Ling, T.-W., Ram, S., Li Lee, M. (eds.) ER 1998. LNCS, vol. 1507, pp. 240–254. Springer, Heidelberg (1998)
29. Silverstein, M.: Linguistic Theory: Syntax, Semantics, Pragmatics. Annual Review of Anthropology 1, 349–382 (1972)
30. Boneau, C.A.: The Effects of Violations of Assumptions Underlying the t Test. Psychological Bulletin 57, 49–64 (1960)
31. Kutner, M.H., Nachtsheim, C.J., Neter, J., Li, W.: Applied Linear Statistical Models, 5th edn. McGraw-Hill/Irwin, Boston (2005)

Barriers to Modularity - An Empirical Study to Assess the Potential for Modularisation of Java Programs

Jens Dietrich[1], Catherine McCartin[1], Ewan Tempero[2], and Syed M. Ali Shah[1]

[1] Massey University, School of Engineering and Advanced Technology,
Palmerston North, New Zealand
{j.b.dietrich,c.m.mccartin,m.a.shah}@massey.ac.nz
[2] Department of Computer Science,
University of Auckland, Auckland, New Zealand
e.tempero@cs.auckland.ac.nz

Abstract. To deal with the challenges when building large and complex systems modularisation techniques such as component-based software engineering and aspect-oriented programming have been developed. In the Java space these include dependency injection frameworks and dynamic component models such as OSGi. The question arises as to how easy it will be to transform existing systems to take advantage of these new techniques. Anecdotal evidence from industry suggests that the presence of certain patterns presents barriers to refactoring of monolithic systems into a modular architecture. In this paper, we present such a set of patterns and analyse a large set of open-source systems for occurrences of these patterns. We use a novel, scalable static analyser that we have developed for this purpose.

The key findings of this paper are that almost all programs investigated have a significant number of these patterns, implying that modularising will be therefore difficult and expensive.

1 Introduction

Object-oriented software engineering has been used successfully in large scale projects for almost three decades. However, there have been challenges arising in large and complex software systems. The use of core object-oriented concepts such as classes, interfaces and name spaces is not sufficient to address many of the problems encountered when trying to achieve quality attributes such as maintainability, openness and scalability. To address these issues, several new technologies have been introduced in recent years to facilitate modularisation. This includes frameworks such as OSGi [4] and its derivatives such as Declarative Services [4], Eclipse [1] and Spring Dynamic Modules [6], and the several Java Specification requests [2] aiming to add modularity support to Java such as JSR277, JSR291 and JSR294. Similar trends exist in other programming languages and platforms. Given that there is a very successful "killer application" (Eclipse) and emerging standardisation (OSGi and the JSRs), many vendors will

G.T. Heinemann, J. Kofron, and F. Plasil (Eds.): QoSA 2010, LNCS 6093, pp. 135–150, 2010.
© Springer-Verlag Berlin Heidelberg 2010

consider refactoring existing, monolithic systems into a new modular architecture. Recently, this has been done by several vendors offering application servers, including Oracle/BEA (WebLogic) and IBM (WebSphere) [21]. The question that arises is how difficult it is to refactor existing systems to take advantage of these new component models.

OSGi and related dynamic component frameworks define modules ("bundles") by combining several existing Java language features, namely name spaces (packages), containers (libraries, aka jars), and class loaders. These modules declare their capabilities and requirements using meta data. This meta data can then be used to dynamically link ("wire") modules together. This has numerous advantages. In particular, it supports evolving applications through rewiring, and prevents DLL-hell style problems, as version constraints can be expressed as part of the meta data.

In OSGi and similar frameworks, modules can control the visibility of packages through `Export-Package` and `Import-Package` declarations. This implies that packages should not be scattered across different modules, and should be used to combine related functionality. This differs from the semantics associated with packages in the original Java language specification where packages were merely used as unique name spaces. Also, this adds another layer of encapsulation enforced by the component framework using the class loader (and not the compiler). It is therefore desirable to have loose coupling between name spaces so that they can easily be separated into different modules that own them. For instance, if there are name spaces NS1 and NS2 with a single dependency from (a type within) NS1 to (a type within) NS2, then the program can be easily refactored into two bundles B1 and B2 such that B1 contains NS1 and B2 contains NS2. The refactoring does not even have to change source code, it only has to change build scripts (creating bundles from class files) and has to create the respective bundle meta data to ensure that NS2 is visible for the bundle containing NS1. A common reason for doing this is to separate the life cycle of the two name spaces - being in separate bundles means that they can evolve separately. To achieve this, it is desirable to have good **name space separability**. We use this term to quantify how easy is it to separate name spaces through simple refactorings that can be (semi-) automated.

Many dynamic component models also use the separation of abstract types and implementation types. This separation facilitates service-oriented programming where service implementation providers are dynamically associated with service consumers through dependency injection [14] techniques. In particular, this enables the dynamic swapping of service providers with minimal impact on the service consumers. This approach is common in OSGi based applications like Eclipse, where applications that consume services define these services through interfaces associated with extension points. Other components providing these services then provide implementation classes through extensions. Other OSGi extensions such as Declarative Services and Spring Dynamic Modules use similar mechanisms. To take advantage of these platforms, interfaces and implementations need to be separated, and the dependencies between them must be minimised. We use the term **interface separability** to measure how easily this can be done. Examples for refactoring that can be used to separate interface and implementation are the use of design patterns such as factory and dynamic proxy [15], and dependency injection.

We propose to use pattern analysis to quantify name space and interface separability of systems. For this purpose, we define a set of patterns which compromise separability. These patterns can be seen as antipatterns or smells in that they may represent design flaws. The detection of these patterns also reveals refactoring opportunities that can be used as starting points for architectural refactorings of systems from monolithic to modular architectures.

The rest of this paper is organised as follows. We discuss related work in section 2. In section 3, we discuss the methodology we have adopted. In particular, we present a scalable static analysis tool we have developed to analyse large sets of complex programs. In section 4, we discuss the individual patterns used to analyse systems for name space and interface separability. We then describe the experiment setup, the data set and the analysis results in section 5. We finish our contribution with some conclusions.

2   Related Work

The term code smell appears to have been coined by Kent Beck and has been made popular by Fowler's book [13]. Code smells illustrate symptoms that might indicate deeper problems. Often, code smells are used as starting points for code refactorings. Closely related to code smells are antipatterns [23]. While early work on smells and patterns has focused on the analysis of source code, many of these concepts can also be applied to software architecture [24]. One driver for this development is the integration of architectural practises into agile development life cycle models [28]. Research into code-level antipatterns and smell detection has resulted in a set of robust tools that are widely used in the software engineering community, including PMD [11] based on source code analysis, and FindBugs [20] based on byte code analysis. PMD is particularly interesting, since it supports the declarative specification of antipatterns using XPath expressions that are evaluated against the abstract syntax tree (AST) of programs.

A closely related area is the detection of design patterns [15]. Several solutions have been proposed to formalise design patterns in a platform-independent manner, a good overview is given in [35].

In [16], the authors describe a set of architectural smells using a format similar to the original gang of four pattern language [15]. These smells are different from ours, and the definitions given by the authors do not seem to be precise enough for tool-supported detection.

Our analysis is based on the dependency graph extracted from programs. This approach has been investigated by several authors. JDepend [3] is a tool that extracts dependencies between classes and packages from Java byte code and calculates metrics that can be used to quantify the quality of the system design. It also detects circular dependencies. Lattix [32] is another tool used to analyse the dependency graph of a program, represented as a dependency structure matrix (DSM). A variety of functions are available to help organise the matrix in a form that reflects the architecture and highlights patterns and problematic dependencies.

We have investigated in our previous work [12] the potential of the Girvan-Newman clustering algorithm [18] to detect refactoring opportunities in dependency graphs. Other work based on cluster analysis includes [33] and [26].

A number of graph query languages have been proposed in the literature, for both general and specific contexts. GraphQL [19] is a general query language for graphs that supports arbitrary attributes on vertices, edges, and graphs. It is based on graph structures that are composable, using the notion of a formal language for graphs. A graph *motif* can be either a simple graph or composed of other graph motifs by means of concatenation, disjunction, and repetition operators, defined in the context of graphs as opposed to strings. A graph *pattern* is a graph motif plus a predicate on attributes of the motif. GraphQL has a similar algebraic system to SQL, but the algebraic operators are defined directly on graphs. SPARQL [30] is a query language and data access protocol for the Semantic Web. SPARQL is defined in terms of the W3C's RDF data model and will work for any data source that can be mapped into RDF. SPARQL is an SQL-like language whose features include basic conjunctive patterns, value filters, optional patterns, and pattern disjunction. It works primarily via constraints on single vertices, it does not support path constraints. TAX [22] (Tree Algebra for XML) is used for manipulating XML data, modelled as forests of labelled ordered trees. TAX is an extension of relational algebra and is complete for relational algebra extended with aggregation. It uses a pattern tree to match interesting nodes. The pattern tree consists of a tree structure and a predicate on the nodes of the tree.

The existing tool most closely aligned to the purposes of our analysis is Cro-coPat [9]. CrocoPat is an effective system to query and manipulate relations that can be extracted from programs. All queries but CNS used in our analysis can be expressed in CrocoPat. In particular, [9] contains definitions of two of the queries we are interested in, DEGINH and STK. CrocoPat is based on Binary Decision Diagrams (BDDs), and known for its excellent performance. CrocoPat's language (RML) is a full programming language with syntax elements such as conditionals and loops, based on first order logic. CrocoPat queries return facts for a certain predicate symbol. Paths cannot be directly represented in Cro-coPat. However, reasoning about paths in CrocoPat is supported through the higher-order transitive closure predicate TC. In our analysis, we require the ability to arbitrarily constrain the lengths of paths when matching instances of our queries. For instance, this feature is needed when querying for circular dependencies between packages, and when we are interested in the actual dependency paths, not just in the packages that are the start and end points of these paths.

The static analysis tool that we have developed, GQL4JUNG, and its method of deployment, is described in detail in the next section. Our experiment suggests that GQL4JUNG is faster than Crocopat for computing instances of queries, and requires significantly less memory. The reasons for this are the use of an observer-based API in GQL4JUNG and the fact that CrocoPat is a purely relational language. In particular, complex terms (such as the package of a class node) can only be computed by looking up association tables (predicate extensions). The details of the benchmarking experiment can be found on the GQL4JUNG project site[1].

None of the existing analysis tools fulfilled all of our requirements. In particular, we required a tool that made available a solid implementation open enough to allow integration of domain-specific heuristics, supported scriptability to analyse large sets of programs in batch mode, and had support for path constraints and aggregation conditions.

In recent years corpora-based empirical studies have become more prevalent, largely due to the fairly widespread availability of open-source software. These studies have had a variety of goals. For example, open-source systems have been used for metric validation (e.g. [10]), for studying the appearance of powerlaw distributions [8], and how features of a language are used in practise, such as use of multiple dispatch [27], inheritance [37] and unused design decisions [36].

There have also been a number of studies attempting to characterise common idioms in software, such as micro-patterns [17] and more recently nano-patterns [34]. Our study differs in that we target idioms that have a negative impact on software quality. Other studies with similar goals include characterising the cyclic structures in dependence graphs [25].

3 Methodology

In order to analyse programs for occurrences of patterns, we have developed the tool GQL4JUNG ("graph query language for Jung ")[2]. This tool can be used to execute graph queries for graphs represented in JUNG [29]. These queries describe motifs representing patterns in the dependency graph. The dependency graphs are relatively simple. For a given program, each type (class, interface, enum etc.) is represented as a vertex. Properties such as the container (in Java, this is usually a jar file or a folder), the name space (package), abstractness and the kind of the type (class, interface, annotation etc.) are represented as vertex annotations. The edges represent relationships between types, annotated with relationship types. Only three types of relationships are used: uses, extends and implements. Extends and implements relationships are used to represent inheritance, all other references such as type references in methods or variables are represented as uses relationships.

The graphs can be extracted from different sources such as byte code and source code of programs written in different programming languages. For our analysis, we have extracted graphs from Java byte code using the dependency finder library [38]. Graphs built from byte code are slightly different from graphs

---

[1] http://code.google.com/p/gql4jung/wiki/GQL4JUNGvsCrocoPat
[2] http://code.google.com/p/gql4jung/

built from source code. In particular, relationships defined by the use of generic types are missing due to erasure by the Java compiler. References to static final numeric fields (constants) are also not visible as the Java compiler replaces these references by the respective values.

The dependency graphs investigated represent the *runtime* characteristics of systems, and the results of this investigation describe the *runtime modularity* of systems as opposed to their *design time modularity*. However, we believe that these graphs are very similar to graphs extracted from source code and that therefore most of the results presented here also apply to design time modularity.

GQL4JUNG graph queries are written using a combination of XML and the MVEL2 [7] expression language. This has several advantages. Queries are easy to parse and very expressive due to the expressiveness of MVEL. In particular, complex expressions and terms can easily be written in a syntax similar to Java. MVEL expressions are used to define constraints on paths and vertices. These expressions can then be directly compiled into Java byte code.

An example query definition is shown in listing 1. A query consists of vertex - (`<select>`) and path roles (`<connectedBy>`), constraints (`<constraint>`) and aggregations (`<groupBy>`). Constraints are boolean expressions referencing either vertex or path roles. Path role definitions have optional `minLength` and `maxLength` attributes restricting the length of the paths. Given a query $Q = \langle VR, PR \rangle$ with vertex roles VR and path roles PR and a graph $G(V, E)$ consisting of vertices V and edges E, a binding is a pair of functions $\langle inst_V, inst_P \rangle$, where $inst_V : VR \rightarrow V$ and $inst_P : PR \rightarrow SEQ(E)$. That is, a binding associates vertex roles with vertices and path roles with sequences of edges. Moreover, the vertices and edge sequences associated with roles by a binding must satisfy all the constraints defined in the query, including the `minLength` and `maxLength` constraints for paths.

Aggregation elements (`<groupBy>`) are expressions defining an equivalence relationship between bindings. Bindings are considered as equivalent if and only if the evaluation of the `<groupBy>` expressions for the bindings of the roles referenced in the expressions yields the same results. Aggregation allows the distinction between instances and variants. Instances are classes of bindings modulo equality defined by the aggregation clauses. Usually, instances are represented by one selected binding. All other bindings in this class represent variants of this instance. By defining appropriate aggregation clauses, potentially large result sets can be pruned to a manageable size by removing pattern occurrences that are non-essential variations of other occurrences. Empirical results show that this is quite effective, see table 1 for details. The query shown in listing 1 describes a pattern where a supertype depends on a subtype. The aggregation clause (line 11) defines that two bindings are variants of the same instance if the super type is the same.

Finally, annotation elements (`<annotate>`) can be used to define instructions to be executed before queries are evaluated. These instructions are names of Java classes that can be instantiated using reflection. The purpose of annotations is to add annotations to vertices and edges before the query is executed.

Queries can then refer to those annotations. This is used in the CNS query (see below). Here, an annotation is used to run a script that annotates vertices with cluster information. The script uses the Girvan-Newman algorithm [18]. Using annotations in queries has the advantage of performing computationally relatively expensive pre-processing on demand, only for queries that actually use the respective annotations.

```
 1 <motif name="subtype_knowledge">
 2     <select role="sub"/>
 3     <select role="super"/>
 4     <connectedBy role="inherits" from="sub" to="super">
 5         <constraint>inherits.type=='extends' ||
 6          inherits.type=='implements'</constraint>
 7     </connectedBy>
 8     <connectedBy role="uses" from="super" to="sub">
 9         <constraint>uses.type=='uses'</constraint>
10     </connectedBy>
11     <groupBy><element>super</element></groupBy>
12 </motif>
```

Listing 1. Subtype knowledge (STK)

Complex, real-world programs generally give rise to large dependency graphs, often with 10000 or more vertices, whereas the number of roles in our smell-based queries remains uniformly very small. The worst-case time complexity for query execution is $O(n^k)$, where n and k are the number of vertices in the dependency graph and the number of roles in the query, respectively. This worst-case time complexity is a consequence of the NP-hardness of the subgraph isomorphism problem, which is essentially the problem that we must solve each time we successfully find an instance of a query motif in a dependency graph.

In practice, the running time for query execution depends on the actual size of the search space required to successfully map the roles of the query to vertices in the dependency graph. The challenge is to reduce this search space as far as possible and to explore it in the best order.

The following techniques are used in GQL4JUNG to address these issues:

1. Before the query is executed, a scheduler orders the constraints so that selective constraints are resolved first. This keeps the derivation tree narrow.
2. When the query engine computes paths to connected vertices, a straight forward breadth first search is used. However, the path constraints are enforced immediately to prune the search tree.
3. Queries can be executed with an *instances-only* flag. If this flag is set, only one member of each aggregation class will be computed. In many application scenarios, this is sufficient. In this case, the constraint resolver can use back jumping instead of back tracking and large parts of the search tree can be pruned. This leads to significant improvements in query performance.

4. The query has an observer [15] API. This means that observers are notified when results are found and can process results while the engine is still searching. If results are only counted, an observer that only increases a counter can be used, resulting in very modest demand for memory.

4   Patterns

4.1   Overview

As discussed in the introduction, there are two properties that facilitate the modularisation of systems: interface and name space separability. We have identified the following patterns that compromise these properties:

1. Abstraction Without Decoupling (AWD) - affects interface separability
2. Subtype knowledge (STK) - affects interface separability
3. Degenerated inheritance (DEGINH) - affects interface separability
4. Clusters in name spaces (CNS) - affects name space separability
5. Cycles between name spaces (CDNS) - affects name space separability
6. Cycles between containers (CDC) - flaw in existing modularisation

These patterns can easily be formalised in GQL4JUNG. We discuss each of these queries in the following subsection. We will not provide a formal definition for each query for space reasons. The interested reader can find the query definition in the open GQL4JUNG repository [3]. Instead, we will use a simple visual syntax to represent patterns. Vertex roles are represented as boxes. Path roles are represented by arrows connecting boxes. These connections are labelled with either *uses* (uses relationships) or *inherits* (extends or implements relationships). They are also labelled with a number range describing the minimum and maximum length of paths. If type roles have property constraints, these constraints are written within the box in guillemets.

4.2   Abstraction without Decoupling (AWD)

An Abstraction Without Decoupling (AWD) pattern exists when a client has a uses dependency on an abstract service and also on an implementation of that service. This means that in order to change the service implementation that is used, the client's code must be changed. Had the client depended only on the service and not the implementation, the implementation could have been changed without any impact on the client. This is a example where interface separability has been violated — there is no separation between the implementation and the client. The pattern is shown in figure 1.

This pattern can often be removed by using dependency injection — instead of hard-coding the dependency to the service implementation, it is stored externally and injected at runtime. In particular, this is desirable if there are alternative

---

[3] http://gql4jung.googlecode.com/svn/tags/r0.4.2/queries/

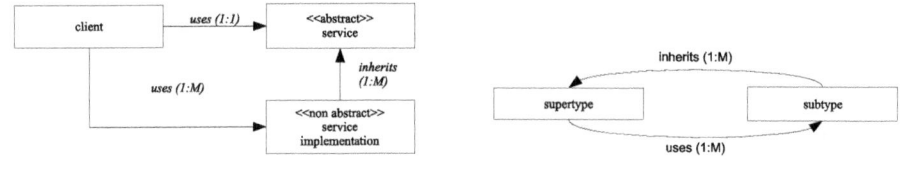

Fig. 1. AWD   **Fig. 2.** STK

service implementations available or if service implementations evolve and have to be upgraded at runtime.

This pattern often occurs when fields are declared using abstract types (such as `java.util.List`) and default values (such as `java.util.Vector`) are used. Sometimes, the low complexity of services does not warrant the full separation of service and implementation references. In Java, inner classes are often used to provide service implementations. This can be captured in a refined version of AWD, Abstraction Without Decoupling With Inner Class Exception (AWDI). AWDI has an additional constraint indicating the the service implementation must not be a member of the client.

For both AWD and AWDI, aggregation is defined modulo the client and the service role. This means that different occurrences are considered as variations of the same instance if client and service are the same but the service implementation or some of the reference paths are different.

4.3   Subtype Knowledge (STK)

In this pattern [9], types use their subtypes. The formal definition of this query is given in listing 1, a visual representation is given in figure 2. The presence of STK makes it difficult to separate interfaces and implementations into different modules. In particular, this would imply circular dependencies between modules containing super- and subtype. Moreover, instability in the (generally less abstract) subtype will cause instability in the supertype, and the supertype cannot be used and understood without its subtype. Aggregation is defined with respect to the supertype.

There are uses of design patterns that result in STK. Examples are singletons [15] where the singleton class itself is abstract, and the default instance is an instance of a subclass. This is sometimes used in conjunction with the AbstractFactory [15] pattern in order to install a global default factory for a certain service.

4.4   Degenerated Inheritance (DEGINH)

Degenerated inheritance [9] (figure 3) means that there are multiple inheritance paths connecting subtypes with supertypes. For languages with single inheritance between classes like Java, this is caused by (multiple) interface inheritance. The presence of DEGINH makes it difficult to separate sub- and superclasses.

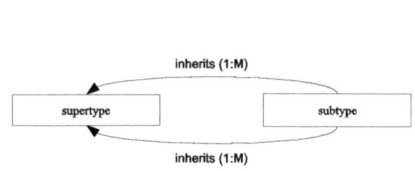

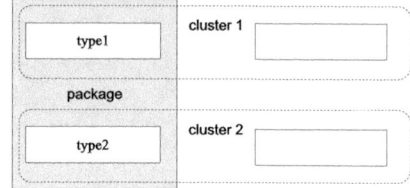

Fig. 3. DEGINH   **Fig. 4.** CNS

In particular, this may cause versioning problems if a class inherits from an interface via several separate intermediate classes or interfaces that are stored in different modules. If these modules are units of versioning, the interface version depends on the resolution algorithm used by the component model, and is difficult to predict by the author of the class. Aggregation is defined with respect to the super type.

4.5   Clusters in Name Spaces (CNS)

Clusters in name spaces (figure 4) are evidence that name spaces can be split to facilitate modularisation. Our clustering script is set to detect only existing, independent clusters, that is, each cluster here is simply a connected component of the dependency graph.

Having multiple clusters in packages is problematic as it might be desirable to move some types to a certain module, and other types to a different module. If modules own name spaces, this creates a conflict. However, if these types were in different clusters a name space could easily be split. Therefore, clusters in name spaces obfuscate obvious modularisation opportunities. Aggregation is defined with respect to the name space where the clustering occurs.

This pattern occurs often when miscellaneous packages are used to combine code that does not fit into other packages. An example is the Java `java.util` package. It contains unrelated functionality such as the collection library, support for internationalisation and localisation (i18n), time and date, and the observer pattern.

4.6   Cycles between Name Spaces (CDNS)

Cycles between name spaces glue name spaces together. This means that these name spaces can not be deployed and maintained separately. This is a classical, well-understood antipattern, and good tool support is available to find instances of this pattern. The definition used here (figure 5) is stronger than the usual definition of circularity. A cycle consists of a path connecting type vertices. The path itself is not necessarily circular, and the first and the last vertex are not necessarily the same. However, start and end vertices have to be in the same name space NS1, while there is at least one vertex in the path in a different name space NS2. This definition is stronger than just having (possibly disconnected) dependencies between NS1 and NS2, and NS2 and NS1. In CDNS, both

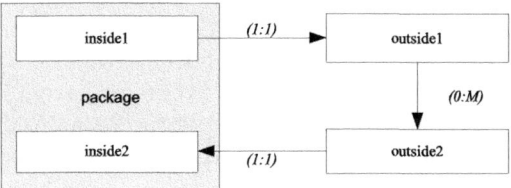

Fig. 5. CDNS

dependencies are linked together. This means that the circular dependency can not be broken by splitting NS2. The aggregation used in CDNS is defined with respect to the name space where the path starts and ends. The path connecting the two outside nodes has a minimum length of 0. This means that the two outside nodes can be identical, creating a triangular pattern.

4.7 Cycles between Containers (CDC)

Finally, we are interested in circular dependencies between containers (usually jar files). This is defined similarly to CNS by a path consisting of connected types linking a container with another container and then returning to the container where the path started. This means that the dependency can not be broken by splitting the container. To deploy containers separately, some of the the types within the path must be changed to break the cycle. Bindings are considered variants if the container where the path starts and ends is the same.

The visual representation of this pattern is the same as for CDNS, except that the inside nodes are in the same container, not in the same package. In our opinion, CDC is a strong antipattern. The very reason to build containers is to deploy them separately and in different combinations in different contexts. However, this is not possible if containers have circular dependencies.

5   Results

5.1   Programs Analysed

The experiment presented here is based on the qualitas corpus version 20080312 [31]. The corpus contains 206 programs. This includes multiple versions of some programs. In this case, we selected only the latest version of each program in order to avoid over-representation of particular patterns prevalent in certain programs. This resulted in a set of 87 programs analysed. The corpus contains a wide range of widely used systems, including end-user applications like azureus and ArgoUML, libraries like antlr, jung, Xerces and Xalan, and tools such as ANT.

5.2   Overview

The average number of vertices in the dependency graphs is 2781.93, the average number of edges is 13509.74. In average, programs have 161.95 packages and 15.69 jars. The largest programs analysed is the spring-framework 1.2.7. The program has 1013 packages and 91 jars, the respective dependency graph has 16313 vertices and 73400 edges.

Table 1 shows some metrics extracted from the result sets. It is remarkable that for each query there is only a small percentage of programs without any results. CDC seems to be the only exception. However, many programs (24) consist of only a single jar file, and can therefore not contain CDC instances by definition. The still relatively large number of programs with CDC instances was a result we did not expect. It is hard to think of any reasonable justification for this.

Table 1. Result summary

metric	AWD	AWDI	STK	DEGINH	CDNS	CDC	CNS
graphs with no instances	1	1	2	12	4	60	4
max number of instances found	11691	11516	870	187	358	7	257
average number of instances found	2068.06	2032.09	126.05	27.54	56.91	0.87	30.15
max number of variants found	147715	147184	3924	3945	2174436	8841	5214942
average number of variants found	24157.40	23990.17	684.89	451.64	178366.93	277.31	80766.18
average variants/instances ratio	9.35	9.42	5.67	14.19	3328.14	360.94	2647.32
max instances/vertex	1.56	1.55	0.19	0.05	0.06	0.003	0.03
avg instances/vertex	0.69	0.67	0.04	0.01	0.02	0.0002	0.01
max instances/edge	0.27	0.27	0.04	0.01	0.02	0.002	0.02
avg instances/edge	0.14	0.14	0.01	0.002	0.005	0.00007	0.003
average time to compute instances (ms)	19302	19414	1163	234	5909	2625	21269

AWDI was introduced to deal with false positives for AWD. However, the results indicate that there is no big difference between the result sets for these two patterns. There are significantly more instances for AWD/AWDI than for any other pattern. This itself is not surprising since it is rather common to declare variables using an abstract type, but to initialise them by using the constructor of a default type.

The table also contains performance data in the last row. These values have been obtained using system with an Intel Core2 CPU T5600 @ 1.83GHz, 2GB of memory, Ubuntu 9.04 with a 2.6.28-13-generic kernel and the OpenJDK 6b14-1.4.1-0ubuntu7.

5.3 Life Cycle, Program Size and Pattern Density

The results summarised in table 1 are based on the analysis of the latest version of each program represented in the corpus. However, for many programs the corpus contains several versions. The analysis of version ranges shows that the number of pattern generally increases. Table 2 shows the number of pattern instances in the first and the last version for the programs that are represented with more than 5 different versions in the corpus. In most cases, the increase is monotonic. There are a few cases where the instances decrease "locally" between two versions. For instance, the number of AWD instances drops from 177 to 142 from `antrl-2.7.2` to `antrl-2.7.3`. The size of the programs measured by graph size continuously increases for these programs. The increase was significant with one exception (jgraph).

We also looked into the correlation between the number of patterns and the size of the graphs. For most patterns, there is an almost linear relationship. The exception is CDC where the number of pattern instances is too small to detect a trend. Figure 6 shows the number of STK, DEGINH, CDNS and CNS instances by program size. Here, each dot represents the number of pattern instances found for a program of the respective size. The trends for AWD and AWDI, not shown in this graph, are similar, the respective curves are significantly steeper.

The almost linear relationship is surprising. Firstly, we expected smaller programs to have lower numbers of pattern instances relative to their size as having fewer developers should mean that each would have a good understanding of the entire program and would therefore be in a position to avoid obvious problems such as circular dependencies. Secondly, we also expected lower relative numbers in very large programs as we expected that other methodologies and tools (such as simple architectural testing with tools like JDepend) would have been introduced to deal with the complexity of large programs and a larger number of developers in teams. However, surprisingly, neither seems to be the case.

Table 2. Pattern instances at the boundaries of version ranges

program	versions in corpus	version range analysed	Vertex count first	last	AWD first	last	STK first	last	DEGINH first	last	CDNS first	last
antlr	10	2.4.0-2.7.6	51	224	1	154	1	13	1	3	1	3
ant	7	1.5.2-1.7.0	1618	2343	1368	1715	60	115	19	26	27	38
azureus	11	2.0.8.2-3.0.3.4	1145	5378	745	7918	16	232	3	25	60	309
jmeter	8	1.8.1-2.1.1	1959	4223	2347	3248	137	193	26	51	60	117
jgraph	27	5.4.4-5.9.2.1	92	94	110	114	16	18	1	1	5	5
jung	16	1.0.0-1.7.1	132	663	169	842	3	6	8	22	4	13
junit	13	2-4.4	38	154	6	58	1	8	0	0	0	8

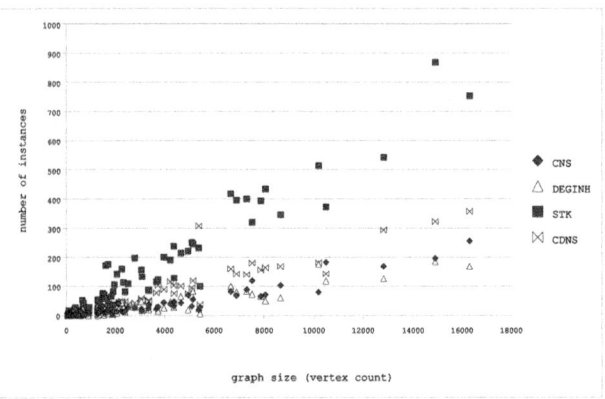

Fig. 6. Pattern instances by program size

5.4   Patterns in Java's Core Libraries

We have also analysed the Java runtime environment (JRE). The graph was built from the rt.jar library taken from SUN's Java SE Runtime Environment (build 1.6.0_05-b13) for Linux. The graph is large, consisting of 16877 vertices and 170140 edges. There are 26555 AWD instances, 26239 AWDI instances, 393 CDNS instances, 1437 STK instances and 184 DEGINH instances. There are however no CNS instances. The last result is mainly due to the presence of the java.lang.Object class connecting the graph. The number of circular dependencies between packages is surprising. It appears that many of these patterns occur in packages starting with sun or com.sun. The unexpectedly high number of patterns in the Java core libraries is particularly interesting as the modularisation of Java itself is currently being investigated (project "jigsaw" [5]).

The reason that this library does not contain instances of CDC is simple - it is only one library. However, there are instances of CDC when other libraries that are part of the JRE are added to the graph. In particular, rt.jar has a circular dependency with jce.jar and jsse.jar. The critical edges are uses relationships from java.net.SecureCacheResponse (in rt.jar) to javax.net.ssl.-SSLPeerUnverifiedException (in jsse.jar) and from java.security.Signature (in rt.jar) to javax.crypto.Cipher (in jce.jar).

6   Conclusion

In this paper we have investigated patterns that compromise the separability of name spaces and interfaces, and therefore hinder refactoring of programs to take advantage of emerging platforms providing support for modular system architectures. We have assessed the scope of the problem by analysing a large set of programs from an open source repository. The results show that the problem is widespread. However, the fact that detection of these patterns can easily be automated, as we have shown, indicates that there is an opportunity to semi-automate the removal of many of these patterns. The necessary refactorings are not restricted to code-level refactorings such as moving classes between name spaces, but would also include refactorings to create or modify build scripts, deployment descriptors and other component meta data.

Creating and cataloguing these refactorings is an interesting challenge for further research. An open question is whether our results can be directly applied to commercial, close source systems. There are some points supporting this conjecture, in particular the fact that software engineers use the same tools and methodologies used in open source software projects. Unfortunately, commercial systems are not readily available for analysis. The main problem is that the licenses of commercial systems usually do not allow byte code analysis.

Acknowledgements

This project has been supported by funding from the New Zealand Foundation for Research, Science and Technology (FRST) for the Software Process and Product Improvement (SPPI) project. The authors would like to thank Gareth Cronin from Kiwiplan Ltd for his input.

References

[1] The eclipse project, http://www.eclipse.org/
[2] Java specification requests, http://jcp.org/en/jsr/overview
[3] JDepend dependency analyser, http://clarkware.com/software/JDepend.html
[4] OSGi™- the dynamic module system for java, http://www.osgi.org/
[5] Project jigsaw, http://openjdk.java.net/projects/jigsaw/
[6] Spring dynamic modules for OSGi™ service platforms, http://www.springsource.org/osgi
[7] Mvel expression language (2009), http://mvel.codehaus.org/
[8] Baxter, G., Frean, M., Noble, J., Rickerby, M., Smith, H., Visser, M., Melton, H., Tempero, E.: Understanding the shape of Java software. In: Proceedings OOPSLA 2006, pp. 397–412 (October 2006)
[9] Beyer, D., Noack, A., Lewerentz, C.: Efficient relational calculation for software analysis. IEEE Transactions on Software Engineering (TSE) 31(2), 137–149 (2005)
[10] Chidamber, S.R., Kemerer, C.F.: A metrics suite for object oriented design. IEEE Trans. Softw. Eng. 20(6), 476–493 (1994)
[11] Copeland, T.: PMD Applied. Centennial Books (2005)
[12] Dietrich, J., Yakovlev, V., McCartin, C., Jenson, G., Duchrow, M.: Cluster analysis of java dependency graphs. In: SoftVis 2008, pp. 91–94 (2008)
[13] Fowler, M.: Refactoring: Improving the Design of Existing Code. Addison-Wesley, Boston (1999)
[14] Fowler, M.: Inversion of control containers and the dependency injection pattern (2004), http://martinfowler.com/articles/injection.html
[15] Gamma, E., Helm, R., Johnson, R., Vlissides, J.: Design patterns: elements of reusable object-oriented software. Addison-Wesley, Boston (1995)

[16] Garcia, J., Popescu, D., Edwards, G., Medvidovic, N.: Identifying architectural bad smells, pp. 255–258. IEEE Computer Society, Los Alamitos (2009)

[17] Gil, J.Y., Maman, I.: Micro patterns in Java code. In: Proceedings OOPSLA 2005, pp. 97–116. ACM Press, New York (2005)

[18] Girvan, M., Newman, M.E.: Community structure in social and biological networks. Proc. Natl. Acad. Sci. USA 99(12), 7821–7826 (2002)

[19] He, H., Singh, A.K.: Graphs-at-a-time: Query language and access methods for graph databases. In: Proceedings SIGMOD 2008, pp. 405–418 (2008)

[20] Hovemeyer, D., Pugh, W.: Finding bugs is easy. In: Proceedings OOPSLA 2004, pp. 132–136. ACM, New York (2004)

[21] Humble, C.: IBM, BEA and JBoss adopting OSGi, http://www.infoq.com/news/2008/02/osgi_jee

[22] Jagadish, H.V., Lakshmanan, L.V.S., Srivastava, D., Thompson, K.: Tax: A tree algebra for xml. In: Ghelli, G., Grahne, G. (eds.) DBPL 2001. LNCS, vol. 2397, pp. 149–164. Springer, Heidelberg (2002)

[23] Koenig, A.: Patterns and antipatterns. JOOP 8(1), 46–48 (1995)

[24] Lippert, M., Roock, S.: Refactoring in Large Software Projects: Performing Complex Restructurings Successfully. Wiley, Chichester (2006)

[25] Melton, H., Tempero, E.: An empirical study of cycles among classes in Java. Empirical Software Engineering 12(4), 389–415 (2007)

[26] Müller, H., Orgun, M., Tilley, S., Uhl, J.: A reverse-engineering approach to subsystem structure identification. Journal of Software Maintenance: Research and Practice 5, 181–204 (1993)

[27] Muschevici, R., Potanin, A., Tempero, E., Noble, J.: Multiple dispatch in practice. In: Proceedings OOPSLA 2008, October 2008, pp. 563–582 (2008)

[28] Nord, R.L., Tomayko, J.E.: Software architecture-centric methods and agile development. IEEE Software 23(2), 47–53 (2006)

[29] O'Madadhain, J., Fisher, D., White, S., Boey, Y.-B.: The jung (java universal network/graph) framework. Technical Report UCI-ICS 03-17, University of California, Irvine (2003)

[30] Prud'hommeaux, E., Seaborne, A.: SPARQL Query Language for RDF. Technical report, W3C (2006)

[31] Qualitas Research Group. Qualitas corpus version 20080312. The University of Auckland (March 2008), http://www.cs.auckland.ac.nz/~ewan/corpus

[32] Sangal, N., Jordan, E., Sinha, V., Jackson, D.: Using dependency models to manage software architecture. In: Proceedings OOPSLA 2005, pp. 164–165. ACM, New York (2005)

[33] Schwanke, R.W.: An intelligent tool for re-engineering software modularity. In: Proceedings ICSE 1991, pp. 83–92 (1991)

[34] Singer, J., Brown, G., Lujan, M., Pocock, A., Yiapanis, P.: Fundamental nanopatterns to characterize and classify java methods. In: Proceedings LDTA 2009 (2009)

[35] Taibi, T. (ed.): Design Patterns Formalization Techniques. Idea Group Inc., Hershey (2007)

[36] Tempero, E.: An empirical study of unused design decisions in open-source Java software. In: Proceedings APSEC 2008, December 2008, pp. 33–40 (2008)

[37] Tempero, E., Noble, J., Melton, H.: How do java programs use inheritance? an empirical study of inheritance in java software. In: Vitek, J. (ed.) ECOOP 2008. LNCS, vol. 5142, pp. 667–691. Springer, Heidelberg (2008)

[38] Tessier, J.: Dependency finder, http://depfind.sourceforge.net/

Evaluating Maintainability with Code Metrics for Model-to-Model Transformations

Lucia Kapová, Thomas Goldschmidt, Steffen Becker, and Jörg Henss

Chair for Software Design and Quality, Universität Karlsruhe (TH), 76131 Karlsruhe, Germany
{kapova,henss}@ipd.uka.de
FZI Forschungszentrum Informatik, 76131 Karlsruhe, Germany
{goldschmidt,sbecker}@fzi.de

Abstract. Using model-to-model transformations to generate analysis models or code from architecture models is sought to promote compliance and reuse of components. The maintainability of transformations is influenced by various characteristics - as with every programming language artifact. Code metrics are often used to estimate code maintainability. However, most of the established metrics do not apply to declarative transformation languages (such as QVT Relations) since they focus on imperative (e.g. object-oriented) coding styles. One way to characterize the maintainability of programs are code metrics. However, the vast majority of these metrics focus on imperative (e.g., object-oriented) coding styles and thus cannot be reused as-is for transformations written in declarative languages. In this paper we propose an initial set of quality metrics to evaluate transformations written in the declarative QVT Relations language. We apply the presented set of metrics to several reference transformations to demonstrate how to judge transformation maintainability based on our metrics.

1 Introduction

Model transformations are often used to transform software architectures into code or analysis models. Ideally, these transformations are written in special transformation languages like QVT [17]. With an observable increase in the application of Model-Driven Software Development (MDSD) in industry and research, more and more transformations are written by transformation engineers. Thus an increasing set of transformation scripts have to be maintained in the near future, i.e., they demand to be understood by other developers, bugs need to be tracked down and removed, and enhancements need to be implemented because of evolving source or target meta-models.

Today there are two main streams of model-to-model transformation languages: imperative (or operational) and functional (or relational) languages. For imperative languages like QVT Operational we can reuse existing literature about software code metrics for imperative, e.g. object oriented, languages. However, for relational model-transformation languages like QVT Relations there is not even a comparable amount of literature. In this paper we report on early experiences gained in our group on applying QVT Relations. They show that understanding relational transformations turns out to be quickly a difficult task. The difficulties increase more than linearly when transformation sizes increase and single relations become more complex.

G.T. Heinemann, J. Kofron, and F. Plasil (Eds.): QoSA 2010, LNCS 6093, pp. 151–166, 2010.

In traditional object-oriented software development *software metrics* are used as a means to estimate the maintainability of code [2]. The estimated maintainability then indicates when the code base becomes too hard to maintain. Software developers take corrective actions like refactorings [7] or code reviews to keep the code in a maintainable state. However, these metrics do not yet exist for relational model transformation languages. Nevertheless, some initial research targets metrics for functional programming languages in general like Lisp or Haskell. Being part of the same language family, some metrics for functional programming languages can serve as a starting point for the definition of metrics for declarative model-transformation languages. In this paper we try to draw upon their ideas in defining our own set of metrics for model-transformation languages.

As an initial step towards estimating the maintainability of functional model transformation languages, we present a set of metrics usable to get insight into the maintainability of QVT Relations transformations. For this, we analysed existing metrics for functional programming languages and combined them with general code metrics (like Lines of Code (LOC)) and complemented them with our own experiences from applying QVT Relations. This set of developed metrics shall finally serve as a basis to judge internal transformation quality and to guide the development of transformation refactorings or review checklists (i.e., a list of bad smells to look for). We evaluated our metrics on the standard model-transformation example given by the QVT standard: the transformation from UML models to entity-relationship models to show that the metrics (a) are computable and (b) give insight into the transformation's internal quality.

The contribution of this paper are metrics to evaluate aspects of the maintainability of QVT Relational transformation scripts. These metrics are described in detail and their ranges of "bad" values are characterized including a rationale explaining which type of maintainability problem the metric detects. An early case study shows the metrics' applicability and initial evaluation results.

The paper is structured as follows. After discussing the properties of transformation languages in Section 2, we give an overview of related work to our approach in Section 3. Section 4 introduces identified quality metrics for transformations and Section 5 illustrates how to systematically compute the values for quality metrics. To demonstrate the applicability of our approach we introduce a case study in Section 6. We discuss the limitations and validity of the approach in Section 7. Finally, Section 8 concludes the paper and highlights future research directions.

2   The Group of Relational Transformation Languages

The goal of our work is to quantify the maintainability of model transformations. Therefore, we start by defining suitable metrics in this context. We identified a lack of quality metric definitions for relational transformation languages in the literature. Hence, in this paper, we focus on model transformations created using QVT Relational (QVT-R), but we assume that our metrics can be applied to model transformations created using other relational transformation languages as well. The main observed difference between relational and operational (i.e., imperative) languages is the fact, that operational transformation languages describe a sequence of statements to create certain output.

In contrast, relational transformation languages only describe the relations between input and output of a transformation in a declarative manner, not the way how it is computed (non-determinism). This results in special characteristics of relational transformation languages which have to be reflected by the metrics to be defined.

2.1   QVT Relational

QVT Relational is part of the QVT standard [17] and used for describing model transformations in a declarative manner. This means the transformation itself is written as a set of relations that shall be satisfied during the transformation process. As QVT Relational is multidirectional, there is no single source and target model but a list of so called candidate models. Each of these candidate models can be chosen as a target of the transformation, identifying the execution direction. When the transformation is invoked in a selected execution direction only the target model is modified such that all relations hold.

```
1  top relation ClassToTable {
2        cn : String;
3        prefix : String;
4        checkonly domain uml c : SimpleUML::UmlClass {
5          umlNamespace = p : SimpleUML::UmlPackage {},
6          umlKind = 'Persistent',
7          umlName = cn
8        };
9        enforce domain rdbms t : SimpleRDBMS::RdbmsTable {
10         rdbmsSchema = s : SimpleRDBMS::RdbmsSchema { },
11         rdbmsName = cn,
12         rdbmsColumn = cl : SimpleRDBMS::RdbmsColumn {
13             rdbmsName = cn + '_tid',
14             rdbmsType = 'NUMBER' },
15         rdbmsKey = k : SimpleRDBMS::RdbmsKey {
16             rdbmsColumn = cl : SimpleRDBMS::RdbmsColumn{}}
17       };
18       when {
19       PackageToSchema(p, s);
20       }
21       where {
22         ClassToPkey(c, k);
23         prefix = cn;
24         AttributeToColumn(c, t, prefix);
25       }
26  }
```

Listing 1. Example of QVT Relational

An example QVT-R transformation is given in Listing 1. A relation has two or more domains, that are given as patterns on the candidate models. The pattern usually includes an object graph pattern, properties and associations between objects and defines a variable binding for each pattern match. By using the same variables in different domain patterns we can define the relation between candidate models. In consequence the target model is modified for each found pattern binding not being fulfilled to the extent that the relation holds. Beyond that, a relation can have *when* and *where* clauses that specify pre- and post-conditions. A relation only has to be satisfied when all precondition relations contained in the *when* clause are satisfied. In a similar manner each relation contained in the *where* clause has to be fulfilled when the relation containing the clause is fulfilled. Furthermore a target domain can be marked as *checkonly*, i.e. the target domain model is only checked for consistency and not modified. Besides this, relations are marked as *enforce* by default, thus insisting on the application of model changes for relations that do not hold. A relation can be marked as top-level. This means that the relation has to hold in any case for a successful transformation, while any non-top-level relation only has to be satisfied when directly or transitively referenced from a *where* clause.

2.2   General Observations on Maintainabilty of QVT-R Transformations

QVT-R can be applied for example in transformations between languages, code generation and incremental or refinement transformations. One main advantage of QVT-R is its brevity and conciseness. In the QVT-R language the structure of transformations is mainly characterised by the interdependencies of its relations. On the other hand relations can be defined in a way that they match overlapping sets of elements. Consequently, this increases complexity in cases when a new relation is introduced and it is influenced by other relations. For example, let transformation T be defined as a set of relations R, $R = \{a, b, c, d\}$. Suppose we want to extend T with a relation e, but e depends on a result of a and a depends on a result of both b and c, while c depends on d. Thus, we first need to understand how relations a, b, c and d are related in order to correctly include e into the transformation. In the case of more complex transformations it is very hard to have all dependencies in mind. Because of this net of dependencies it is hard to say if a new introduced relation conflicts with other relations or influences them in an undesired way. One possible design of relational transformation could be clustering of relations that match or create the same element (clustering of top-level relations). Furthermore, the identification of possible execution paths, how long they usually are and what they dependend on, is a very complex task.

3   Related Work

Quality metrics have been studied already to measure quality (software quality was defined by [3]) of object-oriented software [6,12,19], software architectures [1,21] and design [15]. Metrics to estimate the maintainability of software are mostly based on measuring the size and complexity of code. Depending on the employed programming languages (functional, imperative, etc.) different metrics need to be employed for this task. The most relevant group of metrics for our approach is derived from related work in the area of functional languages, such as the metrics defined by Harrison et al. in [11]. The group of relational transformation languages is related to functional programming languages, therefore we can reuse the existing functional metrics, similar to [22], in combination with some metrics used for object-oriented languages. However, Amstel et al. [22] focuses on model transformations created using the ASF+SDF transformation language. Most of these metrics are, however, quite generic and could be applied to nearly arbitrary functional programming languages. Nevertheless they do not take into account the special character of relational transformations, such as their strong alignment to the source and target metamodels. Still, some of these metrics can be used to measure certain aspects of model transformations written in QVT-R. We adapted some of the metrics to the special requirements of the QVT-R transformation language and extended them by the addition of more specific metrics (especially the group of manual metrics). Furthermore, we automated the gathering of the majority of the metrics presented in this paper.

In [8] initial considerations for transformation metrics based on a classification of transformation features [4] and a goal question metric plan were presented. However, these ideas were still in a very early stage and were not elaborated down to the special needs of different groups of transformation, such as relational transformations. Reynoso et al. [18] analysed how the complexity of OCL expressions impacts the analysability and understandability of UML models. As OCL is also part of QVT-R these findings are relevant for our approach. However, the remaining part of relational transformations, apart from OCL expressions, cannot be analysed using this approach. A special way of gathering a maintainability metric based on the occurrence of frequent patterns within a model or transformation was presented in [14]. The presented metric is based on a pattern mining approach that detects the most frequently occurring constructs. The assumption made in that paper is based on cognitive psychology, which says that the human brain works like a giant pattern matching machine and therefore can process things that re-occur often, more easily. Thus we incorporated this metric into our suite. Using OCL for the definition of metrics was introduced by Abreu in [5]. However, the approach presented there did not cope with metrics concerning the maintainability of transformations at all.

4 Metrics Definition

This section introduces metrics for measuring the quality of model transformations created using relational transformation language, such as QVT-R. For each metric we give a *description*, including a brief *motivation*. We also include the *rationale* behind the metric giving insights in why we believe the metric indicates the maintainability of a transformation. Additionally, we include a way for the *computation* (if possible using QVT-R and OCL) of the introduced metrics.

4.1 Automated Metrics

In this section we will discuss the metrics derived for QVT-R that can be automatically computed. We identified four categories: Transformation Size metrics, Relational metrics, Consistency metrics and Inheritance metrics. In the following sections we will give the names, descriptions and rationales of the automated metrics. Table 1 then gives the computation directions using OCL for the presented automated metrics.

Transformation Size metrics. The size of the transformation has an impact on the understandability of a transformation. The size of a whole transformation can be measured in several ways. The number of *lines of code*, for instance, is a simple metric measuring the pure code size of a transformation. This is comparable to measuring lines of code in programming languages. Comments and blank lines are also included in this metric. The number of code, comment and blank lines can also be viewed separately. Used in conjunction with other metrics we can derive valuable measures of a transformation, e.g. when compared to the number of top level relations.

The *number of relations* is a metric that can be used to derive the degree of fragmentation and modularisation of a transformation. Higher number of relations can be considered better, as it is an indicator for a high degree of modularisation. A high degree of modularisation can support the maintainability of a transformation and also the reuse of a transformation or parts of it. The *number of top level relations* gives a picture about the independent parts of a transformation. A top level relation is a starting point for a transformation and can trigger the execution of other relations. An execution of a transformation requires all top level relations to hold. The ratio of top level relations to non-top level relations shows the rate between independent and dependent parts of a transformation. An interesting metric is *number of starts* defined by the number of top relations without when-clause. A higher number of starts increases the number of possible execution paths and therefore makes the transformation less maintainable. The metric *number of domains* expresses the complexity of a transformation dependent on the number of match patterns. The *number of domains predicates* additionally gives information about the complexity of these patterns. The *number of when-predicates* and the *number of where-predicates* defines how complex the dependency graph between relations is.

The *number of metamodels* in a transformation has an impact on the complexity of the transformation itself and its match patterns. The *size of the metamodel* (defined by a number of classes) on which the relations match elements might also have a great impact on the structure and therefore on the understandability and modifiability of the transformation. The larger the metamodel the larger the set of possible instances of this metamodel. Therefore, more combinations may have to be considered in the match patterns of the relations.

Relational metrics. The size of a transformation relation can be measured in different ways. The OMG specification of QVT states that a relation has one or more domains and that every domain has a domain pattern that consists of a tree of template expressions. The size of a relation can be expressed in terms of its number of domains or the depth of the domain patterns. Additionally, relations can define when and where predicates giving pre- and postconditions. This leads to three different metrics for measuring the size of a relation: *Number of domains , Number of when/where predicates, Size of domain pattern per domain*. Another derived metric, the *ratio between the size of the relations and the number of relations* might also give hints about the maintainability of the transformation itself. However, the direction of the metric (e.g., for better maintainability) remains to be evaluated. For example, having many but small relations helps to understand the transformation punctually, for specific relations. However, grasping the interconnections of many small relations is also a tedious and error-prone task, thus leading to the conclusion that having larger but fewer relations may be also good for maintainability. Still, defining a functional dependency between size and number of relations in a transformation might give hints on the maintainability of the transformation.

The metric *average number of local variables per relation* additionally gives indications on the dependencies within a relation that a developer needs to grasp when trying to understand and modify the relation. A measurement for the complexity of the interconnections between relations is the average number of arguments in the form of its domains and the number of variables that are bound by calls to other relations in when- or where- predicates. These metrics are denoted *val-in* and *val-out*. Note that in QVT-R *val-in* is always the same as *number of domains*. A high number of *val-out* means that a relation is strongly dependent on the context, which might decrease the reusability of a relation.

Relations generally depend on other relations to perform their task. The dependency of a relation R on other relations can be measured by counting the number of times relation R uses other relations or queries. These dependency metrics are denoted *fan-in* and *fan-out*, where *fan-in* is the number of calls to R and *fan-out* is the number of relations that are called by R. A high value of *fan-in* indicates that the relation is reused quite often and therefore is highly reused or somehow more central to the overall transformation. A high value of *fan-out* means that a relation uses a lot of other relations or functions (maybe delegates functionality to library queries), again making the relation more "central". The metric *number of enforce/checkonly domains* expresses a rate of change between the domains of the relation (e.g., source and target domain). The metric expresses the number of possible match patterns by the number of checkonly domains and the level of change provided by a relation (a number of diverse change patterns) by the number of enforce domains. The complexity of a transformation may furthermore be affected by the *number of OCL helpers* and *number of lines/restricted elements per OCL query*, which encapsulate more complex behaviour.

Consistency metrics. A high degree of inconsistency in the transformation is a reason for confusion during development and may lead to reusability and transformation completeness problems. To detect an inconsistency in a transformation we introduce a number of consistency metrics. An example of inconsistency could be a relation that was not completed during development. Such a relation could be identified as a relation without domains, with only one domain or with domains without predicates. Therefore, we defined the metrics *number of relations without domains*, *number of relations with singular domains* and *number of domains without predicates*. An additional metric for the detection of incomplete relations is the *number of unused variables*. Unused variables pollute the code and complicate navigation within the transformation.

The already introduced consistency metrics are easy to automate. Another quite generic but still interesting metric is *number of clones*. However, the automation of this metric is a research field by itself. This metric identifies code duplicates, which are, as in other fields of code maintainability, candidates that impact maintainability of the code.

Inheritance metrics. QVT-R transformations can extend each other and override relations from parents. Inheritance metrics measure the level of inheritance of the transformation and its complexity. The *balance* metric shows size and distribution of transformation functionality between children. This metric is calculated as a ration between a number of relations, domains and equations per child transformation in comparison to the average.

In a similar way as in object-oriented programming the dependency of children on their parents can be measured by counting the *number of transitive parents per child* and *number of direct/transitive children per parent*. Based on these metrics and the fan-in and fan-out metrics we can get a view of the dependencies between relations in the different transformations (create a dependency graph). The metric *number of overrides* gives information on how many relations from a parent transformation were overridden by a child relations. The larger this value gets, the more effort has to be invested into understanding which parts of the transformation hierarchy are actually used (combination of non-overridden (inherited), overridden and additional non-inherited parts).

4.2   Manually Gathered Metrics

In the following, we describe metrics that are not gathered fully automated but require manual or semi-automated analysis to determine the actual value of a metric.

Similarity of relations (frequent patterns). The *Similarity of relations (frequent patterns)* indicates how many similar patterns can be found in a transformation. A large part of the complexity of a transformation and on an model abstract model of the transformation comes through the need to understand patterns that occur within these models. The more complex a transformation is the harder it is to maintain it. Thus, to be able to grasp the complexity of transformations, we propose to emulate human information processing through pattern mining on models. Human analysis of software products is conducted either top-down or bottom-up according to [16]. Using a top-down approach the analyst tries to apply his/her knowledge about design and domain to classify the software product under analysis. In order to do this he/she tries to gain an overview of the whole application. He/She will then successively pick selected software segments and determine their relevance for his current mental model of the software. Using a bottom-up approach the analyst will start reading comments of source code or other software artifacts. The control flow of certain sections will then be inspected sequentially and arbitrary selected variables will be traced throughout the flow. Especially in declarative transformation languages this is a difficult task as there is no explicit control flow. The information gained will be integrated to a mental software model which is the opposite to the top-down approach. Masak [16] notes that top-down analysis is being conducted more often by experts whereas bottom-up analysis is being used more often by novice analysts. These findings give strong indication that experts may have abstract mental patterns at hand which are being used for analysing the software product whereas novices must resort to documentation. If analysability is measured in terms of time to analyse parts of a software product the required time will be low if the analysed parts dominantly adhere to the expert's patterns. On the other hand the time will be very high, if the expert can apply only a few of his/her patterns or the software heavily differs from patterns known to him/her. These general observations were also stated for visual patterns in [20] which is why we propose to incorporate them into an analysability metric.

This metric can be computed by using the frequent pattern mining algorithm presented in [14] to identify possible frequent patterns. From these candidates the relevant patterns can be selected and their similarity can be estimated. However, the result of these pattern mining is mostly a superset of frequent patterns as they would be found by a human. Thus, manual selection needs to be performed to see whether each of the most frequent patterns is really a pattern that occurs as repeating structure in the transformation or if it is just the result of constraints on e.g., the transformation metamodel. For example, in QVT Relations a frequent pattern that is the result of the language concept would be that each relation domain has a root variable which refers to a meta-class that is contained in the package referred to by the domains typed model (see [17] for the QVT Relations metamodel). However, this construct in inherent to QVT relations and is not a frequent pattern that would be relevant for the analysability of a transformation. Thus, this metric cannot be computed fully automatically but needs an additional manual filter action. For example, a result of this metric could be that 30% of all relations of a transformation employ a pattern involving the matching or creation of a certain tree structure consisting of specific types of model elements within the source or target model. As humans are pretty good in pattern matching, a developer would then be able to recognise this combination over and over again thus helping him/her to more easily understand these 30% of relations.

Number of relations that follow a design pattern. The *Number of relations that follow a design pattern* may be another important indicator for transformation maintainability. However, the determination of this metric is a tedious manual task as a design pattern is an abstract concept. It may occur in a form that can only vaguely be identified. The number of design patterns employed in the transformation may be a strong indicator on how good a transformation can be understood by external readers. However, as the area of transformation development is still quite immature only few design patterns have been identified yet. To determine this metric we need to count the number of design patterns and their occurrences within the transformation. For example, if a transformation uses the *Marker-Relation Pattern*[9] throughout its whole implementation and a developer knows what that pattern is used for he or she can grasp the meaning of the transformation more easily.

Type Cut Through Source/Target Metamodel. The metric *Type Cut Through Source/Target Metamodel* represents the rate of overlapping rules with respect to the transformation's metamodels. The type cut concerning a metamodel is the set of patterns that match instances of the same parts of a metamodel. In the UML to RDBMS example from the QVT standard (from which an excerpt in shown in Listing 1) the type cut concerning the meta-class UmlClass would be all those relations that contain a pattern that matches any UMLClass. The greater this overlap is, the more attention has to be paid when patterns of relations are modified in order to not lose coverage of possible instances of the metamodel.

To compute this metric we need to count the number of relations that overlap over the same part of a metamodel. For example, Relations a, b and c can all match instances of the same meta-class m. Thus the overlap rate concerning class m would be 3. Finding type cuts that only refer to a certain element of the metamodel, such as one meta-class m

can be done straight-forward. However, it might be more interesting more fine-grained patterns that are matched using several different relattions. How such a detailed type cut can be identified remains target to future research.

5   Computation of Metrics

The automated metrics described in section 4.1 can mostly be expressed as OCL expressions on the QVT-R meta-model. These OCL expressions can be used to count the number of elements of a specific type, for instance the number of relations a transformation has. The expressions have to be evaluated in the context of a transformation or a relation depending on wether a transformation local or relation-local metric is calculated. Table 1 shows the OCL expressions used for calculating the metrics. To bring these metrics together, relation local metrics can be aggregated by calculating an average.

```
1  query countSubExps(templ:QVTRelation::TemplateExp) : Integer
2  {
3  if (templ.oclIsTypeOf (QVTTemplate::ObjectTemplateExp))
4    then templ.oclAsType(QVTTemplate::ObjectTemplateExp).part->iterate(p:QVTRelation
         ::PropertyTemplateItem; acc:Integer = 1|  acc + countSubExps(p.value.
         oclAsType(QVTRelation::TemplateExp)))
5    else
6      if (templ.oclIsTypeOf (QVTTemplate::CollectionTemplateExp))
7      then countSubExps(templ.oclIsTypeOf (QVTTemplate::CollectionTemplateExp).member
           .oclAsType(QVTRelation::TemplateExp)))
8      else
9        1
10     endif
11  endif
12  }
```

Listing 2. Query function for calculating the domain predicate count

For more complex metrics like the domain pattern tree depth it was necessary to write more complex OCL query functions. Listing 2 shows an OCL query function for recursively counting the nodes of a domain pattern tree. To easily apply all metric expressions and query functions, we developed a QVT-R transformation that transforms a QVT transformation to a special metrics model. The metrics metamodel allows for compact storage of metrics for every relation in a transformation and for the transformation itself. Moreover, it is possible to store the aggregated values that are also calculated by our metrics transformation. Furthermore, for measuring the lines of code we utilised common methods used for programming languages. We distinguished whitespace, pure comment and code lines. Figure 1 shows the workflow for retrieving the metrics.

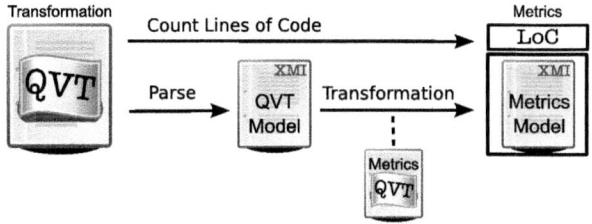

Fig. 1. Computation of metrics workflow

6 Case Study

In this section, we demonstrate how the introduced metrics give insight into the quality of transformations. We illustrate the applicability of our metrics generation approach and discuss the results. For this purpose, we present a case study based on an evaluation of three different transformations.

MOM (Message-oriented-Middleware) Completion Transformation. This refinement transformation integrates performance-relevant details into software architectural models. These details are woven as additional subsystems into the model of architecture. The MOM completion transformation is dependent on the input from a mark model [4] that configures how the actual architecture model should be refined. The configuration, defined by the mark model, provides the variability to the transformation. For example, if a connector is to be refined by message-passing the mark model can provide information about the type of messaging channel, e.g., using guaranteed delivery. For further details on this transformation we refer to [13,10]. Because this transformation is partially generated (includes copy relations for all metamodel elements, these relations are generated by the Ecore2Copy Transformation) we analyse this transformation twice: once with generated part and once without. The source and target model of this transformation are based on an underlying component-based metamodel with the size of 110 classes. This transformation is used as a representative of the group of quite complex transformations.

Ecore2Copy Transformation. This transformation is a so called Higher-Order Transformation (HOT), as it generates another transformation. This specific HOT is used to generate a default copy transformation for a given metamodel by producing a copy relation for each class and each property of the given metamodel. This is required because there is no copy operator in QVT Relational. For further details on this transformation we refer to [9]. The source model of this transformation is the Ecore metamodel having 31 classes and target metamodel is the QVT Relations metamodel itself with the size of 110 classes. This transformation is used as a representative of the group of medium-complex transformations.

UML2RDBMS Transformation. This transformation is presented in the QVT specification as an example relational transformation [17]. The UML2RDBMS transformation

Table 1. Automated metrics

Name	OCL expression
Transformation t	
Number of relations	`t.rule → size()`
Number of top level relations	`t.rule → select(oclAsType(QVTRelation::Relation).isTopLevel) → size()`
Number of starts	`t.rule → select(oclAsType(QVTRelation::Relation).isTopLevel` `and oclAsType(qvtrelation::Relation).when → isEmpty()) → size()`
Number of when	`t.rule → iterate(r:qvtbase::Rule;sum:Integer = 0|` `sum + r.oclAsType(qvtrelation::Relation).when → size())`
Number of where	`t.rule → iterate(r:qvtbase::Rule;sum:Integer = 0|` `sum + r.oclAsType(qvtrelation::Relation).where → size())`
Number of metamodels	`t.modelParameter → size()`
Number of OCL queries	`t.ownedOperation → size()`
Relation r	
Number of domains	`r.domain → size()`
Number of enforced domains	`r.domain → select(isEnforcable) → size()`
Number of checkonly domains	`r.domain → select(isCheckable) → size()`
Number of when-predicates	`r.when.predicate → size()`
Number of where-predicates	`r.where.predicate → size()`
Number of local variables	`r.variable → reject(v	TemplateExp.allInstances().bindsTo.includes(v)) → size()`
Val-In	see number of domains
Val-Out	`Set{r.when} → including(r.where).predicate → collect(p	collectVariableArguments` `OfRelationCallExps(p)).variable → asSet() → size()`
Fan-In	`RelationCallExp.allInstances().referredRelation = r`
Fan-Out	`Set{r:when} → including(r.where).predicate → collect(p	collectRelationCallExps(p))` `.referredRelation → asSet() → size()`

Table 2. Automatically calculated metrics

	GenMOM-Completion	MOM-Completion	Ecore2-copy	UML2 RDBMS
Lines of Code	7582	1304	473	239
Clean code	5789	1104	416	181
Comments	220	65	13	4
Number of relations	488	23	17	8
Number of top level relations	330	12	8	3
Number of starts	99	1	1	1
Number of OCL queries	20	21	1	1
Number of when-predicates	233	13	9	5
Number of where-predicates	221	5	12	13
Number of metamodels in transformation	3	3	3	2
Average number of domains per relation	2.11	4.652	2,76	2,5
Average number of domain pattern nodes per relation	2.63	14.78	11.529	2
Average number of when-predicates per relation	0.9	1.7826	1	0.63
Average number of where-predicates per relation	0.49	0.87	1.82	1.63
Average number of local variables per relation	0.001	0.478	1.05	2.375
Val-in per relation	2.63	14.78	11.529	2
Val-out per relation	2.3	4.45	3.66	3.12
Fan-in per relation	1.12	1.67	1.34	0.78
Fan-out per relation	1.02	1.34	1.2	0.7
Average number of checkonly domains per relation	1.04	2.09	0.714	1
Average number of enforce domains per relation	1.08	2.5652	2.47	1

transforms UML class models into RDBMS tables. The minimum UML source metamodel contains 6 classes and the target RDBMS metamodel has a size of 18 classes. This transformation is used as a representative of the group of very simple transformations.

The results of this case study have shown that the generated transformation (Gen-MOMCompletion) in contrast to the transformation without the generated parts (MOM-Completion) has a higher number of small relations. Additionally, the complexity of match patterns is not high and the complexity of pattern matching is distributed on a number of relations (Figure 2). Thus, we see how the rate of domain pattern nodes per relation decreases significantly if the simple copy rules are added.

Transformation MOMCompletion, intuitively categorised as a complex transformation, shows a much higher values in average domain pattern tree depth as well as the average number of domains and when-predicates per relation(Figure 3). Interestingly, the number of where-predicates increases diametrically opposed. This may indicate that different approaches for defining the overall transformation have been employed. Moreover, where-predicates indicate a somehow "forward" (thus also more imperative) executed transformation whereas more when- predicates indicates a more declarative way of the whole transformation design. Which of these designs is more maintainable remains to be evaluated. However, using these metrics a connection between these findings could be underlined.

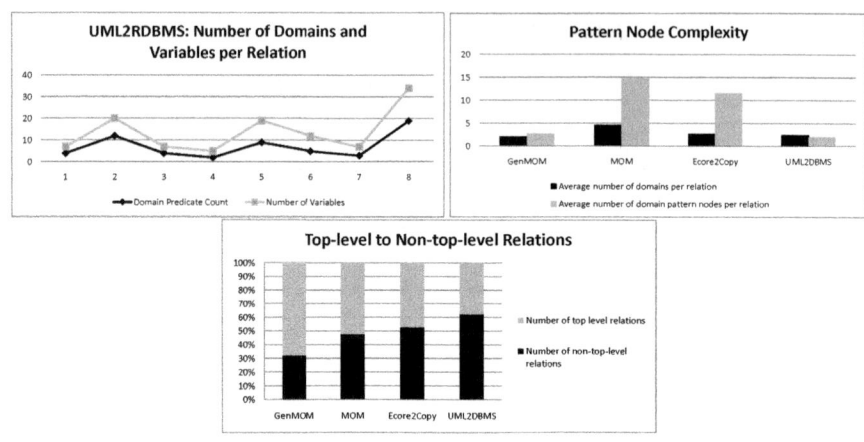

Fig. 2. Results: Transformation Complexity

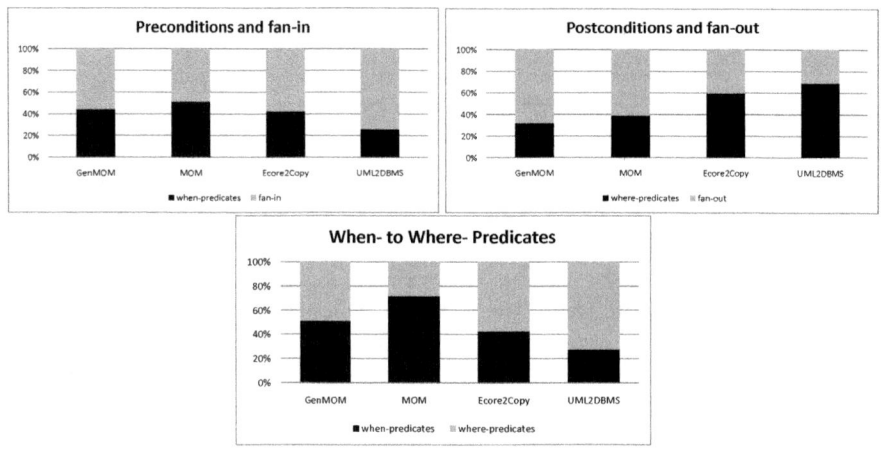

Fig. 3. Results: Relations Dependencies

The ratio between the number of top level relations and non-top level relations is the smallest in case of the generated transformation (1:1). This means a higher utilisation of top level relations. The generated transformation takes an advantage from a higher number of execution paths possible in the transformation and is not tuned to limit the number of starts in order to support maintainability. This also makes sense as the parts generated for the copy transformations are not intended to be maintained manually anyway.

In general, our observation is that roughly half of the relations are top-level relations. We can distinguish a pattern showing that a transformation was written manually by a human based on the number of starts as it seems natural for a human mind to consider only one execution path.

7   Limitations and Validity

The definition of metrics with the goal to estimate quality attributes, such as maintainability, always comes with the wish to indicate whether a lower or a higher value of a metric is better or worse. However, this decision cannot be made without a sound validation of the "meaning" of a metric. For example, having a low number of relations, at first glance, seems to be good for maintainability whereas a high number seems to be bad. On the other hand, if these few relations are very long they may be harder to maintain that more but smaller relations. Thus, in this paper we only identified what could be possible indicators that may resemble maintainability of transformations. We intentionally did not decide, for most of our metrics, which "direction" of a metric is good or bad concerning maintainability. We leave it to future work to determine and evaluate this meaning. Thorough empirical evaluations need to be performed in order identify how meaningful each metric is.

8   Conclusions and Future Work

In this paper we presented an initial set of code metrics to evaluate the maintainability of QVT Relational transformations. However, such metrics could be applied to different relational transformations, they play important role when considering architecture refinement transformations. We demonstrated the use of these metrics on a set of reference transformations to show their application in real world settings. The presented metrics help software architects to judge the maintainability of their model transformations. Based on these judgments, software architects can take corrective actions (like refactorings or code-reviews) whenever they identify a decay in maintainability of their transformations. This results in higher agility when changing metamodels of software architectures or their platforms, which together with metamodel build basis for transformation definition. Future work is twofold. First, the identified metrics need to be incorporated into tools which indicate the code quality while developing the transformations in an IDE. Examples of such tools for object-oriented languages are Project Usus or Checkstyle . Second, the metrics must be empirically validated to study the extent to which they indicate decay in maintainability of transformations written in QVT Relational. Further some additional metrics could be identified as needed during this process, e.g. such as metrics for recursive relations and transformation cycles.

References

1. Becker, S.: Quality of Service Modeling Language. In: Eusgeld, I., Freiling, F.C., Reussner, R. (eds.) Dependability Metrics. LNCS, vol. 4909, pp. 43–47. Springer, Heidelberg (2008)
2. Becker, S., Hauck, M., Trifu, M., Krogmann, K., Kofroň, J.: Reverse Engineering Component Models for Quality Predictions. In: Proceedings of the 14th European Conference on Software Maintenance and Reengineering, European Projects Track (2010)
3. Boehm, B.W., Brown, J.R., Lipow, M.: Quantitative evaluation of software quality. In: ICSE 1976: Proceedings of the 2nd international conference on Software engineering, pp. 592–605. IEEE Computer Society Press, Los Alamitos (1976)

4. Czarnecki, K., Eisenecker, U.W.: Generative Programming (2000)
5. Brito, F., Abreu.: Using ocl to formalize object oriented metrics definitions. Technical report, FCT/UNL and INSC (2001)
6. Fenton, N.E.: Software Metrics: A Rigorous Approach. Chapman & Hall, Ltd., London (1991)
7. Fowler, M., Beck, K., Brant, J., Opdyke, W., Roberts, D.: Refactoring: Improving the Design of Existing Code (1999)
8. Goldschmidt, T., Kuebler, J.: Towards Evaluating Maintainability Within Model-Driven Environments. In: Software Engineering 2008, Workshop Modellgetriebene Softwarearchitektur - Evolution, Integration und Migration (2008)
9. Goldschmidt, T., Wachsmuth, G.: Refinement transformation support for QVT Relational transformations. In: 3rd Workshop on Model Driven Software Engineering, MDSE 2008 (2008)
10. Happe, J., Friedrich, H., Becker, S., Reussner, R.H.: A Pattern-Based Performance Completion for Message-Oriented Middleware. In: Proceedings of the 7th International Workshop on Software and Performance (WOSP 2008), pp. 165–176. ACM, New York (2008)
11. Harrison, R., Samaraweera, L.G., Dobie, M.R., Lewis, P.H.: Estimating the quality of functional programs: an empirical investigation. Information and Software Technology 37(12), 701–707 (1995)
12. Henderson-Sellers, B.: Object-oriented metrics: measures of complexity. Prentice-Hall, Inc., Upper Saddle River (1996)
13. Kapova, L., Becker, S.: Systematic refinement of performance models for concurrent component-based systems. In: Proceedings of the Seventh International Workshop on Formal Engineering approches to Software Components and Architectures (FESCA 2010). Electronic Notes in Theoretical Computer Science (2010)
14. Kübler, J., Goldschmidt, T.: A Pattern Mining Approach Using QVT. In: Paige, R.F., Hartman, A., Rensink, A. (eds.) ECMDA-FA 2009. LNCS, vol. 5562, pp. 174–189. Springer, Heidelberg (2009)
15. Lange, C.F.J.: Phd thesis: Assessing and improving the quality of modeling a series of empirical studies (2007)
16. Masak, D.: Legacysoftware. Springer, Heidelberg (2005)
17. Object Management Group. MOF 2.0 Query/View/Transformation, version 1.0 (2008)
18. Reynoso, L., Genero, M., Piattini, M., Manso, E.: Assessing the impact of coupling on the understandability and modifiability of ocl expressions within uml/ocl combined models. In: 11th IEEE International Symposium on Software Metrics, September 19-22 , p. 10 (2005)
19. Rubey, R.J., Hartwick, R.D.: Quantitative measurement of program quality. In: Proceedings of the 1968, 23rd ACM national conference, pp. 671–677. ACM, New York (1968)
20. Solso, R.L.: Cognitive Psychology. Allyn and Bacon (2001)
21. Stammel, J., Reussner, R.: Kamp: Karlsruhe architectural maintainability prediction. In: Proceedings of the 1. Workshop des GI-Arbeitskreises Langlebige Softwaresysteme (L2S2): Design for Future - Langlebige Softwaresysteme, pp. 87–98 (2009)
22. van Amstel, M.F., Lange, C.F.J., van den Brand, M.G.J.: Metrics for analyzing the quality of model transformations. In: Paige, R.F. (ed.) ICMT 2009. LNCS, vol. 5563, pp. 239–248. Springer, Heidelberg (2009)

Good Architecture = Good (ADL + Practices)

Vincent Le Gloahec[1,3], Régis Fleurquin[2], and Salah Sadou[3]

[1] Alkante SAS, Rennes, France
v.legloahec@alkante.com
[2] IRISA/Triskell, Campus Universitaire de Beaulieu, Rennes, France
regis.fleurquin@irisa.fr
[3] Valoria, Université de Bretagne-Sud, Vannes, France
salah.sadou@univ-ubs.fr

Abstract. In order to ensure the quality of their software development process, companies incorporate best practices from recognized repositories or from their own experiences. These best practices are often described in software quality manuals that do not guarantee their implementation. In this paper, we propose a framework for the implementation of best practices concerning the design of the software architecture. We treat the case of architecture design activity because it's the basis of the software development process. Our framework enables on the one hand to describe best practices and on the other hand to check their application by designers. We present an implementation of our framework in the Eclipse platform and for an ADL dedicated to Web applications. Finally, we give an example of use from the context of our industrial partner.

Keywords: Best Practices, Design, Software Architecture Quality.

1 Introduction

The software architecture plays a fundamental role in modern development processes. Throughout a project, it can serve as a baseline against which the various stakeholders analyze, understand, build their decisions, and evaluate the software [1]. The languages (Acme [2], xADL [3], ByADL [4], UML as an ADL [5]) used to elaborate architectures highlight concepts (such as connectors, components, etc.) that meet two requirements: (i) be enough expressive to represent all targeted systems, and (ii) allow the architect to focus his attention on key issues such as information hiding, coupling, cohesion, precision, etc. Architecture Description Languages (ADL) direct and sometimes compel the architect to comply with some relevant and universally recognized rules in the target area. Thus, they restrict the form of representable architectures by excluding undesirable ones. The aim is to produce architectures with good quality properties.

However, these languages are designed to allow the representation of architectures that answer various type of needs. Thus, some architectural motifs can be considered useful in some contexts and avoided in others. The quality of architecture is not absolute but is estimated according to each project's requirements (cost, schedule, quality of service, etc.) [6] that sometimes are conflicting. So, the

G.T. Heinemann, J. Kofron, and F. Plasil (Eds.): QoSA 2010, LNCS 6093, pp. 167–182, 2010.
© Springer-Verlag Berlin Heidelberg 2010

quality of an architecture is the result of a compromise. The language must be tolerant and not unduly restrict the range of possibilities to let free the creativity of architects. Consequently, the use of an ADL alone, as elegant as it may be, can not guarantee obtaining an architecture that meets the quality requirements desired for a given project.

Best language Practices (BPs) found in the literature, such as modeling processes [7] [8], styles [9], patterns [10] and metrics can then provide an essential complementary tool. Based on the specific context of the project, they will help to direct the architect toward the subset of relevant models among those allowed by the language. In this sense, BPs help the architect to limit the area of choice thanks to a language restriction adapted to the project. They help to increase the effectiveness of development in terms of quality and productivity. Additional BPs specific to an application domain, a technology or a managerial and cultural context may also emerge from projects within companies. Properly used in a project, these best language practices constitute the expertise and the value-added of a company. This valuable capital of knowledge guarantees to a company the quality of its architectural models and thus allows to satisfy its customers, to stand out, and to solicit labels and certificates [11]. In other words, to be competitive.

Unfortunately, we show in section 2 of this paper that due to a lack of an adequate formalism to document this knowledge, companies that try to capitalize on this knowledge use informal documents, often incomplete, poorly referenced, and sometimes scattered. This leads to an inadequate and ineffective use and sometimes loss of best language practices. This loss decrease the quality of the designed architectures. We rely for that on a study conducted with an industrial partner that uses a dedicated ADL for Web applications. We propose a language (section 3) and a software platform (section 4) that allow respectively to document and to enact these BPs for any graphical ADL. In this way, we ensure the durability and reuse of knowledge, as well as a constant verification of the application of best language practices. We then show, in section 5, how this language can be used to document some BPs for web applications coming from our industrial partner. In the same section, we show also how these practices can be integrated in their ADL tool (AlCoWeb-Builder). Thus, this helps developers to respect the best language practices defined in their own companies, without changing their working habits. Finally, we describe related work in section 6 before concluding in section 7.

2   Problem Statement

In this section, we show the interest for a company to make productive its language practices. We rely on a study undertaken in one of our industrial partners: the Alkante company[1]. We begin by presenting the development environment (language, tool, best practices) developed by this company for designing the architecture of its applications. Then, we present the difficulties it faces in some

---

[1] Alkante is a company that develops Web applications (www.alkante.com).

of its developments. The analysis of the causes of these difficulties highlights the interest to capitalize and automate best language practices.

2.1   Development Environment

In the context of rich Web application development, Alkante has defined an ADL (referred to as AlCoWeb) to help design the architecture of its applications [12]. This ADL is an UML profile. The UML language has been chosen mainly because the version 2.0 of the UML specification contains most of the abstractions needed to design rich Web applications with hierarchical entities. Alkante develops mainly Geographical Information Systems (GIS) with the help of a component-oriented framework composed of PHP and Javascript code artifacts. Thus, when designers define the architecture of their applications, they need to deal with entities such as modules, pages, forms, html controls and raw PHP scripts. In order to manipulate those specific entities in the AlCoWeb ADL, they have been defined as stereotypes dedicated to the specific Alkante's architecture. In this profile, we can found stereotypes such as <<AlkModule>>, <<AlkHtmlForm>>, <<AlkHtmlButton>>, etc.

Based on the AlCoWeb ADL, Alkante has developed a complete model-driven architecture platform called AlCoWeb-Builder. This tool allows the designers to model and assemble Web components to create large applications. Components are designed hierarchically and incrementally using component assemblies and connectors. Once atomic and hierarchical components have been designed, they are made available as components off-the-shelf and can be reused to build larger artifacts, like an authentication form or a geographical Web service for example. AlCoWeb-Builder is a graphical editor, build upon several frameworks of the Eclipse platform. It also comes with a code generation facility. Based on a template system, this tool allows to generate the code of designed Web applications, as illustrated in Fig. 1.

Using this ADL in many projects, the company has identified over the years some language practices. For instance, to ensure a complete code generation, the architecture of Web applications should be very specific. Thus, the quality assurance manager (QAM) of the company has defined a dedicated BP in the form of a complete process, documented in a quality manual.

The core of this BP consists of the following steps:

1. Create one and only one module: a module represents the root container of an architecture. At the implementation level, it corresponds to a physical folder that will embeds the code artifacts of the designed Web application;
2. Create one and only one application container in the module: the module component must contain a single application container. This component is the central piece that represents the business logic of the Web application and also provides services for inter-application communications;
3. Create pages in the application container: a page component directly maps to a Web page. In the AlCoWeb ADL, pages are considered first class entities for building the presentation tier of Web applications. Consequently,

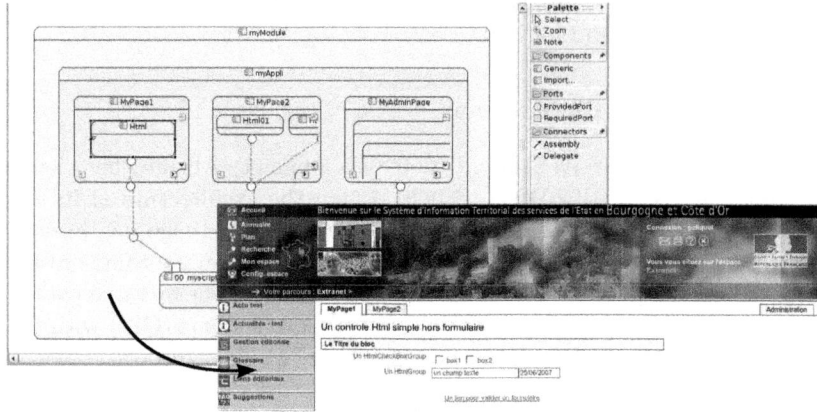

Fig. 1. Design example with AlCoWeb-Builder and the resulting Web interface

the application container must contain at least one page component for the architecture to be valid. At runtime, pages are responsible for the general layout of their sub-components;

4. Create forms in pages: each page must contain at least one HTML form component. This component is always required to build a valid Web page. This architectural decision has been made because dynamic web pages intensely use forms to submit user's data to a web server;

5. Create HTML controls associated with forms: basic and advanced HTML controls (buttons, lists, calendars) must belong to a form component. For the sake of simplicity in the design of Web applications, all HTML controls without exception must be systematically placed in a form;

6. Create scripts: finally, script components represent code artifacts in charge of the rendering of dynamic Web pages. Scripts can be connected directly to page components, and also use the application container to call services from external applications. Without those components, even if the rest of the architecture is valid, the Web application could not be rendered in a client browser.

The QAM in charge of the definition has added some other BPs in the quality manual. Many of them take the form of modeling rules that need to be checked to ensure the quality of a final architecture. These BPs ensure things such as naming conventions or the way components can be put together.

2.2 Recurrent Problems

The MDA approach allows Alkante's team to ease their development effort through components reuse at the model level, and to automate, as possible, code generation and deployment. Although this approach reduces development costs, they observed on occasion that some architectures had not been properly designed.

Some architectures led to errors in the generated code. A major drawback of code generation is that it is difficult to find, from the generated code, the origin of the errors in an architecture. Consequently, developers take a long time to repair. A causal analysis has shown that these errors result from faults made during the component assembly stages when building large applications, while atomic and small hierarchical components are mostly modeled correctly. As AlCoWeb is a hierarchical language, the code generation engine expects the architecture to be designed hierarchically, where HTML forms must be contained in a page, pages must be contained in the root application component, and so on. If this constraint is not respected, the generated application won't be usable. The BP cited above should have guarantee the respect of this constraint. Clearly, this BP has not been correctly applied or not applied at all.

Another recurrent problem concerns the way components must be assembled. All basic and some more advanced HTML controls – more than 30 components, such as buttons, expanded lists, tabs, calendars, etc. – are available as components off-the-shelf. By default, all those components are designed to provide a service named `getHtml()`, which returns the HTML code of the component. At runtime, stacked calls of this service on a hierarchical component allows to produce the complete HTML code of a complex and rich Web page. However, structural components that form the basis of the architecture – e.g. modules, application containers, and scripts – must be designed from scratch by the developers. To design a valid architecture, each `getHtml()` service of `<<AlkHtmlPage>>` components must be delegated to the parent application container (using a delegate connector from a page's provided port to one provided port of the application component). Then, those provided services must be connected to a required port of a script component using an assembly connector. As for the composition of hierarchical components, the non respect of this specific assembly leads to a poor quality of the architecture that results in the generation of unusable Web applications. Again, this problem results from the non-application or misapplication of a BP, yet documented in the quality manual.

2.3   Discussion

The source of the two problems cited above is the non-compliance with some of the BPs outlined in the quality manual. Further causal analysis shown that the root cause has always been one of the followings:

1. Involvement of new designers who did not know when and how the documented practices should be applied. This problem occurs because most of the documented practices do not describe precisely their application context and some of them are ambiguous;
2. Some BPs become fastidious when the architecture complexity grows (for instance, inducing the same manual verification but on numerous model elements), thus developers have ignored or partially applied them;
3. Some BPs are complex and consequently manually error prone (for instance, inducing many verifications on several model elements);

4. When a project is subject to significant time constraints, developers have chosen to ignore some BPs in order to respect the deadline.

To remedy this, we must make productive the BPs. They must be enforced in the used tools (editor, transformations, and code generator). We can try to "hard-code" the BP in the tools suite (if possible by the tool). But, we believe it would not be a good solution. Firstly, tools change over time. We do not want to have to re-code all the BPs each time a tool change. Secondly, BPs evolve too. Each time a BP change, we have to do the corresponding changes in the tool's code. Thus, we must separate the BP definition from the tools.

We advocate that the BPs become first class entities when using an ADL language. Thus, the language will be adapted to fit a particular context (developer, project, company, application domain, etc.). In this way, each company can contextualize a general purpose language to its own needs.

Consequently, to produce quality products, a language should not be reduced solely to its three components (abstract syntax, semantics, and concrete syntax). Indeed, as we emphasized throughout this section, companies often define their own best practices which enrich the language to fit a specific context. The remaining of the paper introduces our approach for the definition and application of best language practices at the early stage of design of software architectures.

3   Best Practices Description Language

The language we introduce in this section, called *GooMod*, contains some properties needed for the description of best design practices. In this section we show how we have done to identify these properties and then we describe the abstract syntax and semantic of the *GooMod* language.

3.1   Identified Properties

Architectural design is a particular case of modeling activity. However, there is a rich literature on best practices for modeling activity. Thus, we made a survey on best practices in modeling activity in order to identify their characteristics and forms. Through literature we observed three types of best modeling practices: those that are concerned only with the form (style) of produced models, those that describe the process of their design, and those that combine both. As the third type is only a combination of the first two, we limited our study to examples covering the former types. For the first type we found that the best practices for Agile Modeling given in [9] are good examples. In [13], Ramsin and Paige give a detailed review of object-oriented software development methods. From this review we extracted properties concerning the process aspect of BPs. For the sake of brevity, we can't go further on this study in this paper. Interested reader may found more detail on the dedicated Web page[2].

---

[2] http://www-valoria.univ-ubs.fr/SE/AMGP

Thus, we have identified the following properties:

Identification of the context: to identify the context of a BP, the language must be able to check the state of the model to determine whether it is a valid candidate for the BP or not.

Goal checking: to check that a BP has been correctly applied on a model, we must be able to check that the status of the latter conforms to the objective targeted by the BP. At the BP description language level, this property highlights the same need as the one before.

Description of collaborations: a CASE tool alone is able to achieve some parts of a BP's checking. However, some BP cannot be checked automatically and the tool would need the designer's opinion to make a decision. In case of alternative paths, sometimes the tool is in a situation where it cannot determine the right path automatically. Thus, a BP description language should allow interactions with the designer.

Process definition: a process defines a sequence of steps with possible iterations, optional steps, and alternative paths. A BP description language should allow processes to be defined with such constructs.

Restriction of the modeling language: several good practices based on modeling methodologies suggest a gradual increase in the number of manipulated concepts (e.g., each step concerns only a subset of the modeling language's concepts). Thus, the BP description language should allow the definition of this subset for each step.

The documentation of a BP associated with a design language requires a description that is independent of any tool; indeed, a BP is specific only to the language. It describes a particular use of its concepts. It should not assume modes of interaction (buttons, menus, etc.) used by an editor in order to provide access to these concepts. Therefore, a BP must be described in a way that can be qualified as a Platform Independent Model (PIM) in Model-Driven Engineering (MDE) terminology (see next section). Ignoring this rule would lead QAM to re-document the BPs at each new version or tool change. The *GooMod* language contains all properties described above and offers a way to document BPs independently of any editor. To introduce the *GooMod* language we present its abstract syntax then its semantic.

3.2   Abstract Syntax of the GooMod Language

The abstract syntax of the *GooMod* language is given in Fig. 2. The process part of a BP is described as a weakly-connected directed graph. In this graph, each vertex represents a coherent modeling activity that we call a step. Arcs (identified by *Bind* in our meta-model) connect pairs of vertices. Loops (arcs whose head and tail coincide) are allowed, but not multi-arcs (arcs with the same tail and same head).

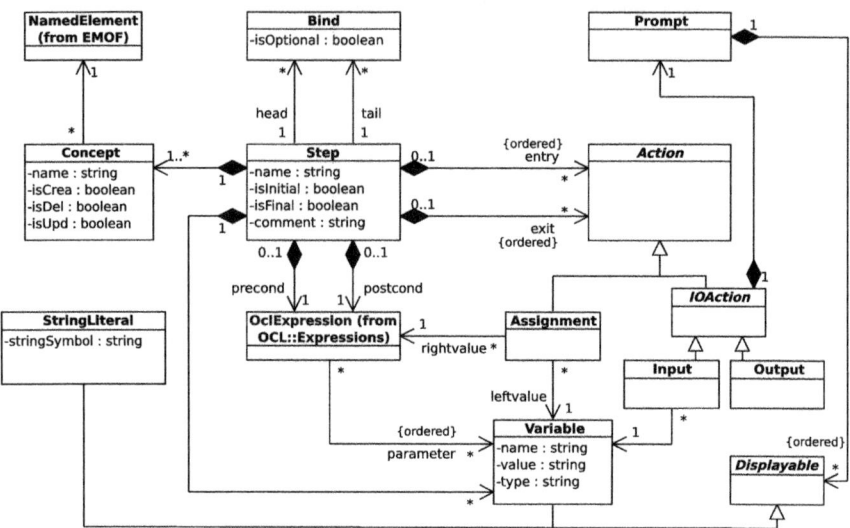

Fig. 2. GooMod Meta-model

A step is associated with four elements: its context, its associated design style, the set of language concepts usable during its execution, and a set of actions. The *context* is a first-order formula evaluated on the abstract syntax graph of the input model before the beginning of the step. We call this formula a *pre-condition*. The design style is a first-order formula that is evaluated on the abstract syntax graph of the current model to allow designer to leave from the step. We call this formula a *post-condition*. The set of the *usable language concepts* is a subset of the non-abstract meta-class of the abstract syntax (described in a MOF Model) of the targeted design language.

Because some BP require the establishment of a collaboration between the system and the designer, we have included the ability to integrate some actions at the beginning (*entry*) and/or at the end (*exit*) of a step. The possible actions are: output a message, an input of a value and the assignment of a value to a local variable. Indeed, at each step, it is sometimes necessary to have additional information on the model that only the designer can provide (goal of *Input* action). Conversely, it is sometimes useful to provide designers information that they can not deduce easily from the visible aspect of the model but the system can calculate (goal of *Output* action). This concerns introspection operations that can be achieved with MOF operators at pre- and post-conditions level. Hence, the usefulness of variables associated with steps to hold results. Thus, actions allow interaction with the designer using messages composed of strings and calculated values.

Steps are also defined by two boolean properties: *isInitial* and *isFinal*. At least one step is marked as initial and one as final in a graph. Finally, an arc can be marked as optional, meaning that its head step is optional.

3.3   Semantic of the GooMod Language

Semantically, the graph of a BP is a behavior model composed of a finite number of states, transitions between those states, and some *Entry/Exit* actions. Thus, a BP is described as a finite and deterministic state machine with states corresponding to the steps of the BP's process.

At each step, the elements that constitute it are used as follows:

1. Before entering the step, the pre-conditions are checked to ensure that the current model is in a valid state compared with the given step. Failure implies that the step is not yet allowed;
2. If the checking succeeds, then before starting model edits a list of actions (*Entry Action*), possibly empty, is launched. These actions initialize the environment associated with the step. This may correspond to the initializing of some local variables or simply interactions with the designer;
3. A given step can use only its associated language concepts. In fact, each concept is associated with use type (create, delete, or update).
4. When the designer indicates that the work related to the step is completed, a list of actions (*Exit Action*) will be launched to prepare the step's environment to this end. With these actions the system interacts with the designer to gain information that it can not extract from the model's state;
5. Before leaving the step, the post-conditions are checked to ensure that the current model is in a valid state according to the BP rules.

Leaving a step, several transitions are sometimes possible. These transitions are defined by the *Binds* whose tail is this step. A transition is possible only if the pre-condition of the head step of the concerned *Bind* is verified by the current state of the model. If several next steps are possible, then the choice is left to the designer. A *Bind* can also be defined as optional. In this case, its tail step becomes optional through the transition it defines. Thus, the possible transitions of the tail step are added to those of the optional step, and so on.

4   Implementation of GooMod

To implement the *GooMod* language, we developed a complete platform for the management of BPs, starting from their definition at the platform independent model (PIM) level up to their enactment at the platform specific model (PSM) level. Figure 3 illustrates the platform and its PIM-PSM separation. This section describes both levels and their associated tools.

4.1   PIM-Level: Modeling BPs

The PIM level of the *GooMod* language allows description of BP independently of the used design tool. This level is implemented thanks to the **BP Definition Tool** (see top of Fig. 3). This tool is designed for QAM in charge of the definition of BP that should be observed in a company. Our graphical editor, designed using

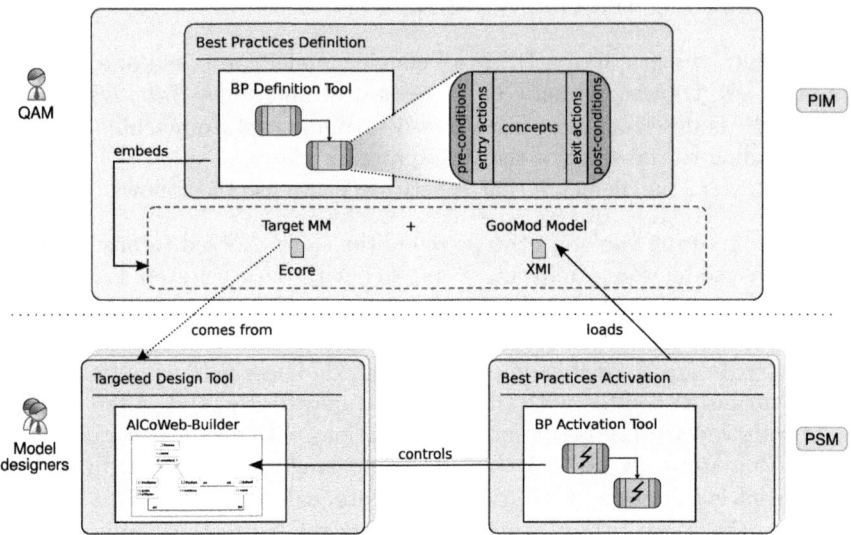

Fig. 3. GooMod platform general architecture

the Eclipse Graphical Modeling Framework[3] (GMF), allows the representation of
BPs in the form of a process. Such a process is represented by a path in a graph.
Each node of the path is a step. The BP Definition tool uses the meta-model of
the target language as its input. At each step of the process, the BP Definition
tool allows for the selection of a subset of manipulated concepts from the target
language, as well as the definition of a set of OCL pre- and postconditions, and
actions before entering and exiting the step.

4.2   PSM-Level: BPs Enactment

The PSM level aims to attach the definition which is done at the PIM level with
a specific design tool. For that, our platform is composed of two parts:

BP Activation Tool: that aims to link a BP model defined with the BP Definition tool to a target design tool. It controls the enforcement of the BP
process.

Targeted Design Tool: which is the end-user design tool where the BP will
be performed. This tool is not intended to be modified or altered directly,
but will be controlled by an external plugin, which in our case is the BP
Activation Tool.

A targeted design tool can be, for instance, the AlCoWeb-Builder tool (see
bottom-left of Fig. 3), which allows Alkante's designers to model the architecture of their Web applications. However, our approach is not limited to this

---

[3] See Eclipse Modeling Project (http://www.eclipse.org/modeling)

design tool. Indeed, the BP Activation tool has been designed to interact with any Eclipse GMF-generated editors. If the first feature of BP Activation is to enact a process and check the elaboration of models, the second feature consists of controlling some parts of the targeted design tool. At each step of modeling, only the editable concepts of the current step are active. Based on the extension capabilities of the GMF framework, the BP Activation tool dynamically activate/deactivate GMF creation tools of the targeted design tool according to the editable concepts allowed for this step. With this approach, we are able to control any GMF editor within the Eclipse platform. To tackle the problem of how to interact with other design tools, we plan to elaborate a mapping meta-model so that QAM could map editable concepts with the creation features (buttons, actions, items) of the design tool.

5   Case Study: Alkante's BP

In the following we present how to define the BP presented in section 2 and how to apply it during a design process.

5.1   Formal Description of BP

The *GooMod* language allows to represent the different steps of this BP in the form of a process. The steps are described with the help of the BP Definition tool as depicted in Fig 4.

The process defines an iteration that allows to create multiple pages and their content. Indeed, once a script has been added, the designer will either be able to continue through the process or to iterate by adding new pages. The dashed arrow between *"Add Form"* and *"Add HTML Controls"* represents an optional transition, thus making the latter step optional. This indicates that adding HTML controls to forms is not necessary to produce a valid Web application in this specific context.

The QAM in charge of the definition of this BP is able to detail each step of the process by adding some rules that need to be checked to ensure the quality of the final architecture. For each step, the QAM can define both pre- and post-conditions that will ensure that models will be well-constructed. Those constraints are given using the OCL language. Besides defining constraints, the

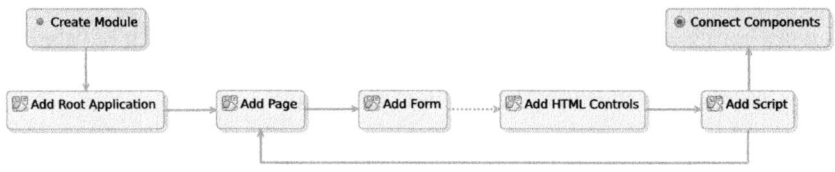

Fig. 4. Process part of Alkante's BP for building Web applications architectural models

QAM adds entry and exit actions that allow the designer to collaborate with the system by means of inputs and/or outputs. Those actions are described using a script-like syntax, where it is possible to declare variables and input/output operations. In addition, each step comes with a list of editable concepts that are used to follow the defined process. In the Alkante's BP, each step is associated with a list of meta-classes of the AlCoWeb language: *Component* and *Port* for each step except the last one, and the meta-class *Connector* for the last step (*Connect Components*), thus allowing to connect components with each other.

For example, here is a complete description of the step *"Add Form"*:

Pre
```
description: at least one page must be present
context: Component
inv: Component.allInstances()->select(c:Component |
        c.stereotype='AlkHtmlPage')->notEmpty()
```

Entry
```
output("You have to create at least one form per page.")
output("Make sure to respect the graphical guidelines.")
```

Concepts
```
[{"Component","cud"}, {"Port","cud"}]
```

Exit
```
input($response, boolean, "Did you respect the graphical guidelines?")
```

Post
```
description: each form must be contained in a parent page
context: Component
inv: Component.allInstances()->select(c:Component |
        c.stereotype='AlkHtmlForm')->notEmpty()
     and
     Component.allInstances()->select(c:Component |
        c.stereotype='AlkHtmlForm').owner.stereotype='AlkHtmlPage'
     and
     Component.allInstances()->select(c:Component |
        c.stereotype='AlkHtmlPage')->forAll(page |
           page.ownedForms->size() >= 1)
     and OclQuery_graphicalCheck() = true
```

The pre-condition checks that before entering the step, the model contains at least one page. The entry action is used to inform the designer about the constraint related to this step (at least one form per page) and recommendation about graphical guidelines. The syntax used to describe editable concepts is given in the form of two strings: the first is the name of the concept, the second is composed of the first letters of the authorized behaviors. In our case, "cud" means "create, update and delete". In the above example, the exit action is used to ask the designer to check whether the graphical guidelines are respected. The post-condition is used to check that the model contains at least one form per page and that the graphical guidelines were respected. In the BP Definition tool, all the rules listed above are editable using advanced editors and content assistants, so that designers don't have to manipulate the syntax given in this example.

5.2   BP in Action

When developers starts designing architecture models with AlCoWeb-Builder, they first load the *GooMod* model defined by the QAM, and then launch the

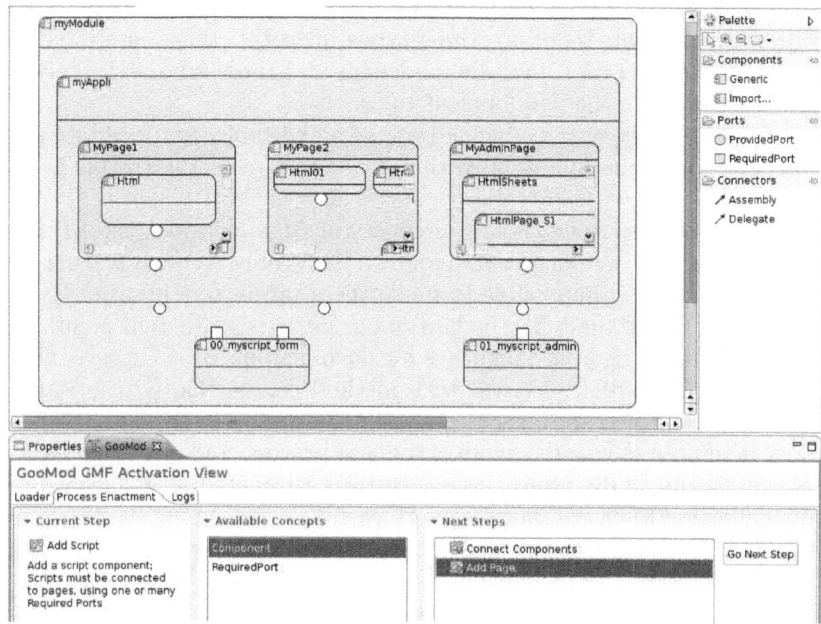

Fig. 5. Applying best practices in AlCoWeb-Builder

controlled editing process. The bottom of Fig. 5 shows the current state of the
BP Activation tool: the current design step is *"Add Script"* (on the left), allowed
editable concepts for this steps are *Component* and *Port* (in the middle), and
the right part shows the next available steps. As we can see, the BP indicates
that we have the choice to go back to the *"Add Page"* step, or to go ahead to
the last step of the process to finish the design of the Web application.

In the company, the *GooMod* platform is used differently depending on skills
and experience of developers. Novice developers systematically use the platform,
whereas experts prefer to make verifications at key steps of the design process.
Indeed, novices are not fully aware of all the practices that have to be respected
to produce a quality architecture, therefore they prefer to be guided through
the whole design process. This reinforces our idea that a tool must be flexible
enough to adapt to the most users. The *GooMod* platform has been designed
accordingly.

The reader may find other examples of use of the *GooMod* platform through
screencasts at `http://www-valoria.univ-ubs.fr/SE/goomod`.

6   Related Work

Best practices management is a particular case of Knowledge Management. This
domain aims to identify, gather and capitalize on all used knowledge (including

BP) to improve companies performance [14]. Thus, in the domain of BP for software development, there are three types of works: those interested in BP archiving, those interested in their modeling, and those who seek their implementation directly in the development tools.

Several works suggest introducing processes and tools that facilitate storage, sharing, and dissemination of BP within companies (e.g. [15], [16]). They advocate in particular the use of real repositories allowing various forms of consultation, thus facilitating research and discovery of BPs. However, the BP referred to by these systems are documented and available only through textual and informal. It is therefore impossible to make them productive in order to control the use within CASE tools. To the best of our knowledge, there is no other work on the definition of rigorous languages for documenting BPs. However this field can benefit from works concerned with method engineering ([7], [8]) and software development process [17]. Indeed, a BP is a particular form of development method. It imposes a way to run an activity, a process, and also imposes a number of constraints on the proper use of language concepts. Language engineering and its definition tools are therefore very useful.

With CASE tools, several works suggest encouraging, even requiring, the respect of certain BP. The domain that had produced good results in recent years is the one that focuses on the automation of BP concerning detection and correction of inconsistencies. These include, in particular, the work presented in [18], [19], [20] and [21]. They propose adding extensions to modeling tools, such as Eclipse or Rational, that are able to intercept the actions of designers and inspect the information system of the tools in order to detect the occurrence of certain types of inconsistency. The inconsistencies treated by these works are various, but they remain on the analysis of syntactical consistency of models expressed in one or more languages, which is already quite complex. Sometimes they address the problem of what they call methodological inconsistencies, i.e., the detection of non-compliance with guidelines relating to how the language should be used. However, these works involve BP with a much smaller granularity than those we are dealing with.

In the domain of software architectural modeling, Acme has been proposed as a generic ADL that provides an extensible infrastructure for describing, generating and analysing software architectures descriptions [2]. This language is supported by the AcmeStudio tool [22], a graphical editing environment for software architecture design implemented as an Eclipse Plug-in. AcmeStudio offers the possibility to define rules (invariants and heuristics) to check whether an architectural model is well formed. However, rules have to be defined directly at the design stage and are embedded in the architectural model. This limits the portability of the solution to another tool and the expressiveness of BPs. In our approach, we prefer the definition of such rules to be at the PIM level, so that they can be reused and remain independent of any tool. The *GooMod* platform can be easily adapted to work with AcmeStudio, since this tool is an Eclipse-based graphical editor. In this way, it could propose features not available in AcmeStudio: support for a process representation of the design activity, better understanding of the ADL through the manipulation of only valuable concepts at each design steps, and ways to collaborate dynamically with designers.

7   Conclusion

To produce softwares with high quality, a company must first ensure that its architecture is of high quality. To achieve a desired level of quality, the use of an ADL alone, as elegant as it is, is not enough. It should be used with best practices to get good solutions depending on the context of use. Through the use of best practices, designers avoid reproducing well-known errors and follow a proven process. But the quality has a cost related to two aspects: the capitalization of these best practices and roll-backs in case of non compliance with them.

With our approach, quality assurance managers are able to define, in a formal description, their own design practices based on books, standards and/or their own gained experience. Since these descriptions are formal, they become productive in tools. They can be automatically applied by designers to produce high quality architectures. Thus, we provide not only a way to capitalize best practices, but also a means to check their compliance throughout the design process to avoid costly roll-backs.

Our approach provides to architects, directly in editing tools, a collection of BPs. This automation relieves the architects of much of manual verifications. Consequently, they do not hesitate to activate them when needed. They can also choose the BPs to use, depending on the given context, their own skills and type of the project.

As a continuation of this work, we plan to provide a best practice management tool that allows the quality assurance manager to optimize BPs use. In addition of defining BPs, this tool should help to involve designers in projects (process + human), with management of access rights and temporary permissions of violation. Finally, it must allow the generalization of individual BPs to make them usable by all designers. This last point will enable the company to go up from the level of individual know-how to the level of collective know-how.

References

1. Erdogmus, H.: Architecture meets agility. IEEE Softw. 26(5), 2–4 (2009)
2. Garlan, D., Monroe, R.T., Wile, D.: Acme: architectural description of component-based systems, pp. 47–67 (2000)
3. Dashofy, E.M., van der Hoek, A., Taylor, R.N.: A comprehensive approach for the development of modular software architecture description languages. ACM Trans. Softw. Eng. Methodol. 14(2), 199–245 (2005)
4. Di Ruscio, D., Malavolta, I., Muccini, H., Pelliccione, P., Pierantonio, A.: Developing next generation adls through mde techniques. In: 32nd International Conference on Software Engineering, ICSE 2010 (to appear, 2010)
5. Medvidovic, N., Rosenblum, D.S., Redmiles, D.F., Robbins, J.E.: Modeling software architectures in the unified modeling language. ACM Trans. Softw. Eng. Methodol. 11(1), 2–57 (2002)

 6. Bass, L., Clements, P., Kazman, R.: Software architecture in practice. Addison-Wesley Longman Publishing Co., Inc., Boston (1998)
 7. Henderson-Sellers, B.: Method engineering for OO systems development. Commun. ACM 46(10), 73–78 (2003)
 8. Gonzalez-Perez, C., Henderson-Sellers, B.: Modelling software development methodologies: A conceptual foundation. Journal of Systems and Software 80(11), 1778–1796 (2007)
 9. Ambler, S.W.: The Elements of UML(TM) 2.0 Style. Cambridge University Press, New York (2005)
10. Buschmann, F., Meunier, R., Rohnert, H., Sommerlad, P., Stal, M.: Pattern-oriented software architecture: a system of patterns. John Wiley & Sons, Inc., New York (1996)
11. Gratton, L., Ghoshal, S.: Beyond best practices. Sloan Management Review (3), 49–57 (2005)
12. Kadri, R., Tibermacine, C., Le Gloahec, V.: Building the Presentation-Tier of Rich Web Applications with Hierarchical Components. In: Benatallah, B., Casati, F., Georgakopoulos, D., Bartolini, C., Sadiq, W., Godart, C. (eds.) WISE 2007. LNCS, vol. 4831, pp. 123–134. Springer, Heidelberg (2007)
13. Ramsin, R., Paige, R.F.: Process-centered review of object oriented software development methodologies. ACM Comput. Surv. 40(1), 1–89 (2008)
14. Stewart, T.A.: The Wealth of Knowledge: Intellectual Capital and the Twenty-first Century Organization. Doubleday, New York (2001)
15. Fragidis, G., Tarabanis, K.: From repositories of best practices to networks of best practices. In: 2006 IEEE International Conference on Management of Innovation and Technology, pp. 370–374 (2006)
16. Zhu, L., Staples, M., Gorton, I.: An infrastructure for indexing and organizing best practices. In: REBSE 2007: Proceedings of the Second International Workshop on Realising Evidence-Based Software Engineering. IEEE Computer Society, Los Alamitos (2007)
17. OMG: Software Process Engineering Meta-Model, version 2.0 (SPEM2.0). Technical report, Object Management Group (2008)
18. Biehl, M., Löwe, W.: Automated architecture consistency checking for model driven software development. In: Mirandola, R., Gorton, I., Hofmeister, C. (eds.) QoSA 2009. LNCS, vol. 5581, pp. 36–51. Springer, Heidelberg (2009)
19. Egyed, A.: Uml/analyzer: A tool for the instant consistency checking of uml models. In: 29th International Conference on Software Engineering, ICSE 2007, pp. 793–796 (2007)
20. Hessellund, A., Czarnecki, K., Wasowski, A.: Guided development with multiple domain-specific languages. In: Engels, G., Opdyke, B., Schmidt, D.C., Weil, F. (eds.) MODELS 2007. LNCS, vol. 4735, pp. 46–60. Springer, Heidelberg (2007)
21. Blanc, X., Mounier, I., Mougenot, A., Mens, T.: Detecting model inconsistency through operation-based model construction. In: ICSE 2008: Proceedings of the 30th international conference on Software engineering, pp. 511–520. ACM, New York (2008)
22. Schmerl, B., Garlan, D.: Acmestudio: Supporting style-centered architecture development. In: ICSE 2004: Proceedings of the 26th International Conference on Software Engineering, pp. 704–705. IEEE Computer Society, Washington (2004)

Author Index